P9-CIT-859

What Happened to Goldwater?

By the same author

Barry Goldwater: Freedom Is His Flight Plan
How to Win an Election

Stephen Shadegg

What Happened

The Inside Story of the 1964

to Goldwater?

Republican Campaign

Holt, Rinehart and Winston
New York Chicago San Francisco

Published simultaneously in Canada by Holt, Rinehart and Winston of Canada, Limited.
Library of Congress Catalog Card Number: 65-25403
First Edition

Designer: Ernst Reichl
87837-0115
Printed in the United States of America

To

Barry Goldwater, a great American,
. . . with affection and admiration

Preface

This book is the record of the emergence of Barry Goldwater as the acknowledged spokesman for the conservative cause and of his overwhelming defeat for the presidency in 1964.

In politics, defeat and victory are both transitory. Ideas and understandings carefully articulated endure to affect and enrich the lives of succeeding generations. The millions of Americans who gave their commitment to a cause, which in their view was identified with the preservation of the proper relationship between man and his government, made a substantial contribution to the future of the Republic.

Let history assess the blame if such must be done. That is her task, not mine. It is my assignment to report, not to condemn—to give credit to those who labored—to provide an understanding for those who are puzzled, and to reassure those who sensed what took place but were never told.

Let the twenty-seven million Americans who bravely shared Goldwater's defeat take knowledge that indeed there was a cause. Let the Republic understand that it must recover from the frivolities and the invectives which obscured that cause.

These pages are written by one who believes the choice which was promised in 1964 and never validated must be offered again, that one day a judgment must be made on the great issues which were whispered but never spoken in 1964.

My political association with Barry Goldwater commenced in 1952, when he asked me to manage his first campaign for the United States Senate, and continued until the early spring of 1962. The circumstances which prompted the Senator to select a new manager for his presidential effort are related in chapter five of this book. Although I had no voice in the strategy or planning of the "Goldwater for President" effort, I was privileged to serve as one of six Regional Directors on the staff of the Republican National Committee during the 1964 campaign. And what I have written is the reflection of my long and intimate association with the man who was nominated by the Republican party for President.

Political campaigns are always attended by an element of hysteria. I regret that it has been impossible to mention all of the hundreds of thousands of volunteers who labored in the precincts and the headquarters across this nation. I have endeavored to deal honestly and objectively with the characters and events recorded on these pages. Political and business reprisals are not uncommon. To avoid this I have cloaked one character with anonymity and given the fictitious name Dr. Charles Wiggamore Kelley to another.

I am grateful to my wife, Eugenia, whose editing has helped to clarify what has been written, to Toni Nelson and Kathy Young, who typed and retyped these pages, and to the volunteers who worked so valiantly in their attempt to achieve a political victory which they believed would help preserve the Republic.

I am indebted to Dean Burch, John Grenier, Wayne Hood, Sam Hay, Dick Herman, Sam Claiborne, Chuck Lichenstein, Don Dornan, Rus Walton, Lee Edwards, Jim McKenna, Peter O'Donnell, Dick Kleindienst, Doug Whitlock, Clif White, and many others who graciously granted my requests for interviews after the election. Their comments, amounting to more than ninety thousand words, strengthened my own understanding of what happened to Goldwater and provided the necessary cross-reference so vital to a writer whose ambition is to make his work a true reflection of the events of a period which may come to be regarded as the most significant political decade of the twentieth century.

Part One

The Man from Arizona

1

In November, 1952, the Democrats in Arizona outnumbered Republicans three to one. Yet Barry Goldwater, a political neophyte, defeated a two-term incumbent Democrat to become the first Republican to represent Arizona in the United States Senate in twenty-six years. In this, his first attempt at statewide political office, Goldwater received the votes of more than fifty thousand registered Democrats.

Six years later when the Senator ran for re-election, his plurality was five times as great as that of the 1952 victory. In November, 1958, more than eighty thousand registered Democrats crossed the party line to re-elect a Republican.

As his party's candidate for the Presidency in 1964, Goldwater lost the election to Lyndon Johnson by almost sixteen million votes. A substantial number of registered Republicans crossed the party line to support the Democrat nominee, and Johnson won the Presidency by the largest percentage of total popular vote of any candidate in United States history.

Goldwater did carry Arizona, but his margin of victory was less than half the plurality of that first election and about one-tenth the magnitude of his 1958 victory. In the suburbs, where Goldwater conservatism was supposed to be strongest, his candidacy was brutally rejected. In the Midwest—heartland of traditional Republican power—Goldwater failed to carry a single state. His popular vote was almost eight million less than the total given to Richard Nixon in 1960. And the man who had enjoyed the affection of millions of Republicans prior to his official announcement on January 3, 1964, emerged in November as the target of Republican animosity.

To find a political parallel to the Johnson landslide and the Goldwater defeat it is necessary to go back to 1936 when Alf Landon, running against the popular incumbent Franklin D. Roosevelt, was able to carry only two states.

No candidate for the Presidency on the Republican ticket ever received such broad-scale financial support. More than one and a half million Americans contributed in excess of thirteen million dollars to Goldwater's campaign. In addition, more than five hundred thousand individual citizens joyously gave their time to the cause, laboring in the precincts across the nation. At least 75 per cent of those qualified to vote in 1964 were called on and solicited by members of this vast volunteer army.

Incumbent politicians prosper in periods of peace and tranquility, draw their strength from a stable economy, benefit as world conflicts lessen. In the spring of 1964 the odds should have favored a challenger. Castro's Communist Cuba threatened the peace of the Western Hemisphere. Our position in Southeast Asia was steadily deteriorating. The NATO alliance was crumbling because of United States insistence on a multination nuclear defense. The Bobby Baker scandal was an unanswered question; the budget was out of balance; the debt had been increased. There were riots in the streets of New York City and Philadelphia; property was destroyed, and the innocent were being injured.

The long rumored animosity between Attorney General Robert Kennedy and the man who had succeeded his brother was verified when Johnson bluntly ruled out any consideration of Bobby as a vice-presidential candidate. This action was widely accepted as an affront to the Kennedy followers, one which would be remembered in November.

Goldwater had been the overwhelming favorite at the San Francisco convention. He enjoyed the support of Republicans in every section of the country and received some delegate votes from every state with the exception of Alaska, Maine, New Hampshire, and Oregon. More than a year earlier, in May of 1963, the *U. S. News and World Report,* in an article discussing potential Republican candidates, revealed that Goldwater was named by party leaders in twenty-three states with 208 electoral votes as the candidate who would run best in their own state. And on June 14th, *Time* magazine put Goldwater's picture on its cover and said categorically: "If the Republican national convention were to be held today, Goldwater would almost certainly be its presidential nominee."

In San Francisco the nation's Republicans, with a few notable exceptions, were confident they had named a fighting candidate—a man who had a real chance to win. Even those who recognized the difficulty of unseating an incumbent President believed Goldwater would do better than any other man who had been suggested to head the ticket.

As the television computers flashed their totals on that Tuesday evening in November, a chorus of disappointed, bewildered partisans voiced the question: What happened to Goldwater?

As the manager of Goldwater's first campaign for the United States Senate in which he won an improbable victory and as the director of his successful effort for re-election in 1958, I shared the optimism of thousands of Republicans. I had seen Goldwater tame a hostile audience with his reasonable, friendly response to antagonistic questions. I had watched him develop a consistent, and to my mind appealing, conservative political philosophy. He possessed to a greater degree than any other politician I have ever seen—with the exception of John Kennedy—that quality of charisma which enables a speaker to arouse a crowd to wild enthusiasm. Over the years it has been my privilege to participate in the campaigns of thirteen different contenders for the United States Senate. Goldwater was by far the most cooperative, most effective candidate I had ever managed.

In the years between elections I had watched him deal with the dissidents in his own party; I had seen him unite warring factions, and I knew the dedication of his followers.

As a regional director for the Republican National Committee, charged with the responsibility of coordinating the Goldwater campaign in ten western states, I concluded early in September that Goldwater would lose in 1964. But I was not prepared for the magnitude of that loss.

Apologists for the Goldwater campaign—National Chairman

Dean Burch in particular—now insist that no Republican candidate could have defeated Lyndon Johnson. Thousands of Republicans cling to the belief that Goldwater could have, indeed should have, done much better as the leader of Republican hopes.

The year 1964 opened with a promise of opportunity for Barry Goldwater and the Republican party. The nation, which had made no attempt to conceal its grief over the assassination of President John F. Kennedy, had turned from its tears to the promise of Christmas and the advent of a new year. The great homogenized society of the Republic, responding to the imperative of history, looked toward the future.

The Johnson administration made a frantic attempt to deny existing uncertainties. They promised business would be better in 1964, cold-war tensions would lessen, living would be richer and easier and less taxing in the fourth year of the sixth decade of the twentieth century.

The people had suffered the loss of a President and had made the transition to a new chief of state under the quieting anesthetic of a genuine grief. Where Kennedy had been exciting and upsetting, the homely, undramatic words of Lyndon Johnson were soporific—almost but not quite overpowering the strident clamor of criticism which had been aimed at the New Frontier.

The Kennedy administration had been distinguished by charm, wit, and elegance. The Kennedy family took possession of the great mass media. Television, news magazines, daily papers, fashion columns—all capitulated to the charm of the Kennedys, and they in turn exploited this happy surrender.

When the Kennedy legislative program bogged down in Congress, the Kennedy popularity seemed to increase with the people. Even the blunders at the Bay of Pigs failed to produce a marked reaction against the President. When the left-wing fanatic, Lee Harvey Oswald, murdered the President of the United States in Dallas, he at the same time deprived the Democrat party of much of its political appeal and all of its charm.

In November, 1960, the defeat of Richard Nixon had been followed by the sound of the starter's gun signaling a race to identify and proclaim a new leader for the Republican party. Under the vigorous chairmanship of Congressman William E. Miller the faithful courageously commenced to enlist the troops and storehouse the ammunition which could bring victory in 1964.

National frustration over the constant advance of the Communist world had been translated into a number of activist groups. American foreign policy—commencing with Yalta—was eagerly and intelligently discussed in living rooms and meeting rooms from Schenectady, New York, to Salinas, California. A new dimension was being injected into the traditional political scene. The one descriptive, all-embracing term selected by those who opposed the New Frontier was conservatism.

Barry Goldwater was the prophet and the voice of conservatism. But Nelson Rockefeller—the attractive, able chief executive of New York state—was widely regarded as the most acceptable Republican spokesman.

When Rockefeller was re-elected governor of New York in 1962, his margin of victory showed some decline in his popularity. But being first over the finish line is what really counts. Nixon lost his race for the governorship of California, and even those who cherished a warm personal regard for the former Vice-President agreed that 1964 would be a contest between Rockefeller and Kennedy.

To be sure, there was some sentimental support for the Senator from Arizona as the party's presidential nominee. But the old pros were inclined to dismiss these murmurs as nothing more significant than a proper sense of gratitude for a hard-working, loyal Republican Senator. Nevertheless, the fact that a Republican from a nominally Democrat western state with only five votes in the Electoral College could be seriously considered to head the national ticket suggested that the strength of the Republican party was moving from its traditional anchors on the eastern seaboard.

Sales of the Senator's *The Conscience of a Conservative* increased. His three-times-a-week newspaper column, *"How Do You Stand, Sir?,"* which commenced with one newspaper, the Los Angeles *Times* in January of 1960, had spread to more than 148 daily papers by 1962. His new book, *Why Not Victory?*, was given a warm reception.

Nelson Rockefeller's divorce in March of 1963 and his remarriage in May of that year provoked an immediate reassessment of the presidential potentials. The politicians who had argued that the breakup of the Rockefeller family would be no great liability lost most of their enthusiasm for the New York governor when his remarriage to Mrs. Murphy was announced.

Goldwater's supporters became bolder. An organization which had been formed in secrecy in 1961 to draft Goldwater for the nomination moved into the open and recruited additional support. By early November, 1963, the pollsters were reporting that Goldwater was the overwhelming favorite of Republican county chairmen. His personal popularity was 45 per cent on the national scale.

Look magazine ventured to suggest that Goldwater could beat Kennedy and backed up that opinion with the results of a survey. In the same week Kennedy died, the *New York Times* treated the Goldwater candidacy in a favorable and encouraging manner. Immediately after the tragedy in Dallas, Goldwater's position was questioned by some of the political columnists. But those who pretended to believe that Oswald's rifle bullet had brought death to the challenger as well as the champion had no alternative candidate to suggest.

When Barry Goldwater promised the nation "a choice not an echo," he was aware of the odds against victory. He believed that he might be carried into the White House by the very evident enthusiasm of the highly vocal conservative groups. At worst he expected to capture more than 45 per cent of the popular vote and assist in the election of a substantial number of Republicans to the House and Senate.

In some quarters the Senator's long delay in making known his intentions was viewed with suspicion. There was a suggestion of uncertainty, of indecision, which was translated by some into a belief that Goldwater was reluctant to seek the nomination. Only twice in this century had an incumbent President been defeated—Taft, through the defection of Theodore Roosevelt, who formed a third-party movement, and Hoover, who was the victim of a great depression. On Election Day Lyndon Johnson would have been President for less than one full year. He had moved into the White House following a tragedy in an atmosphere of sympathetic good wishes, and he announced his intention to attempt to carry out the Kennedy legislative program. Whatever the Congress did in 1964 could not rationally be blamed on Johnson.

Standing on the patio of his hilltop Phoenix home, Goldwater promised: "This will not be an engagement of personality—it will be an engagement of principle." He emphasized the virtue of individual liberty. He described the year 1964 as that moment when "we must face up to our conscience and make a definite choice." He said, "Let there be a choice right now and in clear, understandable terms."

Goldwater described the Democrat party as favoring the extension of governmental power. He offered to spell out the basic philosophical division which he believed separated the two parties.

In the preconvention months from January to mid July, Goldwater steadfastly refused to make any derogatory or personal comments about the other Republican contenders—Rockefeller, who was first in the field; Vice-President Nixon who, until the final day of the convention, appeared to be a hopeful; Henry Cabot Lodge, the 1960 vice-presidential candidate; Senator Margaret Chase Smith of Maine; and Governor William Scranton of Pennsylvania.

These were the preliminaries. In the battle for the championship the high promise of a campaign based on issues rather than personalities was forgotten. The pledge to spell out the issues in understandable terms was never completely redeemed. James Marlow, writing from Washington, D. C., for the Associated Press, described the effort: "On top of everything else, he [Goldwater] made a kind of empty campaign. He criticized the Democrats but was dim on what he would do himself." Jack Steele, writing in the *New York World-Telegram,* said: "I've never observed a presidential campaign in which so many mistakes were made."

On October 30th, the *New York Daily News* opened an editorial with these words:

When Barry Goldwater was nominated we had bright hopes that the Arizonan would put on a skillful, high-powered campaign which would draw many vital issues sharply between him and President Johnson. Goldwater is right in most of his positions on governing the U. S.—keeping the country prosperous, regaining national prestige, and rolling back Communism. We do not like Johnson's extreme welfare statism, his pie-in-the-sky promises, his sanctimonious excuses for such as Walter Jenkins, or his flabby attitude toward Communism. Also we detest beyond words the campaign of vilification which Johnson's backers and flunkies have mounted against Goldwater. But the Goldwater campaign has been so clumsily conducted and the Senator has made so many unfortunate remarks in public that one wonders how capable a President he would be.

The elaborate and skillful organizational operation which had swept aside all of Goldwater's opponents for the nomination seemed to disintegrate after San Francisco.

Scores of incumbent Republican congressmen were drowned in the Johnson tidal wave, including such members as Brotzman of Colorado, Bromwell and Jensen of Iowa, Snyder of Kentucky, Beermann of Nebraska, Martin of California, Wilson of Indiana, McClory of Illinois, Knox of Michigan, Wyman of New Hampshire, Wharton of New York, Schenck of Ohio, Short of North Dakota, and Foreman of Texas. In the state of Washington, Westland, Horan, and Stinson were all defeated. Harrison of Wyoming and Derounian of New York, along with Chenoweth of Colorado and Van Pelt of Wisconsin, were rejected.

A host of promising Republican candidates for the Senate were defeated—John Wold in Wyoming, Bud Wilkinson in Oklahoma, Robert Taft in Ohio, Paul Laxalt in Nevada, and Ernie Wilkinson in Utah. Yet, at the beginning of 1964, Barry Goldwater and those who supported him had good reason to hope that he would become the thirty-seventh President of the United States.

As chairman of the Republican Senatorial Campaign Committee for a total of six years, Goldwater had appeared before friendly audiences in almost every section of the country. He was admittedly the best fund raiser the Republican party ever had. He was the man who had unselfishly withdrawn his name from consideration in Chicago in 1960 and called for unity and hard work. He had made hundreds of speeches in support of the Nixon-Lodge ticket, and even the critics who disagree with and downgrade everything Goldwater stands for will attest to his great personal charm.

Goldwater survived defeat in New Hampshire, moved irresistibly forward through the primaries of Indiana, Illinois, and Nebraska, lost Oregon by default, carried California by the barest of margins, and dominated the San Francisco convention.

The most partisan of Lyndon Johnson's followers rate him as a poor television personality. The Democrat national convention in Atlantic City was totally devoid of any drama or conflict. And the selection of Hubert Humphrey, although pleasing to the ADA wing of the party, was offensive to the sizable conservative segment.

Johnson suffered by comparison with the glib, rapid-fire, commanding personality of the man whom he had succeeded. He had managed to amass a sizable personal fortune in an industry which is regulated by the federal government. His image as a wheeler-dealer politician was strengthened in September when Senator John Williams of Delaware tossed further fuel on the Bobby Baker scandal.

Experienced politicians can discover in the conduct of the Goldwater campaign a long list of tactical and strategic errors. National Chairman Dean Burch, not without some reason, ascribes Goldwater's defeat to the unfair treatment accorded to the Senator by the press. The Rockefeller-Romney faction insists that disaster was inevitable because of the candidate's allegiance to the conservative philosophy.

There is some support for the argument that the American people, unable to face another change in the Presidency in so short a time, merely followed their charitable inclination to give Lyndon Johnson a term of his own.

Yet to many observers Goldwater the presidential candidate was somehow different from the man who had earned their affection in prior years. The warm, outgoing, reasonable personality was concealed behind a stern and rigid mask. The man who was supposed to be the master of television appeared ill at ease and uncertain on that medium. In the words of one of his oldest and closest Arizona associates, "Goldwater sounded shrill."

The votes have been counted. History will determine whether or not the November choice was a happy decision. The debate over the outcome will be renewed in 1968 and perhaps at four-year intervals thereafter. No amount of examination after the fact will alter what has been done—"The Moving Finger writes; and, having writ, Moves on." . . . Yet the serious, concerned citizen, anxious to contribute to our representative form of government, must at least attempt to find an answer to that vexing question: What happened to Goldwater?

Was his nomination the mistake which subsequent events seem to indicate?

Is conservatism dead, outmoded, no longer useful?

Were Goldwater's ideas totally unacceptable? Was he the captive of a militant, fascist, uncompromising minority?

What happened to Barry Goldwater?

2

Most of Goldwater's detractors cling tenaciously to the notion that perverse fate—aided and abetted by a handful of willful radicals—procured the Goldwater nomination. Such a reconstruction ignores the significant political polarities which had been developing in this country since the late 1930's.

The innovations of the New Deal, the Fair Deal, and the New Frontier were bitterly resisted by diverse groups for a variety of reasons. All who opposed the expansion of central authority were classified as conservatives. Supporters of change appropriated the liberal label.

Through a series of fortuitous circumstances, rather than as the result of any advance planning, Barry Goldwater became the man on the surfboard, riding the wave of growing conservative power. His first successful election was assisted by a series of events beyond the control of any individual political figure. The war in Korea was going badly. The Truman administration suffered from the scandals of mink coats and deep freezers. The Republicans nominated an extremely popular war hero, and Eisenhower's appeal was personal rather than political.

As a freshman senator, Goldwater hoped to be named to serve on the Interior Committee, a natural aspiration for a new member from an arid state which is dependent for its prosperity on the federal reclamation system. There was no place for Goldwater on Interior. In response to a request from Senator Robert Taft of Ohio, he agreed to an assignment on the Labor Committee. But he was not very happy about it.

"Arizona doesn't have any labor problems," Goldwater argued

correctly. In 1952, industry was less important than agriculture, copper, or cattle to the state's economy.

His committee position brought Goldwater in contact with Mike Bernstein, a veteran Capitol Hill lawyer, who, after graduating from the New York University Law School and completing military service in World War II, was appointed as a legislative attorney in the Department of Labor in 1946. Bernstein earned promotion to the position of senior attorney on the staff and general counsel to the National Labor Relations Board. When Eisenhower was elected and the Republicans took control of Congress, Senator H. Alexander Smith of New Jersey became chairman of the Labor Committee and named Bernstein majority counsel.

Goldwater was immediately impressed with Bernstein's comprehensive understanding of the complexities of the labor problem. He was dismayed and intrigued by the continuing violent struggle between labor and management. He had long believed the union movement was good for the American working man. Now he discovered the cynicism of certain labor leaders and the brutal mechanisms by which some union bosses were exploiting the workers with the same disregard for the individual that had once characterized management.

Goldwater's appearance on the Washington scene coincided with a period of sudden growth and expansion of his native state. Between 1946 and 1955 the population of Arizona doubled. The state's wide, open spaces, mild climate, and long underdeveloped resources were suddenly recognized. This new interest in Arizona was translated into new interest in the junior senator from Arizona. Goldwater's dynamic personality, ruggedly handsome appearance, and personal concern in the new developments that were to become the hallmark of that decade lifted him almost immediately out of the class of the ordinary.

Goldwater was a jet pilot in a jet age, a ham radio operator in a period when the electronic miracle of television was being born, and a better than average student of anthropology. He was an authority on the Arizona Indians. He had explored the mysteries of the Colorado in a rubber boat.

In a way denied to most new members of the Senate, Goldwater came to Washington with a national acceptance. In the depths of the Great Depression, Goldwater had taken over the family department stores and built a reputation as a merchandiser which spread throughout the entire dry-goods industry. As a pre-Pearl Harbor veteran of World War II he had formed friendships with military leaders and servicemen all across the nation. As the husband of Peggy Johnson, an heiress to the Borg-Warner fortune, he enjoyed a social acceptance in the highest industrial and financial circles.

The liberal character of the national administrations from 1933 to the present day is partially the result of the support given to the cause by the liberal intellectuals. For years the conservatives lagged behind. But by 1952 management was busily engaged in providing its spokesmen with the same kind of solid intellectual support which had long been available to the other side.

The leader in this new effort was Dr. Charles Wiggamore Kelley, a brilliant, witty Ph.D. Goldwater and Kelley were drawn together by the Senator's new interest in the problems of labor and management. Quiet-voiced, knowledgeable, forty-three-year-old Kelley represented the management of an enlightened industrial giant. He became Goldwater's friend and confidant.

The successful public figure who achieves power and fame is frequently pictured as a man who has marched forward on a predetermined course. The fortunate accidents which anoint some men with fame while denying recognition to others are conveniently overlooked.

Lady Luck was standing in the wings when the Senate created a select committee for the purpose of investigating labor and management abuses.

Goldwater, low man on the totem pole in seniority and a member of the minority party, would not, under normal procedures, have been named to this blue ribbon investigating panel. But Senator William A. Purtell of Connecticut asked to be excused, and Goldwater became one of the two Republicans on the Labor Committee to receive appointment to the Select Committee to Investigate Improper Activities in Labor-Management Relations, a body which soon became identified as the McClellan Committee in deference to its chairman, Arkansas Senator John McClellan.

In every session of the Congress there is only a limited number of dramatic confrontations. Members of the press, radio and television, eager to escape the dull routine of most legislative hearings, prick up their ears, lick their lips in anticipation, and prepare to shoot the works whenever a special committee is created.

Democrat members on the McClellan Committee were Sam J. Ervin of North Carolina, Pat McNamara of Michigan, and a young senator from Massachusetts, John F. Kennedy, who was able to arrange the employment of his younger brother, Bobby, as special counsel. Jimmy Hoffa of the Teamsters had attracted considerable attention as the result of alleged strong-arm tactics. There was evidence to support the claim that organized crime had invaded the waterfronts. The bitter and prolonged UAW strike against the Kohler Manufacturing Company of Wisconsin was being given headline attention in the nation's newspapers.

Bobby Kennedy focused the investigation on the Teamsters Union and its president, Hoffa, who had been bitterly critical of Walter Reuther, the UAW chieftain, who believed Hoffa was plotting to gain control of the entire union movement. The animosity between Hoffa and Reuther was both personal and ideological.

Goldwater, along with Senators Carl Curtis of Nebraska and Karl Mundt of South Dakota, wanted to investigate the UAW-inspired strike against the Kohler plant. He charged that the Kennedys were deliberately protecting Walter Reuther.

In the course of the hearings Goldwater received more than fifteen thousand letters from rank-and-file union members complaining about what they called the dictatorial tactics of the UAW chief. This was the genesis of the widely publicized Goldwater-Reuther feud.

Guy Nunn, the official radio spokesman for the UAW, who was then doing a daily broadcast from a Canadian station aimed at the Detroit-area listening audience, took up the cudgels against the Arizona Senator.

As tempers rose, Goldwater challenged Walter Reuther to a

televised debate. And then, with an independence characteristic of his public life, qualified the challenge by insisting that he be permitted to pay personally for his half of the time. Unrealistic? Quixotic? To be sure. But in the eyes of his Arizona constituency, completely consonant with the fearless independence of a politician ready and willing to face any issue.

Service on the McClellan Committee was not the only springboard which helped to bounce Barry Goldwater from the platform of a freshman senator high into the air as a national public figure. In 1954 he was chosen to head the Senatorial Campaign Committee, which is independent of the Republican National Committee and devoted exclusively to providing support for Republican senatorial candidates.

The committee had long been presided over by venerable Victor Johnson, a man who through the years has demonstrated a magnificent capacity for collecting funds to be used in the election of Republican senators. Goldwater and Johnson became fast friends, and the Senator from Arizona embarked on speaking tours aimed at those constituencies where Republicans hoped to win in 1956.

With a popular, Republican, incumbent President seeking re-election, a spokesman for the Senatorial Campaign Committee enjoyed a readymade welcome. At first Goldwater's speeches were more distinguished by their sincerity than by their eloquence. But a man on his feet in front of a crowd must either improve or retreat permanently to a seat in the spectator section.

Goldwater discovered that Midwest audiences responded when he declared his devotion to the Constitution. They applauded his criticism of the expanding federal bureaucracy, the increased federal indebtedness, and the foreign-aid program which was giving American dollars to support nations within the Communist orbit.

Through his friendship with Dr. Charles Kelley, Goldwater had been introduced to the brilliant conservative philosopher and writer, Dr. Russell Kirk. Kirk, a disciple of the English political philosopher Edmund Burke, helped Goldwater to articulate his instinctive, intuitive support of conservative principles.

Traveling the country on behalf of Republican hopefuls did little to increase Goldwater's strength at home, but it was the foundation for his well-developed, widespread acquaintance with Republicans at the local level which figured so prominently in the party's decision in San Francisco ten years later.

Goldwater's smashing re-election victory in Arizona in 1958 was unquestionably the turning point in his public career. To continue in public life, every politician must be re-elected when his term expires. But in this case, the 1958 victory did much more than guarantee his presence in the Senate for an additional six years. He won in a state where the registration was two and a half to one against his party. He won in a year when the Republicans lost strength in the Congress, and he won on his own. No critic could successfully suggest that he rode into office this time on the coattails of a popular presidential candidate.

When Goldwater asked me in May of 1952 to manage his first campaign for the Senate, he was aware of the odds against his winning and was prepared to accept defeat philosophically. In January of 1957, when he asked me to start working on his re-election effort, he was determined to win.

Political campaigns which blossom into victory in the normal eight- or ten-week period prior to the November decision require meticulous advance planning. What we did in Arizona and what is necessary in every successful political race is detailed in my book *How to Win an Election.*

By comparison, the 1952 effort had been a spur-of-the-moment, understaffed operation. Hoyt Pinaire, a young man who was comptroller of the Goldwater stores, was treasurer and paymaster of that first effort. Mrs. Jack Harris, Goldwater's long-time personal secretary, had handled the scheduling. Brooks Darlington, an unpaid volunteer, wrote the press releases. It was my responsibility to do everything else. We prepared the speeches in my office. We wrote the scripts for radio and television. We wrote and I recorded all the radio commercials. We produced campaign cards and campaign literature, and because most observers in Arizona believed there was no chance for a Goldwater victory, there was little interest in what we were doing.

In 1957 hundreds of people wanted to help the incumbent Senator win re-election. Harry Rosenzweig, Goldwater's boyhood friend, took charge of raising the money. Bert Fireman, a capable columnist attached to the Phoenix evening newspaper, was employed on a part-time basis to write press releases. An office was opened at a convenient location, staffed with a secretary and clerical help.

In the world of politics an opportunity for a candidate to run against an unpopular situation or personality not involved in the direct contest is always welcome. The UAW, meeting in Miami, Florida, in the spring of 1958, announced that its number one political objective for 1958 would be the defeat of Senator Barry Goldwater of Arizona. We believed this was a political situation demanding exploitation. Walter Reuther had few friends in Arizona. Union membership was largely confined to the construction trades—craft unionism rather than the political structure of eastern industry. It was decided that Goldwater would aim his campaign against the dictation of the eastern union bosses and would treat his actual opponent, the same Ernest McFarland he had beaten in 1952, as a secondary figure.

McFarland had ousted the incumbent Republican governor in 1954. He had been re-elected in 1956 by an overwhleming plurality. He was an affable, hard-working campaigner with many friends and the power of the state patronage system at his disposal. At least two-and-a-half times as many Democrats as Republicans could be expected to vote. In the winter form book, McFarland should have been an easy winner.

Our strategy was first to arouse general indignation against some of the obvious sins of the labor bosses and then, as the underdog, capitalize on the drama of the lone knight on the white charger attacking the twin evils of out-of-state influence and union excesses.

It is traditional to open an Arizona campaign shortly after Labor Day. Goldwater formally commenced his drive for re-election in Prescott, Arizona, September 10th, 1958, standing on the same Court House steps where he was to launch his campaign for the Presidency six years later.

The Senator asked his audience to remember the situation the Republicans had inherited in 1952: the Truman scandals; the uncertain foreign policy which had sent five hundred million human beings behind the Iron Curtain between 1945 and 1952; the Korean War which had cost 122,000 American lives.

He said:

> The drums and the bugles are silent, the call for Minutemen to spring to action is almost a forgotten phrase from our history books, science is supreme.
>
> We have penetrated the space age. We are talking of sending a manned rocket to the moon. The magnitude of the destructive forces of the atom is almost too great for us to grasp. We are prosperous, apathetic, contented and self-indulgent.
>
> We consume aspirin by the million pounds monthly. We take alcohol and stimulants to pep us up, and Miltown to slow us down. We are all frantically engaged in a race to get somewhere but that goal is no longer clear before us.
>
> We seem to have lost our way, to have deserted those moral principles which gave force and direction to the first faltering years of the American Republic.
>
> If we stop for a moment, if we listen carefully tonight, we can hear the drums of Valley Forge, we can hear the bugles on Heartbreak Ridge calling you and calling me to action and to sacrifice. This time the arena is not a bloody battlefield with mortar fire and star shells, but a battle for the minds of men to be settled for the moment in the ballot boxes on Election Day.

The speech in its entirety is a most descriptive outline of what Goldwater hoped to make the 1964 presidential campaign. He recited his record as "a Republican opposed to the Super-State," pointing out, "In the Congress I've not been a me-too Republican. When conscience has demanded it, I have spoken out against the policies of my own administration. I have fought for a balanced budget and that budget has been balanced for four of the five years of the Republican leadership."

He reported how the Republicans under Dwight Eisenhower

had rebuilt the nation's military strength, equipped the Strategic Air Command with jet bombers, commissioned the first fleet of nuclear submarines, improved the training programs for military service.

He said he had voted against foreign aid but had given his support for increased Social Security benefits for all categories of recipients and increased Social Security taxes to finance these benefits.

Goldwater won that contest by more than thirty-five thousand votes in a year when the Republicans were losing twelve seats in the Senate. His victory attracted the attention of the national press, and in a very real sense, this was the beginning of his rise to prominence as a national politician.

When Goldwater returned to Washington for the session which opened in January of 1959 he was treated with new respect by his colleagues and by the press. He became ranking minority member of the Labor Committee, moving from position four to position number one, and from number six to number three on Interior and Insular Affairs.

Mike Bernstein approached Goldwater with a suggestion: "Why not spell out the conservative concern for members of the great middle class?" Mike argued that management had its champions in the Congress, union members and union bosses were well represented, but the whitecollar workers, the independent businessmen, and the small farmers were being neglected. "They," he said, "are the forgotten Americans."

Bernstein, with some assistance from Goldwater, prepared a stirring speech. "The Forgotten American" became a part of the Goldwater conservative manifesto. The press played up the speech. The Senator's office was deluged with requests for copies. The year was beginning auspiciously.

As a result of his service on the McClellan Committee and his position on the Labor Committee, Goldwater was invited to participate in administration councils. When the Kennedy-Erwin Bill came up for debate in April, he made headlines as the only member of the Senate to vote against what was widely touted as a reform measure beneficial to both labor and management.

Bernstein believes that Goldwater was actually representing the administration's opposition to the measure. But if this is true, the man in the White House had failed to communicate his disapproval to any other Republican senator. According to Goldwater, the President was angered by his action. At a White House function Eisenhower demanded to know why Goldwater had voted against the measure. The Senator replied that it was an inadequate bill, one which would not correct any of the abuses disclosed by the McClellan hearings, offered no protections against secondary boycott, and was, in his view, a fraud.

Inspired by this conversation, Eisenhower ordered a real investigation of the measure and shortly thereafter appeared on television to condemn what he called an inadequate labor bill.

On September 3rd the Senate reversed itself. By a vote of 95 to 2 the Kennedy-Erwin Bill was rejected and the Landrum-Griffin Act passed in its place. Every knowledgeable politician in America recognized that Barry Goldwater was the one man responsible for this legislative turnabout.

Goldwater's re-election in 1958 produced still another benefit. The incumbent senators, particularly those who were up for re-election in 1960, insisted that Goldwater again become chairman of the Senatorial Campaign Committee. There were ten incumbents ranging in shades of political belief from Clifford Case of New Jersey, an avowed liberal, to Carl Curtis of Nebraska, a vocal conservative. Among others were Leverett Saltonstall of Massachusetts, John Sherman Cooper of Kentucky, and Margaret Chase Smith of Maine.

These politicians were not at all concerned about Goldwater's ideological allegiance. They wanted his help because he had demonstrated an ability to win, a know-how which they believed would be helpful in their own contests.

Goldwater asked me to come to Washington to explain the techniques we had employed in the Arizona victories. When I had finished my presentation, a number of senators requested that I be engaged as a special consultant to the Senatorial Campaign Committee.

In completing this assignment I traveled over a hundred thousand miles, visited most of the states where there were Republicans up for re-election, and provided all the candidates with detailed, day-by-day instructions on timing, advertising, organization, recruitment of support, and all the other activities which are necessary to winning elections.

In the campaign of 1964 thousands of die-hard Goldwater fans exhibited vocal animosity toward those Republicans classified as middle-of-the-road or liberal. In this action they rejected the example Goldwater had set throughout his entire public life. He was a Republican. He supported Republicans. He detested hyphenated labels. His enemies were the collectivists in the Democrat party.

3

When the first session of the Eighty-sixth Congress adjourned, Goldwater's performance in the Senate and out on the hustings had attracted the support and earned the admiration of such early conservative voices as William F. Buckley, Jr., editor of *National Review;* Russell Kirk, author of *The Conservative Mind;* Clarence Manion, former Dean of the Notre Dame School of Law; and a sizable number of earnest, working Republicans.

In November, 1959, the Western Republican Conference was held at the Biltmore Hotel in Los Angeles. Both Rockefeller and Goldwater were scheduled to address the gathering. Rockefeller was greeted with courteous applause. The delegates gave Goldwater a thundering ovation.

In his speech Goldwater said:

> For twenty-five years the apostles of the welfare state have been busy transforming that stern old gentleman in a top hat, cut-away coat and red, white and blue trousers from a symbol of dignity and freedom and justice for all men into a national wet nurse, dispensing a cockeyed kind of patent medicine labeled "something for nothing"—passing out soothing syrup and rattles and pacifiers in return for grateful votes on Election Day.

He remarked that Senator John Kennedy, who was then obviously campaigning for the Democratic nomination, had recently observed that Americans had gone soft. In answer to this, Goldwater said: "And now, like the over-indulgent guardians who have spent the child's inheritance catering to adolescent whims and desires, they are naïvely amazed at what their over-indulgence has produced."

He presented his view that the Republican party was a conservative party committed to a free state, limited central power, and a balanced budget.

The editors of the *Los Angeles Times* took notice of what Goldwater had to say. The head of the Chandler clan invited the Arizona Senator to return to Los Angeles for a visit with the editorial board so they might explore his views.

Goldwater did return, and over a long and pleasant luncheon the *Times* men probed the mind of the Senator from Arizona. As a result of this meeting, Nick Williams, the managing editor, invited Goldwater to write a column for southern California's most influential newspaper.

Goldwater discussed the project with me in Phoenix in December and asked if I would like to try my hand at writing the series. He said: "I won't have the time to do it, and I'm not that kind of a writer anyway."

It was agreed that Goldwater would select the subjects and I would do the actual writing.

On January 17, 1960, the *Times* described the forthcoming column with these words:

> The decade of the sixties should be the most dynamic in the world's modern history. The *Times,* believing that what we do and what we think in the next ten years will forever shape the destiny of the United States, also believes that only the most analytical thinking can preserve the essence of the way of life that we have always called American.
>
> That is why, beginning next Sunday, on our editorial pages the *Times* will present a three-times-a-week column written especially for the *Times* by the leading conservative thinker in American public life, United States Senator Barry Goldwater.
>
> The *Times* is proud to publish the opinions of the Republican Senator from Arizona. In the struggle for men's minds he has won victories where the odds seemed insurmountable. He thrives on debate because he believes—and practices—what he preaches. And the *Times* believes that debate is the surest way of charting our path through this decade of destiny.

In May and June of 1964 the *Times* gave its editorial support to Governor Nelson Rockefeller. Goldwater was deeply hurt. He believed this newspaper, of all the publications in the country, had understood and supported his aspirations for a conservative administration.

Goldwater was reluctant to take any money for his by-line as a United States Senator. He felt that in some manner the acceptance of a fee would be to capitalize on an office he honored and respected. The *Times* offered a payment of fifty dollars a week. Goldwater wanted the money given to charity and suggested that we send it to the Prescott Community Hospital. Later on, at my request, we gave the column's earnings to a young lawyer who had decided to enter the Church Divinity School of the Pacific and become an Episcopal priest. At a later date Goldwater ordered the money turned over to Trinity Cathedral in Phoenix for the purchase of some stained-glass windows. When I gave up writing the column at Goldwater's request in May of 1962, it was producing about sixteen hundred dollars a month. In addition to the Arizona recipients and the theological student, a contribution of two hundred dollars a month was given to Goldwater's old school, Staunton Military Academy.

The column was a happy collaboration. Because I had been privileged to work with the Senator throughout the development of his entire public life, I was familiar with his beliefs, his philosophy, and his aspirations for America. In a letter to the editor of the *Times,* which was published before the column started, Goldwater had made it clear that he would assign the actual task of writing the 800-word essays to me.

Dr. Charles W. Kelley and some of Goldwater's other Washington associates viewed this new undertaking as a possible mistake. They argued that in our rapidly changing political world a position which might appear wise today could be a liability at some future time. Goldwater resolved not to comment on any of the daily problems of government or foreign affairs. He reviewed the copy before it went to the newspaper and frequently made suggestions. But in almost two and a half years there was only one occasion when he asked me to kill a column which had been written. This one had reference to the Peace Corps which Goldwater opposed when it was organized. "I've changed my mind about the Peace Corps," he told me on the telephone, "I think it's doing some good, and I don't want to be critical of it."

In April of 1960 Rex Barley of the Times-Mirror Syndicate asked permission to offer the column for sale to papers throughout the nation. By the end of that year Goldwater was appearing in more than eighty daily newspapers, and twelve months later "How Do You Stand, Sir?" was being purchased and published by more than one hundred forty subscribers. Rex Barley told us the column was the fastest selling item he had ever handled. A number of editors, including Jim Brown, publisher of the *Boise* (Idaho) *Statesman,* reported that readership surveys indicated Goldwater was the most popular writer on the editorial page.

While the newspaper column was carrying the Goldwater ideas into millions of homes, another event took place which both enhanced the Goldwater public image and gave some indication of the growing conservative strength in the nation.

Clarence Manion suggested it would be helpful to the cause if the Senator would write a book setting forth in simple terms the basic conservative political philosophy. Manion argued that such a book would strengthen Goldwater's position, exert a beneficial influence on the midsummer decisions the Republican party must make in convention, and serve as an answer to the liberal argument.

Goldwater liked the idea. The book was to be based in general on the content of the speeches he had been making to Republicans across the nation. L. Brent Bozell, brother-in-law of the editor of *National Review* and a conservative intellectual, was enlisted to help with the actual writing.

Manion arranged a contract with the Victor Publishing Company of Sheperdsville, Kentucky, for an initial printing of ten thousand copies. No one envisioned a bestseller. Manion thought the book might have some acceptance among the conservatives on college campuses. Bozell thought his job was to write a simple primer, a guide book to a Utopian conservative society. Goldwater liked the title, *The Conscience of a Conservative,* but doubted the book would have much circulation.

"We are not writing a platform for the Republican party," he explained to me, "but what I hope we can do is awaken the American people to a realization of how far we have moved from the old constitutional concepts toward the welfare state." Under the terms of the contract the Victor Publishing Company acquired almost all the rights to the book. Goldwater, Manion, and Bozell were not looking for royalties; they wanted publication.

Goldwater sent a copy of the manuscript to me as rapidly as the chapters were completed. I suggested only minor changes, and these were not always followed. I have been praised by some commentators for writing the book, criticized by others—notably Drew Pearson. Goldwater was kind enough to say that some of the speeches I had written formed a basis for the book. The truth is, Goldwater and Bozell deserve full credit for the writing. The rest of us made only minor contributions.

The Conscience of a Conservative did arouse the American people. Before the book was out a month it was necessary to print ten thousand additional copies, and by 1964, in hardback and paperback cover, more than three and one-half million copies had been sold.

The publication of this first Goldwater book had a tremendous impact on the political thinking of the American voter. It called attention to the growth of the federal state as "the biggest land owner, property manager, renter, mover, hauler, medical clinician, lender, insurer, mortgage broker, employer, debtor, taxer, and spender in all history." It questioned the propriety of the federal government's appropriating nearly one-third of all earnings every year in the form of taxes.

It was here that Goldwater, speaking of civil rights, said:

> It so happens that I am in agreement with the objectives of the Supreme Court, as stated in the Brown decision. I believe it is both wise and just for Negro children to attend the same school as whites, that to deny them this opportunity carries with it strong implications of inferiority. I am not prepared, however, to impose that judgment of mine on the people of Mississippi or South Carolina or tell them what methods should be adopted and what pace should be kept in striving toward that goal.

In *Conscience* Goldwater called for "prompt, and final, termination of the farm subsidy program," and said, "The only way to persuade farmers to enter other fields of endeavor is to stop paying inefficient farmers for produce that cannot be sold at market prices."

This oversimplification of Goldwater's basic belief was to cost him dearly in 1964. He did, and does, believe it is wasteful to pay a man to produce something which is not wanted or needed. But in the political frame of reference, Goldwater has always argued that the subsidy program should be phased out gradually over a period of years. He says the federal government is responsible for the farmers' present problems and should accept responsibility for moving the farmer back into the free market, even if this should require substantial outlays of federal cash to train the farmer for a new occupation, to move him from his inefficient farm to a new location, and to retire his land from production.

In the book Goldwater expressed disappointment with his own party for not reducing the level of federal spending and described the graduated income tax as "confiscatory, a device intended to level all men to a common income and create an egalitarian society." He called for the abolition of the graduated features of the tax laws, and said: "The sooner we get at the job the better."

Such language is all very well for a theoretical primer on the ideal state, but in a political reference, Goldwater has never been so naïve as to believe the graduated provisions of the tax laws could be quickly or totally eliminated.

When the so-called Liberty Amendment was proposed as a method of abolishing the graduated income tax by amending the Constitution, Goldwater refused his support. He took it as a hopeful sign that Americans were concerning themselves about the tax problem, but he recognized that in the political world of the present such a revolutionary proposal would never be accepted.

In 1964 his aspiration was to stress the stifling effect which the graduated provisions exert upon the economy and to overhaul the tax structure in such a way as to minimize this influence.

Goldwater dealt bluntly with the Communist menace, saying, "If any enemy power is bent on conquering you and proposes to turn all of its resources to that end, he is at war with you, and unless you contemplate surrender, you are at war with him." In 1960 the words in *The Conscience of a Conservative* became a battle cry of freedom for millions of concerned Americans.

When Goldwater appeared before the Republican state convention in South Carolina in the spring of 1960, he went as a Republican committed to the nomination of Richard Nixon. He was hopeful that Nixon would identify with the conservative cause; he had absolutely no thoughts of seeking the nomination for himself. The South Carolina delegates, led by State Chairman Greg Shorey and National Committeeman Roger Milliken, responded to the Senator's dynamic challenge by pledging their delegation to his nomination for the Presidency in Chicago.

Most politicians would have been pleased at this evidence of popularity and confidence. Goldwater was deeply disturbed. He recognized that Richard Nixon had the nomination sewed up. Moreover, he believed that any contests at the convention in Chicago would harm the Republican chances for victory in November. Shorey and Milliken had acted without consulting Goldwater.

The Senator returned to Washington, made an appointment with the Vice-President, and explained how the momentary enthusiasm of the group had gotten out of hand. He told Nixon that he would not solicit support or give any encouragement to those who wanted him to become a serious contender. He also tried to explain to Nixon the amazing growth of conservative sentiment in the United States. He felt the Vice-President would do well to take this into account when the Platform was being written and in any public statements or speeches prior to the convention.

The action of the South Carolina convention placed Goldwater in an embarrassing position. Both Governor Paul Fannin of Arizona and State Chairman Dick Kleindienst had made prior commitments to Nixon.

Goldwater called a meeting of Arizona Republican leaders in his office in Phoenix following the South Carolina action. He explained that while he was personally in favor of the Vice-President, he did not want to go to Chicago without the backing of the

Arizona delegation. "I'd look like a fool to the rest of the country if South Carolina was for me and Arizona was for Nixon." When the party met in state convention, the Arizona Republicans enthusiastically endorsed Goldwater. It was assumed that Nixon would readily understand the reason for this public action.

When we left Phoenix for Chicago on July 17th, a week in advance of the scheduled opening of the 1960 convention, I had three statements in my briefcase—one, a press release to be made on Saturday the 23rd disclosing Goldwater's request that his name not be presented to the convention; the second, a statement he intended to deliver to the Platform committee; and the third, his recommendation that the Republicans consider issuing a brief statement of principles in place of the wordy collection of meaningless promises usually offered in party platforms. Goldwater did not expect the Platform committee to follow his advice, which was patterned after the action we had taken in Arizona in 1958. (In that year the party had issued a simple statement of principles, and the declaration had been well received.)

Two unexpected events occurred in Chicago. In combination they tempered Goldwater's determination not to be a candidate. The first was his appearance before the Platform committee. Goldwater's recommendation was enthusiastically welcomed (though never acted on), and the Senator detected a crystallization of conservative sentiment.

The second unforeseen development was the announcement on Saturday morning, July 23rd, that Nixon had gone to New York to discuss the Platform with Governor Rockefeller.

Goldwater was attending a meeting of the National Finance Committee when the story broke in Chicago. Len Hall, Nixon's campaign manager, was furious. He had not been advised in advance of the conference. Hall had served with distinction as chairman of the Republican National Committee; he had managed the successful re-election of Eisenhower in 1956. He had helped stop the effort to dump Nixon as vice-presidential nominee in that year. From a political standpoint the Nixon-Rockefeller meeting on the eve of the convention was, in Hall's opinion, a serious error.

Nixon was the frontrunner. Rockefeller was a half-official challenger. Had Rockefeller gone to Washington to see Nixon, the meeting would have carried the appearance of a weak contender attempting to reach an agreement with the leader.

When Nixon went to New York his action could be interpreted as evidence of uncertainty—a lack of confidence—and perhaps a willingness to compromise his position. Many of the delegates viewed the New York meeting as a Nixon surrender to the eastern liberal wing.

Goldwater, in an impromptu TV statement, described the get-together as "an American Munich." Then he instructed me not to go ahead with the planned release which would withdraw his name from consideration.

By Saturday afternoon the Goldwater supporters were pressuring the Senator to permit them to solicit delegates in his behalf. They wanted to make a real attempt to name him as the 1960 candidate. The Texas delegation, which had come to Chicago pledged to Nixon, held a special caucus and decided that their delegates could in good conscience vote for another candidate. They did not take formal action to give their support to Goldwater, but the implication was plain.

However, a majority of the delegates were morally and legally committed to Nixon as the result of primaries and state conventions. The Senator realized that to stay in contention and be defeated would give some commentators an excuse to describe this as a rejection of the conservative viewpoint.

Goldwater told those who came to see him that if he could be assured of three hundred votes by Tuesday night he would stay in the race. "We can't win" he said, "but we might make a respectable showing." The Senator refused to visit any of the state delegations or make any personal effort to gain additional votes. "It's my political neck they are putting on this chopping block," he would say, "and I don't know that I like it."

On Wednesday morning Goldwater informed the Arizona delegation that he did not want his name placed in nomination. Then we went across town to the South Carolina headquarters where he made the same statement.

Roger Milliken refused to accept the Senator's decision. "We were instructed by our state convention to vote this delegation for Senator Goldwater, and that's what we intend to do," he insisted.

We finally agreed that Arizona would nominate the Senator, South Carolina would make one of the seconding speeches, and Goldwater would come to the podium and ask that his name be withdrawn from consideration.

We chose Governor Paul Fannin of Arizona to make the nominating speech. I went to a borrowed office in the Loop and commenced writing the words which would place Goldwater's name before the convention. Dr. Kelley was assigned the task of writing the Senator's withdrawal statement.

Goldwater went back to the Blackstone and informed the Nixon camp that he was unable to prevent his supporters from going through the formality of placing his name before the convention. He said he would be on the platform to ask that his name be withdrawn and make a plea for party unity.

Governor Fannin, with less than an hour's preparation, outlined the reasons why the convention should consider naming Barry Goldwater as its 1960 candidate. But it was Goldwater's withdrawal speech which electrified the convention. He began:

> Mr. Chairman, delegates to the convention, and fellow Republicans: I respectfully ask the chairman to withdraw my name from nomination. [There was a roar of protest from the delegates.]
>
> Please, I release my delegations from their pledge to me and, while I am not a delegate, I would suggest that they give these votes to Richard Nixon.
>
> Now, Mr. Chairman, with your kind permission and indulgence, as a conservative Republican I would like to make a few statements that will not take more than a few minutes and I think might help in this coming election.
>
> We are conservatives. This great Republican party is our historic house. This is our home. Some of us do not agree with every statement in the official Platform of our party, but I might remind you this is always true in every Platform of an American political party.
>
> Both of the great historic parties represent a broad spectrum

of views spread over a variety of individual and group convictions. Never have all these views been expressed totally and exclusively in the Platform of either party, but we can be absolutely certain of one thing: in spite of the individual points of difference, the Republican Party Platform deserves the support of every American over the blueprint for socialism presented by the Democrats.

In less than a thousand words Goldwater urged the conservatives to give their enthusiastic support to Dick Nixon, warned that a split in the party would be disastrous, scolded those dissidents who out of pique threatened to stay home, and pledged his personal efforts to the election of the Republican nominee.

In any consideration of the reasons for the Republican loss in 1964, the difference between Chicago and San Francisco demands to be recognized. In Chicago many of the delegates were less than enthusiastic about the winner. But after Nixon's nomination they went home to give effective and determined support to the party's nominee. In San Francisco the delegates who were not enthusiastic about Goldwater went home and, following the examples set by Rockefeller and Romney, withheld their support for the party's nominee.

Goldwater in Chicago added a sense of dignity and purpose to an otherwise drab convention. When he was finished the delegates in the hall responded by giving him an almost unanimous spontaneous demonstration. Those who saw him on television or heard him on radio responded with thousands of letters and telegrams of encouragement and approval. On that evening the drive to nominate Goldwater for the President of the United States began. When Nixon lost in November by a tissue-thin margin to Jack Kennedy, the image of Goldwater emerged to dominate the thinking of hopeful Republicans in every section of the nation.

Part Two

The Draft

4

In politics as in war the propitious time to storm the citadel of the enemy is that moment when leadership is confused or absorbed with some internal conflict. The Republican party was both absorbed and confused in November of 1960.

The election of John F. Kennedy presented a number of vexing problems not readily apparent to the average citizen. With Eisenhower in the White House as a spokesman, the GOP had been able to maintain a position of dominance in the national press, even though its members were outnumbered in both House and Senate. This advantage would disappear with the inauguration of Kennedy.

Candidate Nixon had been sharply criticized for his conduct of the 1960 campaign. A great many influential Republicans—governors, senators, and members of the House—felt they had been ignored by the Nixon strategists. Conservatives charged Nixon's defeat to his close relationship with the liberal element represented by Arthur Flemming, former Secretary of Health, Education and Welfare, and William Rogers, former Attorney General. Nixon was accused of having failed to follow the advice of his campaign manager, Leonard Hall. He had, said his critics, traveled too far and said too little.

National Chairman, Senator Thruston Morton of Kentucky, who had succeeded to the post following the resignation of Meade Alcorn, was up for re-election in 1962, which made it impractical for him to continue serving in the party post. Those members of the National Committee who were not busy licking their wounds from November were busy speculating on Morton's successor.

The Democrats were preoccupied with inaugural plans, savoring the sweetness of a return to power. No one cared very much what the Republicans or any Republican might be planning.

The first meeting dedicated to securing the 1964 presidential nomination for Senator Goldwater was held at the Jefferson Hotel in Washington, D.C., in late November, 1960. Ostensibly we gathered to consider ways of minimizing the recent defeat, but six of the seven men who attended had their eyes on 1964.

In addition to Goldwater, those present were Roger Milliken, Republican national committeeman from South Carolina, the man who had insisted Goldwater be nominated in Chicago; G. R. Herberger of Minnesota and Arizona, a long-time Goldwater supporter and one of the most successful Republican fund raisers; Charles Barr of Chicago, considered the most knowledgeable Republican in the Midwest; Richard Herman, president of Herman Brothers Trucking Company of Omaha, Nebraska, who had successfully directed the 1960 campaign for United States Senator Carl Curtis in Douglas and Lincoln counties; and William R. Spear, former state chairman of Nebraska, invited because of his long experience in Republican politics.

I had called these men together because I believed that if there was to be any chance of nominating Goldwater in 1964, an early start was required.

The Senator was much more concerned about the future of the party than he was about his own position within the party. He insisted we direct our thoughts toward the consideration of a successor to Morton.

"What we ought to do," Goldwater said, "is find a competent, professional party organizer—the more experienced the better—and put him to work."

There was no one in the party who came nearer to meeting Goldwater's specifications than did the successful, professional Republican chairman of Ohio, Ray Bliss. But the national party post was an honorary position, and Bliss was a paid chairman at a salary reputed to be something over $25,000 a year.

"The fact we don't pay our national chairman might be a part of our problem," Goldwater argued.

Without in any way discrediting the contributions made by party chairmen who had given their time without pay, Goldwater insisted the job required the skillful touch of a full-time chairman. There was logic to support Goldwater's contention. We all agreed Ray Bliss would be an excellent choice if he would take on the job.

Goldwater called the Ohio chairman on the telephone. They talked for almost thirty minutes. Bliss was receptive to the proposition, but he did not want to seek the post if there was to be any opposition.

We agreed to contact our friends on the National Committee and urge the election of Bliss as a paid national chairman. We were confident that under his direction the organization work would be carried on without any ideological overtones. From our standpoint, the committee would be neutralized. Its power would not be used to advance Goldwater's candidacy; neither would it be used to help any other potential nominee.

Milliken and Barr were particularly insistent that Goldwater should attempt to retain his post as chairman of the Senatorial Campaign Committee. It would, they said, make it possible for him to visit every area of the country, increase his acquaintance with state and county chairmen, and strengthen his hold on the affections of rank-and-file members of the party.

The Senator was not at all sure that he wanted to continue in the job. To do so meant giving up virtually every hour of his spare time to the task, flying thousands of miles and being charged with failure if the Republicans lost any Senate seats in 1962.

In 1960 every Republican had been re-elected and one new seat had been gained. Goldwater could retire with a batting average of a thousand per cent.

The actual decision would be made by the other Republican members of the Senate. Our effort was aimed at persuading Goldwater to be available for re-election. We were confident most of the members of the class of 1960 would give him their support. Goldwater wanted to wait and see how things shaped up. But he did promise to keep an open mind about the chairmanship.

Despite the opposition of Senator Jacob Javits of New York, Goldwater was re-elected to head this important committee, but we failed in our efforts to put Ray Bliss in charge of the party effort. Internal opposition developed, and his name was never placed before the group. Instead, Congressman William E. Miller of New York was elected national chairman. The Ohio man accepted the decision with good grace, but some of his intimates believe he felt that Goldwater let him down, failed to come through with the promised support at the crucial moment.

After Goldwater became an announced candidate for the presidential nomination in 1964 and the drive was on to secure the support of the Ohio delegation, some Goldwater lieutenants came to the conclusion that Ray Bliss was opposed to the Senator's candidacy. Dick Kleindienst, director of field operations for the Goldwater for President Committee, disputes this claim and states emphatically that Ray Bliss was impartial, that he kept every commitment and was actually instrumental in the final switch from favorite son Governor James Rhodes to Goldwater in San Francisco.

Prior to the Republican defeat in 1960, Goldwater had concerned himself primarily with domestic issues. On November 14, 1960, before the Air War College in Montgomery, Alabama, Goldwater delivered a speech which became the basis for all of his later statements on foreign affairs. The Senator's second book, *Why Not Victory?*, was really an expansion of the Alabama statement.

In preparing for this appearance the Senator turned again to Brent Bozell, a recognized authority on Communist imperialism.

Goldwater took as his premise an assumption that the ultimate objective of American foreign policy must be to help establish a world in which there is the largest possible measure of freedom and justice, peace and material prosperity.

The Senator said America must use its power to resist Communist expansion. He attacked the Kennedy claim that we were in danger of becoming a second-rate military nation as the result of our failure to develop intercontinental ballistic missiles.

Deteriorating United States prestige, which had been one of the principal Kennedy charges, was disposed of in this paragraph:

Prestige is a measure of how other people think of you—well or ill. But contrary to what was implied during the campaign, prestige is surely not important for its own sake. Only the vain and incurably sentimental among us will lose sleep simply because foreign people are not as impressed by our strength as they ought to be. The thing to lose sleep over is what people, having concluded that we are weaker than we are, are likely to go off and do about it.

Goldwater touched on the Castro regime and argued that this Communist government must be eliminated. He suggested we should take responsibility for all of Africa and proceed on a long-range program of education in government, economics, agriculture, and industry which would one day elevate the African to a position where he would be capable of governing himself.

Goldwater said the proposals for disarmament being advanced by the Communists were offered only because of America's superior military capability. He said that to give away our advantage would be to weaken the American defense in the face of a determined enemy.

To state publicly that we "favored disarmament" was giving our enemies a propaganda weapon which Goldwater suggested might some day be used against us. He reminded his audience that after we had voluntarily suspended the testing of nuclear weapons, the Russians had callously resumed testing when it suited their over-all strategic purpose.

He said the United Nations "has its useful functions, but the formulation and conduct of American foreign policy is not among them."

Soldier Goldwater, the Air Force brigadier general, detesting the thought of war, spoke bluntly and frankly to his fellow officers who might one day be called upon to defend America against enemy aggression.

In the 1964 campaign, Goldwater suffered greatly because the Democrats charged him with being trigger happy and said he would take the nation to war to solve our foreign problems. The Montgomery, Alabama, speech, considered in its entirety, becomes a thoughtful, authoritative program for peace through strength.

"Free institutions and free governments are being challenged," Goldwater said, "by an implacable foe dedicated to their destruction. If we renounce in advance the right to resist Communist aggression with military strength," he argued, "we have in effect lost the battle and are merely waiting to arrange the terms of surrender."

In December, 1964, Harry Truman's Secretary of State, Dean Acheson, speaking at Amherst College, echoed the thoughts Goldwater had first voiced to that audience in Alabama. Acheson said:

> But you will say—surely the opinion of the world has condemned the use and threat of force. . . . does this not give us firm ground on which to stand? Well, does it? . . . Is it moral to deny ourselves the use of force in all circumstances when our adversaries employ it under handy excuses whenever it seems useful . . . ? It seems to me not only a bad bargain but a stupid one.

The Acheson statement was widely applauded by many of the same voices who in the 1964 campaign attacked Goldwater for his "warlike attitude."

Goldwater said, in this, his first lengthy discourse on foreign policy:

> Peace is a worthy objective. But if we must choose between peace and keeping the Communists out of Berlin, then we must fight.
>
> Freedom in the sense of self-determination is a worthy objective. But if granting self-determination to the Algerian rebels entails sweeping that area into the Sino-Soviet orbit, then Algerian freedom must be postponed.
>
> Justice is a worthy objective, but if justice for the Bantus entails driving the government of the Union of South Africa away from the West, then the Bantus must be prepared to carry their identification cards yet awhile longer.

Prosperity is a worthy objective, but if providing higher standards of living gets in the way of producing sufficient guns to resist communist aggression, then material sacrifices and denials will have to be made. It may be, of course, that such objectives can be pursued consistent with the policy designed to overthrow communism. My point is that where conflicts arise, they must always be resolved in favor of achieving the indispensable condition for a tolerable world—the absence of Soviet Communist power.

In this speech the Senator offered his listeners a real choice, not between war and peace but between a foreign policy designed to protect American interests as opposed to a foreign policy consisting primarily of reaction to events after the fact.

The press, lost in its admiration for the Kennedy victory, scarcely noticed what Goldwater said that November in Alabama. But his supporters studied the message, and their enthusiasm increased. It is interesting to speculate on what might have been the outcome in 1964 had the Goldwater campaign speeches been as carefully developed as the Goldwater statement on foreign policy delivered in 1960 to his comrades-at-arms.

Goldwater refused to give his blessing to the men who met at the Jefferson Hotel for the purpose of making him the 1964 Republican candidate. But the Senator's refusal, or reluctance—or perhaps it was superior political wisdom—did not lessen the determination of these men or affect their admiration for the Arizona Senator. On October 18, 1961, eleven months after that first meeting in Washington, twenty-two men from across the nation met at the Avenue Motel on South Michigan Avenue in Chicago. Of the original group, only Barr and Milliken were able to make the meeting.

Because I was then volunteer state chairman of the Republican party in Arizona and publicly identified as the manager of Goldwater's political activities, it seemed unwise for me to go. Certainly any premature disclosure of our ambition would have met with well-organized and probably effective opposition. It has been argued elsewhere that Goldwater actually received the nomination in 1964 by default, that is, the moderates and liberals did not organize behind a single candidate because they grossly underestimated the strength of Goldwater sentiment.

But in a very real sense Senator Barry Goldwater was nominated for President by the men who met in Chicago thirty-three months in advance of the Republican convention. This was the nucleus which produced the Draft Goldwater movement—twenty-two men from sixteen states bringing a variety of political experience to their selfassigned task.

Their names would not have attracted any great public attention even if their purpose had been known. Robert Morris, currently with the University of Dallas, one-time candidate for the Senate from New Jersey; David A. Nichols, chairman of the Maine State Republican Committee; Leonard E. Pasek, Kimberly-Clark Corporation, Neenah, Wisconsin; Speed Reavis, Jr., of Little Rock, Arkansas; John Keith Rehmann, of Des Moines, Iowa; William A. Rusher, publisher of *National Review;* Gregg D. Shorey, Greenville, South Carolina, former state chairman of the Republican Committee; Charles Thone, Lincoln, Nebraska, chairman of the Republican State Central Committee; Frank A. Whetstone of Montana, former Republican national committeeman; Congressman John M. Ashbrook of Ohio; Charles R. Barr of Chicago; James H. Boyce of Baton Rouge, Louisiana; Congressman Donald C. Bruce of Indianapolis; Robert F. Chapman, chairman of the South Carolina Republican party; Ned Cushing of Kansas, past chairman of the National Young Republicans; Sam Hay, former chairman of the Milwaukee county committee, Wisconsin; Robert E. Hughes, state treasurer of Indiana; Robert Matthews of Indianapolis; G. H. Milliken of Greenwich, Connecticut; and Roger Milliken of Spartanburg, national committeeman of South Carolina; Attorney Roger Allan Moore, general counsel for Republican committee of Massachusetts; and F. Clifton White of Rye, New York.

The lost cause, the forlorn hope, is celebrated in literature and history. It is doubtful if the circumstances of that Chicago meeting can be duplicated in American politics. The men who came together to nominate the Republican candidate were, in a sense, outside the Republican party because they did not represent its official hierarchy. They could not claim to speak on behalf of any organized segment of our political society.

The popularity of the incumbent Democrat President was becoming a national legend. The Republican party was torn with internal dissension. The candidate they wanted to support had refused to give them any encouragement. And the history of both parties suggested it would be impossible to nominate a candidate from an unimportant western state with only five votes in the Electoral College. Had these men been reasonable politicians, willing to settle for a goal reasonably attainable, they would have adjourned and gone back to their private pursuits.

At that first meeting very little attention was given to the obstacles. They were recognized and then dismissed.

On the positive side, these men were all passionately committed to the conservative political philosophy. They believed it was the destiny of the Republican party to perform as a national conservative political instrument. They found some encouragement in the readily documented growth of conservative thought. There was no guarantee their efforts would or could succeed. But they were compelled to make the effort.

F. Clifton White, a professor of political science who had deserted the classroom for the field of practical politics, was chosen to chair the group. White had once been a candidate for the Republican nomination for Congress in New York State. He had been a leader in the national Young Republican organization. With his partner, Joseph Ely, he conceived the "ECO" program (Effective Citizens Organization) and then persuaded the nation's industrial leaders that it was their responsibility to sponsor political education courses for their employees.

The group had been drawn together by mutual aspiration; Goldwater was their first choice to head the ticket in 1964. But they were all too wise to settle irrevocably on a single course of action. Instead they decided to dedicate their immediate efforts toward the building of a nationwide conservative movement within the Republican party. If men and women of conservative persuasion could be inspired to take an active part as precinct committeemen, county chairmen, members of executive committees, etc., a proper foundation for the campaign of 1964 could be built.

White was instructed to call on Goldwater in Washington and inform him of the group's intention in a general way without revealing their ultimate objective. It was believed Goldwater would denounce any attempt at this time to make him the nominee. But so long as the group maintained the fiction that their ambition was merely to strengthen the conservative cause, the Senator could be expected to give his wholehearted support.

Goldwater, who has always been cursed—or blessed—with an inner compulsion to be completely frank with his close associates, seriously questioned the wisdom of those of us who wanted him to become the Republican standard bearer. He had great respect for the powers of the Presidency. He was geniunely humble at the suggestion that he was the one man to lead the nation out of the wilderness of the welfare state and a foreign policy which appeared to be based upon appeasement.

When those close to the Senator tried to talk to him about the presidential possibility, he frequently became irritable and short-tempered.

Dick Kleindienst says that even after the official announcement was made in January, 1964, Goldwater had difficulty adjusting himself psychologically to the idea that he was the only man in the Republican party qualified to be President. In 1961 the Senator did not even want to talk about it.

The Draft Goldwater group, and that is what it truly was, met again in Chicago in December, and there were some new recruits: Wirt Yerger, chairman of the Republican party in Mississippi; Tad Smith, Texas state chairman; and Governor Don Nutter of Montana. White reported the results of his conversation with the Senator, and it was decided to open a full-time office in New York City. The country was divided into nine regions, with a volunteer coordinator assigned to each geographical section, and a budget of sixty-thousand dollars was adopted for the year 1962.

By the time Congress finally adjourned in the first year of the New Frontier, Goldwater was physically exhausted. He had made more than two hundred speeches in connection with his duties as chairman of the Senatorial Campaign Committee. When he came to the Western Republican Conference at Sun Valley, Idaho, in early September I was shocked by his appearance. He had lost weight, his hair was noticeably grayer, and the lines of fatigue were deeply etched in his face.

Goldwater held a news conference for the benefit of reporters and delivered a scheduled speech at the dinner meeting. Physical fatigue had put out the fire. The audience was polite but not enthusiastic. Those of us who were thinking about 1964 were deeply concerned. It was obvious that Goldwater had been driving himself too hard. After dinner he stayed up half the night discussing Republican problems with Idaho's Governor Bob Smylie. Goldwater had many friends in Idaho as a result of his numerous appearances, his column was in the *Boise Statesman,* and Smylie, who had to run for re-election in 1962, was eager to have Goldwater's advice and support.

When the conference adjourned on Sunday noon, I had the solid assurance of every western state chairman with the exception of two that if Goldwater would consent to seek the nomination in 1964, their state delegations would support him—a promise which was later honored in every state except Oregon and Alaska.

5

When Goldwater arrived in San Francisco following his appearance in Sun Valley, the ship on which he had booked passage to the Orient was strike bound. After five days of waiting for the dispute to be resolved, he canceled the Pacific trip and booked passage to Europe on a Norwegian freighter, the "M. S. Burrard." The vessel had accommodations for only a dozen passengers. The atmosphere was relaxed and casual. For Goldwater it was a magnificent opportunity to rest, to think, and to write.

Early in 1961, the McGraw-Hill Book Company had proposed publication in book form of some of the Senator's newspaper columns. Before the project was fully launched, Goldwater's editor decided it would be more valuable for him to do a book on foreign policy. There were no distractions or interruptions as the cargo vessel pursued its leisurely course down the west coast of North America, through the Panama Canal, and on to Europe. Goldwater, when not stretched out in the sun, spent his time writing.

A rapid two-finger typist, he enlarged and expanded on the ideas first presented before the Air War College. When they docked in Liverpool he sent the manuscript to McGraw-Hill to be edited. The book, *Why Not Victory?,* published early in 1962, was immediately accepted as a valuable addition to current conservative thinking.

The *Wall Street Journal* commented: "In a clear-cut style Senator Goldwater attacks the heart of various world problems, and most of the time his logic is irrefutable."

The *Saturday Review* said: "In Goldwater's book there is nothing of fanaticism . . . it is a reasoned analysis of the failures of foreign policy under the party that he opposes."

The *St. Louis Globe Democrat* recognized Goldwater as a potential standard bearer of the Republican party when it said: "His book is provocative. It should be read by all, even those who don't want to vote for Goldwater for President in 1964."

The introduction is worth rereading by anyone who truly wants to understand why so many Goldwater partisans were both offended and bewildered when the Democrats succeeded in branding their leader as a trigger-happy warmonger during the campaign of 1964.

> I am not calling for return to the naked power of politics of the nineteenth century. I am not asking that we declare hot war on Russia or turn a deaf ear to the pleas of help from destitute nations. I am willing to be as modern as anyone as long as modernism does not constitute a debasing of our traditional values. But if to be modern I must accede to policies that would turn the foreign affairs of the United States over to the United Nations, disarm our great military machine, welcome Red China into the Committee of Nations, give away our food and technical skills to the so-called neutralist nations, and get nothing in return . . . if this is what is meant, then indeed I am not modern and never want to be.

Goldwater returned from England refreshed in body and spirit, eager to formulate his political plans for 1962. The off-year elections for Congress offered a clue as to what might be expected in 1964. To maintain his position of leadership in the Republican party nationally, Goldwater believed it was necessary for the Republican party in Arizona to re-elect Governor Fannin, Congressman John Rhodes, and Attorney General Robert Pickrell.

Arizona's Democrat United States Senator, the honorable and highly respected Carl Hayden, would come up for re-election in 1962. Hayden was eighty-five years old. His wife, Nan, who had been an invalid for about fifteen years, had died, and the Senator was not fully recovered from this emotional shock. Some Hayden intimates believed he planned to retire and would not seek re-election.

Hayden was chairman of the Appropriations Committee, the senior member of the Senate in both age and years of service, and in the Congress seniority is the key to power. We knew that Eugene Pulliam, publisher of the *Arizona Republic* and the *Phoenix Gazette,* and editor William Mathews of the *Arizona Daily Star* would give their support to the long-time Democrat senator despite his age. There are no sure things in politics, but the odds were at least ninety to ten that Hayden would win if he stood for re-election.

This was the problem confronting the leadership of the Arizona Republican party when we gathered at the Hotel Westward Ho in Phoenix in mid December, 1961. Should we run any Republican in the event Hayden announced for re-election? Should we try to win against the odds? Or should we fill the ticket with a lamb willing to be sacrificed, a procedure the party had followed in 1956? We knew that any kind of senatorial effort would siphon money and manpower from other races where our chances for victory were far more promising.

The United States Senate has often been described as the world's most exclusive gentlemen's club. The members understand the need for partisan division on legislative proposals and political philosophy, but there is a generally accepted agreement that a member of the club does not go all out to defeat his colleague regardless of party lines.

Goldwater and Hayden were long-time personal friends, and although Hayden had gone through the motions of supporting a fellow Democrat in 1958, he had not thrown his whole weight into the effort to defeat Goldwater for re-election. There was another long-range reason for suggesting we should let Hayden run unopposed. Arizona's growth is certain to be limited unless a source of supplemental water is found. Since 1920 the state has been trying to secure authority for the diversion of Colorado River water into central Arizona. After years of litigation, the Supreme Court had rendered what appeared to be a favorable opinion. Hayden, as Chairman of the Appropriations Committee, was in a position to help Arizona get that water. If a Republican were to replace Hayden in the Senate after 1962 and the Central Arizona Project failed to pass, our party might be held responsible for frustrating the state's most vital aspiration.

To the practical politician the wisdom of conserving our resources by letting Hayden run unopposed was understood without any argument. But it is most difficult to persuade the rank and file of party members to accept such sophisticated reasoning. Before the meeting ended we took a secret ballot on the three alternatives—run a strong candidate and try to win, run a token candidate, postpone a decision until after Hayden announced his intentions. The third proposition received majority support and settled nothing.

Three days later a Glendale, Arizona, automobile dealer, Evan Mecham, who had been elected to the state Senate from Maricopa county in 1960, announced his intention to seek the Republican nomination for the United States Senate. Mecham had the support of Frank C. Brophy, a national director of the John Birch Society. This activist, anticommunist group had been strongly critical of Hayden's Senate record, and we feared that Mecham would wage a bitter, personal campaign. If he did, the entire Republican slate would suffer.

As state Republican chairman I had tried to explain the subtleties of the problem to Mecham and persuade him not to take any action until the party was in full agreement. He refused to listen.

The popularity of Goldwater and the Republican party was at its peak in Arizona. In my first full year as state chairman (1961) we had raised more than $125,000, enough to pay off the campaign debts hanging over from 1960 and finance the party operation for the balance of 1961, including a special election for a House seat in District Two, vacated when President Kennedy named Stewart Udall Secretary of Interior. In the spring of 1962, we repeated our fund-raising "Dinners with Barry" and produced almost two hundred thousand dollars.

But the Mecham candidacy continued to hang as a shadow threatening Republican party prosperity. In the months following his announcement he had distributed literature carrying a most unflattering picture of Senator Hayden, and many of his supporters were referring to Arizona's respected Democrat as "the senile senior senator."

On Monday morning, March 27th, Goldwater telephoned me from Washington to discuss the problem created by Mecham's candidacy. Hayden had made no official announcement, but it was no secret that he intended to seek re-election if he was still in good health in July, when candidates in Arizona are required to file their nominating petitions. It was this uncertainty which had prompted Goldwater's call. If Hayden did not run, there would be a real possibility of electing a second Republican from Arizona. Goldwater wanted a strong candidate; he suggested that I give some consideration to seeking the nomination myself or interest my predecessor as state chairman, Dick Kleindienst, in making the race.

It was a delicate situation, and I responded by asking the Senator if he intended to run for President in 1964 and, if so, whether he wanted me to run his campaign.

"I honestly don't know what I am going to do," he told me, "but if I do run, yes, I want you to manage the campaign."

"That solves my problem," I told him, "I would rather manage your campaign than run for the Senate."

"Being in the Senate wouldn't preclude that possibility at all," he said; "in fact, it might enhance it . . . you think it over."

It would have been politically expedient, safe and easy, to sit tight. If Hayden made a last-minute decision not to run, the Democrat party had two or three candidates waiting in the wings who could probably have defeated the announced Republican. The prospect of a bitter primary fight for the nomination to run against Hayden was not very appealing. But I was Goldwater's state chairman, and he had recognized what might be an opportunity to gain another seat for the Republican party. When I called him back that afternoon to tell him I had decided to make the race, he suggested I telephone Senator Hayden, whom we both admired, and explain to him that I was becoming a candidate because of my dissatisfaction with Mecham's tactics and that, in the event I won the nomination, my general election campaign would be aimed at the national administration and not at Hayden personally.

I made the call. The old gentleman let me know that he understood what I was trying to do and why I was doing it.

When the notice of my candidacy appeared in the papers, Senator Goldwater was on a speaking tour in Montana and Nebraska. The reporters were waiting for him when he returned to Washington the following Monday. "Had he instructed his Arizona campaign manager to enter the race against Hayden? Did this mean that Goldwater would actively campaign against the state's senior senator?"

Goldwater responded by saying that my announcement was news to him, that he would maintain strict neutrality during the primaries, and that he wished both candidates good luck.

From a political standpoint this statement was both wise and correct. As head of the Republican party in Arizona it would have been highly improper for Goldwater to interfere in a primary contest. Unfortunately for me, his necessary silence was interpreted by many Republicans as an indication of his opposition to my candidacy, and I lost the primary by about ten thousand votes.

In the meantime Hayden filed for re-election, and was unopposed in the primary. A temporary illness kept him from campaigning vigorously in the general election, but he won anyway.

Fannin, Rhodes, and the Republican attorney general, Bob Pickrell, were all re-elected, but the Mecham-Shadegg primary had an unfortunate effect upon party unity. It had been necessary for me to resign as state chairman when I became a candidate, and Dick Kleindienst, who had reluctantly returned to the job, was unable to continue in that post after the general election.

At the party convention called to elect a new chairman, Fannin, Rhodes, and Goldwater supported a southern Arizona cattleman and former member of the state legislature, Keith Brown. Mecham tried unsuccessfully to win the chairmanship, and his supporters were bitter in defeat. The fine sense of cooperation and unity which Goldwater had developed since 1952 was destroyed. The division carried over into the 1964 election, but those details belong in another chapter.

After my defeat Goldwater asked me to go to Oregon to help the Republican candidate for the Senate, and I went.

The off-year elections were inconclusive. The Republicans made no substantial gains, but they did not suffer any expensive losses either. After the administration tempered its position and failed to force "onsite" inspections in Cuba, there was a wave of antiadministration comment. Many Republican leaders believed the bold Kennedy Cuba action had ended in a Communist victory. There was talk that we had agreed to withdraw our missiles from bases in Turkey and Greece and had given Khrushchev a commitment not to mount or support a military invasion of Cuba in return for the removal of the Russian missiles from that island base.

Early in December, 1962, Goldwater came to my home. It was our first face-to-face meeting in more than six months. The Senator was dressed in khaki trousers and a short-sleeved, cotton T-shirt. He carefully avoided discussing events of the primary. We spent thirty minutes in pleasant, unimportant conversation. Finally he told me he had really come to ask if I would manage his campaign in 1964.

"For the Senate or for the Presidency?" I asked.

"I still haven't made up my mind," Goldwater said, "if it's for the Senate, you can do it with one hand tied behind your back. If it's for the big job, it will be that much tougher."

I told him I was eager to help, and before he left for Washington we decided to proceed on the assumption that he would run for reelection to the Senate. "If I change my mind," he said, "you can change your plans."

On February 9, 1963, Goldwater returned to Phoenix, and I went to his home to submit a preliminary draft of the procedures which I believed should be instituted immediately.

"Is it true that you are giving public-relations advice to the Salt River Project?" the Senator asked.

"Yes, it's true," I said.

"In that case, Steve, I don't think I can afford to have you connected with my campaign."

In September, 1962, Arizona Public Service, a private, investor-owned utilities system covering most of the state of Arizona, had launched an attack against the tax-exempt status of the Arizona pioneer reclamation district, the Salt River Project.

When the Arizona state legislature convened in January, 1963, the governor called attention to the fact that the project, the nation's first and most successful reclamation venture, was not contributing its fair share of taxes. In addition to delivering water to two hundred and forty thousand acres surrounding Phoenix, the project had developed a profitable electric utilities system which served thousands of nonfarm customers. Governor Fannin suggested the possibility of putting this utility property on the state tax rolls.

The conflict between these two giants was the renewal of an old dispute. There were good arguments to support both sides of the controversy. My association with the project as public-relations consultant dated back to the early 1940's. I had been serving in a similar capacity in 1957 when I started to work on Goldwater's re-election effort but had resigned to give my full attention to the campaign. Now Goldwater felt he could not be drawn into the controversy either by implication or association.

Ten days later the Senator wired from Washington to say that he had asked Denison Kitchel to serve as his campaign manager. Kitchel, a long-time friend of Goldwater's, was born in Bronxville, New York, and had come to Arizona after graduating from Yale University and Harvard Law School. He had married Naomi Douglas, daughter of Walter Douglas, long-time president of the Southern Pacific Railroad of Mexico. Her uncle, "Rawhide" Jimmy Douglas, had developed the copper empire which is now owned by Phelps Dodge, and Kitchel was a member of the firm which represented this corporation in Arizona. Lewis Douglas, director of the budget in the Roosevelt days and later ambassador to the Court of St. James, is Mrs. Kitchel's cousin. A one-time ardent New Dealer, Kitchel had changed his registration from Democrat to Republican after the 1950 election. His firm handled labor matters for Phelps Dodge and he had been a management witness before the McClellan Committee.

There was speculation in national and Arizona political circles and in the press over the choice of Kitchel as campaign manager. Some writers have suggested Goldwater was angry at me for entering the Senate race. Others have advanced a theory that we had a bitter quarrel over the authorship of the newspaper column, a collaboration which began and ended pleasantly for both of us. The only reason the Senator gave me was that my connection with the reclamation project might become a political liability. I had been retained by the project before Goldwater called on me in December, and I could not, with honor, refuse to carry out that commitment. The dispute was settled in the early spring in a manner satisfactory, or at least acceptable, to all parties, and the great explosion which Goldwater feared would upset both the political and economic patterns in Arizona was avoided.

6

Throughout the full year of 1962 Goldwater was aware of the effort being made by the men who had first met in Chicago in October, 1961. Most of the time he tolerated the movement as an activity helpful to the conservative cause.

When White opened an office, Suite 3505 of the Chanin Building in New York City, Goldwater simply refused to believe that such a small, underfinanced beginning would have any effect on the Republican decision in 1964. Unlike John F. Kennedy, who had eagerly and openly directed the organization which produced his nomination in 1960, Goldwater seemed to go out of his way to play down the possibility of his own candidacy.

The White group, at its second meeting in Chicago, had sought earnestly to find a name for the movement. It would have been a fatal mistake to include "Goldwater" in the title. Yet any phrase which did not carry the Senator's name failed to satisfy. They finally agreed to use no name at all—a decision which had many advantages. A committee without a name presents a difficult target for critics to attack. When Clif White and Rita Bree opened the office in New York, it was identified only by its address.

Most of the budget went for travel and correspondence. There was a time in midsummer of 1962 when it appeared the effort must fold for lack of financial support. White had to pay his travel expenses and the office rent out of personal funds. There was no money to pay a secretary and precious little for postage. William Rusher, publisher of *National Review* and one of the sponsors of that first meeting in Chicago, has described this period as "the group's Valley Forge."

If Goldwater had embraced the idea, adequate financial support would have been a minor problem. If he had firmly rejected the possibility of running for President in 1964, the group would probably have turned its efforts toward the election of conservative candidates to the Congress. In the twilight zone which existed the persistence of the committee becomes almost as remarkable as its ultimate success.

The governor of New York was busily campaigning for the Republican nomination. He had recruited a staff of researchers, speech writers, and political experts—all assembled in his handsome headquarters at 22 W. 55 Street in New York City. His advance men were in the field making overtures to such knowledgeable Republican organization men as Larry Lindemer, onetime state chairman in Michigan; Jean Tool, state chairman of Colorado; and Mort Frayn, the state chairman of Washington. A number of former Eisenhower associates were on the payroll, including speech writer Malcolm Moos.

George Hinman, the charming and urbane national committeeman for New York, traveled the nation cementing old realtionships with Republican party leaders. Those who were not particularly taken with the governor of New York were charmed by Hinman and his gracious wife, Barbara. Rockefeller had the money, the hired talent, and a passionate ambition. The White group had almost no money, no staff, and a candidate who did not want the nomination and did not believe he could be nominated.

The third gathering of the committee-without-a-name convened on April 13, 1962, in the Minnesota north woods. There were some new faces, but not many. The atmosphere was informal and relaxed. As one member remarked at the time, "It was a period when we had to feed on each other's enthusiasm and confidence."

White reported some modest results. He had found sentiment for Goldwater. But how could they tell its real strength when every approach had to be made indirectly, when there could be no mention of their candidate's name, when the committee itself was anonymous?

It was almost spring. Politicians and campaigns were beginning to blossom. The snow would soon melt and with it the nation's indifference toward its governors.

The professionals in the Republican party would be forced to give all of their attention to the immediate problems of November.

If things went badly for Republican candidates, what chance there ever might have been to defeat Kennedy in 1964 would lessen. Uncertainty is the compelling charm of a horse race or a football game or a World Series. There is always an uncertainty about the outcome of a political contest. But to the men who gathered at that northern meeting place where winter was playing its last encore, the spring and everything beyond was beset with an abnormal unpredictability.

The man they had chosen to support had given no indication that he would agree to become a candidate. The money they had sought to fiance their venture had not been raised. The party they sought to re-establish in power was torn by factional disputes. Richard Nixon was seeking to make a political comeback in California. Rockefeller supporters boasted their champion would impress the nation with the magnitude of his re-election victory. These men were not novices playing in a new arena. They were neither innocent nor naïve. They were not seeking power or glory or prestige for themselves. They believed.

They believed their country was in danger; they listened soberly when White reported how the death of Governor Don Nutter of Montana had affected the outlook in the Rocky Mountain region. Nutter had joined the group at the December, 1961, meeting. He was the only Republican governor who had been willing to support Goldwater openly.* And now he was gone, killed in the crash of a faulty National Guard airplane.

Despite all the circumstances which argued against success, the mood at the meeting was optimistic. White reported that Goldwater supporters in the Southwest planned to get together in Phoenix in late May or early June. Among those attending would be John Tyler, the national committeeman from Oklahoma; Tad Smith, state chairman of Texas; Joe Skeen, state chairman of New Mexico; and half a dozen others.

The committee, after two days of discussion, adjourned. Its members went to their respective homes, committed to carry on quietly, to work and wait and hope that the outcome in November would bring an end to uncertainty.

* Fannin of Arizona had not been invited to participate. It was felt his presence might lead to public identification of the Goldwater candidacy.

October with its Cuban crisis and November with the midterm election, which no one could construe as conclusive, brought encouragement in the form of negative results in two races: Nixon lost his bid for the governorship of California; Rockefeller was reelected, but his margin of victory was substantially less than his supporters had predicted. Republicans in the South—Charlton Lyons of Louisiana and James Martin in Alabama, Lyons running for governor and Martin for the United States Senate—had shown surprising strength.

When the committee met in Chicago in December, 1962 (the much-publicized secret meeting), it had more than doubled in size. John Grenier, the youthful state chairman of Alabama whose candidate Martin had come within less than 1 per cent of defeating the veteran Democrat Lister Hill, and Peter O'Donnell, vigorous, thirty-eight-year-old state chairman of Texas, insisted it was time to end the waiting game.

"If Goldwater doesn't want to make up his mind, we will draft him," O'Donnell declared, "and because he might say 'no,' we'll tell him what we're going to do. We won't ask his permission to do it."

There were no dissenting voices. White was instructed to call on Goldwater at the earliest possible moment and inform him that the "Draft Goldwater Committee" intended to conduct a nationwide campaign among Republicans to make him the 1964 presidential candidate.

Three times before the group had met and planned and dreamed without attracting any attention or notice from the press—a rather remarkable achievement. Perhaps those earlier meetings were ignored because the nation's newsmen, who might have heard what was going on, refused to take the effort seriously. It is asking almost too much to believe that not a single reporter anywhere in the United States had been aware of this small buzzing in the ear of the elephant.

The December meeting stirred up the hornets. The columnists and the editorial writers and the TV commentators treated the matter as though they had discovered an incipient rebellion, a threat against the dearly beloved *status quo*. And the secret meeting was not a secret twenty-four hours after the committee adjourned.

When Clif White called on Goldwater in mid January to inform him of what he already knew, the Senator made no attempt to conceal his annoyance.

"I won't be painted into a corner," he told White. "It's my political neck, and I intend to have something to say about what happens to it."

White left the Senator's office convinced that his work had been wasted. The reasons for Goldwater's reluctance were, in White's mind, painfully logical. The Senator's term expired in 1964. If he became a candidate, it would mean relinquishing his Senate seat. The Republican party had carried on a torrid romance with conservative Robert Taft in 1951 and 1952 and then left him waiting at the church when Dewey, Brownell, and Lodge engineered the nomination of Dwight Eisenhower.

True, President Kennedy, in the eyes of the conservative Republicans, had made a number of serious errors. But his personal popularity had increased rather than diminished. And to project the defeat of a popular first-term President was contrary to all the traditions of American politics.

The next logical step—and indeed the only procedure open to White—was to call a meeting of his executive committee to permit the orderly liquidation of more than two years of effort.

Chicago is the convenient hub of most of the nation's major airlines. For this reason the meeting was set for the O'Hare Inn on Sunday, February 17th. What might have been the dismal epilogue of a forlorn hope became instead the almost defiant beginning of an event which will long be debated by men interested in politics.

If Goldwater would not consent to run, they would draft him anyway. The work which had been done in the precinct elections and the county conventions would have to speak for itself. Peter O'Donnell was elected chairman of the Draft Goldwater Committee. It was believed that since O'Donnell was the Texas state party chairman, representing a growing Republican territory with twenty-five votes in the Electoral College, Goldwater would be required to consider seriously the advisability of an outright repudiation.

Clif White was named executive director. Senator John Tower of Texas and Senator Carl Curtis of Nebraska encouraged the movement and promised to help. Congressman John Rhodes of Arizona assured O'Donnell that Goldwater would have the support of a substantial number of respected members of Congress.

On April 8, 1963, the National Draft Goldwater Committee called a press conference in the Mayflower Hotel in Washington, D.C. Clif White and Rita Bree transferred their base of operations from Suite 3505 in Manhattan to a newly opened headquarters on Connecticut Avenue in the District of Columbia.

On the Fourth of July the Draft Goldwater Committee filled the District of Columbia stadium with enthusiastic, cheering Goldwater supporters. The man they hoped to make President of the United States was in Arizona. Tower of Texas predicted victory, and his words were more significant than the attendant press recognized.

On the day it was born the Draft Goldwater Committee possessed considerable political muscle. There were Draft Goldwater chairmen in thirty-three of the fifty states. These chairmen were supported by active committees reaching into a majority of the cities and towns. And now, with the movement out in the open, the support came from where it counted—from precinct committeemen, legislative district chairmen, county leaders, and members of the National Committee.

Politicians speak reverently of organization, issues, a pleasant image, the ability to arouse enthusiasm as essential to victory. Yet the most important ingredient for success at the polls is a sense of timing. The hopeful who announces too early is frequently exhausted before the contest actually begins. The cautious one who waits until it is too late has trouble catching up.

In the twenty-nine-month period between November, 1960, and April, 1963, Goldwater skillfully avoided any commitment to seek the Republican nomination. This was good politics, but Goldwater's motives were not political. His appearance of being an off-again-on-again presidential aspirant was an honest and sincere reflection of his inability to agree with those who were saying that Barry Goldwater was the only Republican who had any chance at all of winning in 1964.

When Peter O'Donnell and Clif White brought the draft movement into the open in the early spring, Goldwater flatly refused any encouragement.

O'Donnell, a hard-driving organizational politician whose experience had been gained winning victories against registration odds in Dallas County, Texas, was not particularly pleased with what he found in Washington. His only avenue of approach to Goldwater was through Senator Tower. On the few occasions when a contact was made Goldwater did not appear to be interested.

As O'Donnell saw it, the Draft Goldwater movement was stuck on dead center. Katharine Kennedy Brown, the long-time national committeewoman of Ohio, had refused to serve as co-chairman. No vigorous effort was being made to collect the financial support which had been promised at the Chicago meeting in December. "We're like a wet noodle," he told friends. "This thing will surprise people if it ever gets started, but right now it isn't started."

O'Donnell was not asking that Goldwater make any public announcement, but he did seek assurances that if the Draft movement successfully enlisted support throughout the nation, Goldwater would become a candidate. Republican regulars were not ready to commit themselves eighteen months before the convention. O'Donnell believed the Goldwater people could go around the party functionaries and enlist the kind of supporters who could put pressure on the hierarchy at the proper time.

Four months before the Draft Goldwater movement was announced in Washington, a group of the Senator's Arizona supporters created a national Goldwater for President Committee with headquarters in Phoenix. The leading movers were all respected citizens, but they were not experienced in politics. This group began to solicit funds, print literature, and grant charters to Goldwater committees around the country. During the early spring the original organizers resigned, and their successors, under the leadership of Jay O'Malley, a nominal Democrat, emerged as a truly effective force behind the Goldwater drive for nomination.

When Kitchel's appointment as campaign director for the Senator's re-election effort in Arizona was announced in February, 1963, his friends expected there would be some immediate local activity. Instead of concentrating on the development of an organization at home, Kitchel went to Washington for a "planning session" with the Senator. And for the next four months he commuted between the nation's capital and his law office in Phoenix.

In midsummer Kitchel moved to Washington, rented an apartment in the same Westchester complex where the Goldwaters lived and opened a campaign office at the Carroll Arms, across the street from the old Senate Office Building.

Did this mean that Goldwater was going to seek the Republican nomination? "Not at all," Kitchel said, "it just means I can be more effective here with the Senator as we work out our plans for 1964."

Knowledgeable observers accepted the disclaimer with a very large grain of salt. Goldwater's nationwide popularity was increasing rapidly. Rockefeller's divorce and remarriage had made the governor of New York a less attractive candidate in the eyes of many Republicans. The day for decision was near.

In this period Goldwater was repeatedly encouraged by his friends in the Senate to enlist the kind of professional staff they regarded as essential to success. The Senator brushed aside such suggestions, saying that it seemed to him he was "doing all right pooping along all by myself."

It is impossible to attempt to identify all of the friends and advisers who were insisting the Senator should become a candidate. Among his earliest supporters in the Senate were Norris Cotton of New Hampshire, John Tower of Texas, Carl Curtis of Nebraska, Karl Mundt of South Dakota, Milward Simpson of Wyoming, and Len Jordan of Idaho. But there were others. On the House side it would be necessary to list John Rhodes of Arizona, Bruce Alger and Ed Foreman of Texas, Bob Dole of Kansas, Melvin Laird of Wisconsin, Robert Michel and Edward Derwinski of Illinois, and Jack Westland of Washington.

Goldwater's senatorial staff, particularly his long-time secretary and confidante, Edna Coerver; his publicist, Tony Smith; and his administrative assistant, Ted Kazy, were supremely confident. They insisted Goldwater could have the nomination for the asking.

Dr. Charles Kelley and Mike Bernstein did not share this optimism. They believed Goldwater might win the nomination, primarily because you cannot beat somebody with nobody and the liberals appeared unable to settle on a single candidate. But Bernstein and Kelley, refusing to let emotion cloud their vision, insisted it would take some kind of a miracle to enable Goldwater to defeat John F. Kennedy.

In this supercharged atmosphere of power politics Kitchel moved with great caution. He refused to go near the Draft headquarters on Connecticut Avenue; he avoided the press. Most of the Republicans he met in these first weeks came away with the impression that Goldwater's new manager was cold, distant, and unapproachable.

"That guy just doesn't like politicians," one national committeeman remarked after being introduced to Kitchel. "He didn't want to hear anything I had to say."

These unfortunate first impressions may have resulted from the fact that Kitchel is hard of hearing. More probably, Kitchel's response was an indication of uncertainty. He had no background in politics to enable him to judge the sincerity of the men who came to see him. In an attempt to overcome this deficiency, Clif White made up what might be called a Political Handicapper's Form Book, giving the pedigree and past performances, titles and connections of all the important Republican politicians. But a book is a poor substitute for long personal acquaintance. Once when a friend advised Kitchel to take a particular problem to Arthur Summerfield and ask for help, Kitchel said, "I'll do it if you say so, but who is Arthur Summerfield?"

The story of this exchange was too good to keep. It went the rounds in Washington. Goldwater's manager did not even know the name of the man who had been Postmaster General under Eisenhower and a successful national chairman of the Republican party.

7

During the summer and early fall of 1963 the Draft Goldwater Committee continued to work in the precincts and in the county and state conventions without any help or encouragement from the Senator or from his campaign manager, Denison Kitchel.

Peter O'Donnell is young, aggressive, and impatient. His understanding of what should be done to win the nomination for Goldwater was based on experience gained in the precincts where the votes are counted. Kitchel, who had passed his fiftieth birthday before becoming involved in any campaign, was cautious and noncommittal. In the secure world he had inhabited as a wealthy corporation lawyer there had always been time to ponder and speculate and theorize. To him O'Donnell's sense of urgency appeared to be almost impetuous. O'Donnell found Kitchel's detachment infuriating. After their first meetings a within-the-organization stalemate developed. Kitchel, who was reflecting Goldwater's reluctance to make a commitment, refused to act on or urge the Senator to accept any of O'Donnell's suggestions. O'Donnell, repeatedly rebuffed, reached the conclusion that Kitchel either would not or could not understand the political moves necessary for success.

Policy prevented Kitchel from consulting with Clif White; his personality blocked the road to O'Donnell. And Kitchel's natural inclination to withdraw into that small group then accepted as Goldwater advisers was encouraged. Mike Bernstein and Dr. Charles Kelley were two dependable members of this group. Through them Kitchel met William Joseph Baroody, Sr.

Forty-eight-year-old Bill Baroody has developed the American

Enterprise Institute, a nonprofit foundation, from a small and uncertain beginning to a position of power and influence behind the scenes in Washington. Baroody, who at one time worked in the Department of Health, Education and Welfare for the Democrats, has built a large and impressive stable of full-time and part-time academicians.

The institute, originally an association, quietly contributes research material to members of Congress. Professor Gerhart Niemeyer, was first brought to the Senator's attention by Baroody. Professor Warren Nutter of the University of Virginia, a recognized expert on Soviet economics, is on the institute staff. Glen Campbell of the Hoover Institute in Palo Alto is an associate. Bud Mote, former administrative assistant to United States Senator Carl Curtis of Nebraska, joined the Baroody group full time in 1962.

Kitchel found Baroody and his coterie of intellectual companions irresistible. In many ways these two men are strikingly similar. Both are slightly under average height; both shy away from publicity—Baroody for professional reasons and Kitchel by nature. Baroody, whose salary from the institute is reputed to be one hundred thousand dollars a year, can indulge himself in a scholarly detachment from the world of practical politics. And Kitchel, who has always been financially able to create an environment to his liking, was fascinated with the theoretical approach to selfgovernment.

Kitchel and his wife became inner members of the select society of the institute and participated in the long evenings of political discussion which took place at Baroody's home. When Arizona visitors called at the Kitchel apartment they were shown a shelf filled with mementos of the Baroody-sponsored intellectual soirees.

Although the institute works primarily for politicians, Baroody will not identify himself either as a conservative or a liberal. On his office wall there is a framed letter written by Hubert Humphrey commending the institute for its assistance to him. With the exception of Ed McCabe, a Washington lawyer who held an administrative post in the Eisenhower administration, and Bud Mote, no one on the paid staff has any extensive political background.

By early fall Kitchel, Baroody, and McCabe were meeting regularly. Sometimes they were joined by the Senator, but more often than not Goldwater's duties in the Senate and his speaking dates around the country prevented him from participating in their discussions.

Being closest to a man who might become President is the next best thing to being closest to the President himself. To maintain this position near the throne, Kitchel, Baroody, and McCabe found it necessary to protect the King from the other members of the Court. Kitchel's personal loyalty to Goldwater cannot be questioned. His admiration for the Senator is almost idolatrous; he believed Goldwater's political instinct infallible. When O'Donnell suggested that the Senator should change his tactics and adopt a new strategy, Kitchel instinctively resisted the suggestion, regarding the advice as an implied criticism of the master. When Dr. Kelley and Bernstein pointed to the obstacles standing in the way of Goldwater's election, their observations were distasteful to the one man who believed until late in the afternoon of November 3, 1964, that Goldwater was destined to be the President.

As the campaign developed after San Francisco, many observers remarked that Goldwater seemed to have deserted his old circle of advisers in favor of a brain trust recruited through Baroody's institute. An event which bears upon this separation and substitution took place in Washington in early September, 1963.

Bill Buckley, the brilliant, articulate spokesman for conservatism and founder of *National Review,* wanted to suggest the creation of a committee of college professors who would endorse Goldwater and who could provide respectable intellectual support for the Senator's position. Buckley contacted Dr. Charles Kelley, and a dinner was arranged. When Buckley and Brent Bozell, the man who helped Goldwater write *The Conscience of a Conservative,* arrived at Kelley's hotel suite, they were surprised to find that Kitchel and Baroody had been included. In addition to the proposal to form an academic committee, Buckley had a second purpose for desiring the meeting. He wanted to put Goldwater in touch with a man who was ready and eager to make a sizable political contribution in cash. The public has been taught to believe that campaign contributions are made by men with evil motives. This is particularly true if the amount involved is more than a few hundred dollars, and candidates want such matters handled with great discretion. The public attitude is paradoxical—campaigns cost millions of dollars, and no candidate could afford to finance the cost personally. Muckraking columnists seem to make a scandal out of even relatively insignificant sums of money, and this offer of cash was not something to be discussed in front of Baroody and Kitchel; so Buckley confined his remarks to an elaboration of the committee idea. A day or so later the *New York Times* printed the following story under the headline: "Goldwater Aides Counter-right . . . :"

> The Goldwater for President ship has just repelled a boarding party from the forces who supposedly occupy the narrow territory to the right of the Arizona Senator.
>
> William F. Buckley, Jr., editor of the right-wing *National Review,* and L. Brent Bozell, who also writes for the magazine, cornered some Goldwater aides the other day. They wanted to join the campaign organization, they said, on the policy-planning level.
>
> Feeling that what their candidate needs least is more support from the far right, Goldwater advisers used an old political dodge. They played dumb. They just could not seem to understand what the *National Review* men were getting at. Mr. Buckley and Mr. Bozell reportedly emerged from the conference with no share of the Goldwater command and wondering if they wanted any.

The *Times* story offended and alarmed both Buckley and Bozell. It seemed obvious someone had talked. But who, and why? The item had the appearance of being an official declaration by Goldwater or Kitchel that the *National Review* people, who had given such strong and early support to the Senator, were no longer wanted.

Bozell, who told me about the incident, said: "It had an aura of authenticity about it which put you off the idea that some wicked old *Times* guy just made it up."

Since neither Buckley nor Bozell intended to join the movement but merely wanted to give occasional help, Buckley telephoned Kitchel to find the source of the leak. The Senator's manager was in California. He insisted that he had not discussed the meeting with anyone. And the fact that he had no intimate newspaper contacts supported his denial.

Dr. Kelley had told one member of the Goldwater staff about the meeting but had not revealed Buckley's proposal or Kitchel's reaction to the suggestion.

When Bill Baroody was asked about the leak, he suggested that perhaps the room had been bugged. Anyone who planted a listening device in Kelley's hotel suite would have required advance knowledge of the meeting, plus an indication that something worth bugging was going to be discussed. Baroody's explanation was defensive and illogical. The *Times* story had been planted by someone who participated in the discussion. After September, Buckley and Bozell had very little contact with the Senator or with his campaign manager.

When Goldwater went to the Western States Republican Conference at Eugene, Oregon, in October, 1963, he was accompanied by Kitchel, Tony Smith, and Karl Hess. Smith had joined the Senator's staff following the 1960 Republican convention. A competent and well-liked newspaperman, he had served on the staff of *Human Events,* a conservative Washington newsletter. Goldwater's emergence as a national political figure prompted some of his friends to suggest that he hire a full-time publicity man, and Smith had been recommended for the job.

Hess, a free-lance writer, had worked for Ralph de Toledano on the *Washington World,* a conservative weekly news magazine financed by Willard Garvey of Wichita, Kansas. He had also contributed to the *American Mercury,* but in 1963 he was associated with the American Enterprise Institute, and Bill Baroody had made him available to write speeches for Goldwater.

The Senator's principal address at Eugene was delivered at

seven o'clock in MacArthur Court. Travis Cross, press secretary to Governor Hatfield of Oregon, estimates that ten or eleven thousand people crowded the university center to hear Goldwater.

It is probable that the Senator and many of the people in the audience were exhausted after a long day of conferences and speeches. Doug McKean of the *Portland Journal* and Merv Schoemaker of the *Oregonian* wrote stories suggesting that the Senator's speech produced an audience reaction something less than wildly enthusiastic.

From MacArthur Court, Goldwater was taken to the fair grounds where delegates to the conference had gathered to enjoy a social hour. The master of ceremonies talked endlessly on the glories of Columbus Day. When the Senator was finally introduced, he responded with some very brief comments, then asked to be excused, saying the National Committee had kept him going day and night, he and his wife were very tired, they were going to the hotel to catch up on their rest. Then he added a flip remark—something to the effect that sleeping with a grandmother could be very restful.

Had the words been said in Arizona where everyone knows and admires Peggy Goldwater (a remarkably young looking grandmother), they would have been accepted and dismissed. Unfortunately, some in the audience took offense, and six months later when Goldwater was seeking support in the Republican primary for the presidential nomination, a number of Oregon Republicans quoted the Eugene statement as their reason for not wanting to vote for Goldwater.

When I went to Portland in mid February, 1964, to help organize the Goldwater primary campaign, I discovered a second unfortunate aftermath of that Eugene appearance. Before he left the fair grounds, Goldwater invited any Arizona Republicans in the audience to his hotel, explaining that he wanted to keep his home fences mended. It was the tagline of this invitation which produced the trouble. There was a suggestion that the refreshments he planned to serve were not nonalcoholic.

Some voters believe public officials should follow a double standard—pretend to be alabaster saints. Whenever a man in public life refuses to maintain the façade of hypocrisy these people react with a phony but violent indignation. Some of those who complained most bitterly about Goldwater's behavior at Eugene did so over a cocktail glass.

Governor Fannin, who was with Goldwater at the fair grounds, puts the blame for the entire incident on Goldwater's staff: "Barry didn't know until we got there that he was supposed to make another speech," Fannin told me, "and by the time we arrived that crowd was in no mood to hear a serious discussion of the problems of state."

According to Fannin, the social hour had started about the time Goldwater was introduced in MacArthur Court. Those who chose to do so had enjoyed something stronger than orange juice. Goldwater was required to speak—without advance preparation—to an audience which might have been willing to be entertained, but was in no mood to listen to a serious message.

There is an old superstition that trouble always comes in threes. Goldwater's Oregon visit seems to bear this out. Smith and Hess brought only a half-dozen copies of the text of the Goldwater major address. A hundred newspaper men were clamoring for copies. Volunteers spent most of the night laboring over typewriters and mimeographs to satisfy the demand.

By the end of October, 1963, Goldwater began to give indications that he intended to seek the Republican nomination. Kitchel expanded his operations at the Carroll Arms office. He announced that all the Goldwater speeches and writings were being put on an electronic memory device. This machine, he told the press, would permit the Senator's staff to give them exact quotations on every subject the Senator had ever discussed.

At another location in Washington, Dr. Kelley directed a small staff geared to political research but this function was kept secret from the press. Kelley believed that if Goldwater were going to run, he would need a complete record of the Kennedy administration and all of President Kennedy's public statements.

Dean Burch, a thirty-five-year-old Tucson lawyer, was hired to serve as Kitchel's administrative assistant. Burch, a native of

Oklahoma, had attended the University of Arizona Law School, then served by appointment on the staff of Arizona's Republican attorney general, Ross Jones.

When Jones was defeated for re-election, Burch moved to Washington and joined Senator Goldwater's staff as a legislative assistant. In 1958 he was promoted to the position of chief administrative assistant to the Senator. During the 1958 campaign Burch was in charge of the Senator's Washington office. He returned to Arizona in the final weeks of that battle and accompanied Goldwater on his speaking tour of Arizona.

In 1959 Burch resigned to enter the private practice of law in Tucson. It is a common practice among members of Congress to maintain offices in their home states, staffed by full- or part-time secretaries. Burch continued his relationship with Goldwater as a part-time assistant for southern Arizona. His move to Washington in early November, 1963, was a clear indication that the Carroll Arms operation headed by Kitchel was concerned with something more than Goldwater's re-election to the Senate.

Nelson Rockefeller made his announcement that he would seek the presidential nomination on November 7th. Goldwater's declaration was delayed by the death of Mrs. Goldwater's mother in Muncie, Indiana. But the decision had been made. Goldwater would run.

Part of the public confusion over the Goldwater decision to run for the Presidency results from the fact that there were two, perhaps three, such decisions. Dean Burch says that when Kitchel asked him to come to Washington the decision had been made. Then in October the Senator officially advised the group which included William Knowland, Kitchel, Baroody, McCabe, Hess, and Senators Curtis and Cotton, that he had decided to run.

Yet when Kennedy was shot in Dallas on November 22nd, Goldwater still had not publicly committed himself. The escape hatch was open. Goldwater's immediate personal reaction was to step out. He had never been victim of that compelling inner drive which forces some men to seek high public office. He was comfortable and at home in the Senate. Re-election would be no real problem, and he was deeply disturbed by the assassination and by all the implications in that act of violence.

There was nothing phony or conventional or put-on about Goldwater's reaction to the assassination in Dallas. That this outrage could have taken place in civilized America was incomprehensible and totally unacceptable. Goldwater and the President had been political antagonists—they were separated by a wide philosophical difference—but their personal relationship, based on mutual respect, had been warm and friendly.

The official blundering which permitted the murder of Oswald before he could be questioned added to the darkness of that hour. Goldwater, who detests violence in any form, who hunts game with a camera not a rifle, whose interest in weapons is that of a marksman and a collector of antique shooting irons, declared a moratorium on politics. He ordered the Draft movement to suspend its operations.

8

If dreams are fragile things with gossamer wings, political candidates and campaigns are no less delicate. All dreamers are acutely responsive to the smiles and scowls of their environment; men and women who aspire to public office are also sensitive.

The politician is required to please and satisfy a thousand different publics. He must correctly sense and identify the sectional, ethnic, chronological, economic, educational, spiritual, and geographical differences which divide his constituency. He must endure unjust criticism with equanimity. When physically exhausted he must present the appearance of fresh enthusiasm. Above all else, he must be sustained by a belief that his victory will benefit those he seeks to serve.

Some men are supported by a limitless ego which blocks off any introspective examinations. Completely confident of their own superiority, they approach public office with the attitude of a prince born to be crowned. Other men, aware of their own limitations, are driven by an overwhelming ambition which enables them to connive, cheat, lie, and ruthlessly destroy their opponents without any sense of guilt.

It has been claimed that Barry Goldwater is the only man in American history to be nominated for the Presidency by a major political party as the result of a genuine draft. This is true. The public—long disillusioned by the many phony drafts of the past inspired by eager office seekers—was correct in the skepticism it exhibited toward the Draft Goldwater movement. But every observer who enjoyed meaningful contact with the Senator from Arizona has described Goldwater's reluctance to be a candidate as genuine.

History suggests that nations and governments survive or fall as the result of seemingly minor incidents, produced in the most part by an error of judgment or a stubborn unwillingness on the part of men who have assayed the shaping of destiny.

The mind of the candidate, the attitude brought by the leader to the contest, may well determine the outcome. Did Senator Barry Goldwater in 1964 fully accept the idea of one day serving as President of the United States? When a slight breath of wind in the leaves of discontent among the Republican delegates suggested such a role in 1960, the Senator angrily rejected the idea of becoming a serious contender for the nomination.

At that November, 1960, gathering in the Jefferson Hotel in Washington he refused to permit the men who were his close friends and long-time associates to initiate any program aimed at his nomination.

When news of the Draft Goldwater meeting held in Chicago in December, 1962, leaked to the press, Goldwater was furious. And when O'Donnell, White, and Company moved from Suite 3505 to a headquarters on Connecticut Avenue and made a public announcement of their intentions, Goldwater's attitude was acutely negative.

Goldwater has been called stubborn, stupid, arrogant, and inept by his detractors. No one has ever accused him of being coy or sly or a practitioner of political double talk and duplicity. Throughout his political life, and particularly during the 1964 presidential campaign, politicians attached to Goldwater winced at his blunt speech, his willingness to take a stand on any issue, his doing the unnecessary, his saying things that need not have been said. No man in public life has been more generously or completely condemned by his critics. But even those to whom his name is anathema have been afraid to accuse him of cowardice, knowing such a charge would be met with derisive disbelief.

No observer is ever commissioned or qualified to claim an understanding of the hopes and fears and beliefs which combine to become the inner thoughts of a fellow human being. It would be a gross impertinence to suggest in these pages that I or anyone else had access to all that was going on in the mind of Goldwater in the years preceding his campaign for election as President of the United States. Yet any real search for an understanding of what happened to Goldwater (in that campaign) without a serious effort to examine the factors which necessarily exerted a powerful influence on Goldwater's thinking would become a superficial ritual.

His attitude of almost reverential patriotism is completely documented. Goldwater's grandfather was a Polish-Jewish immigrant forced to flee the persecution in his homeland. His escape to America took him out of the ghetto. On the western frontier he found an opportunity to become a financial success. Perhaps even more significant, in the new territory of Arizona the Goldwaters were accepted.

The Senator has said, "I had to go back east and leave Arizona before I found out that Jews were somehow different from other Americans."

As a child in a frontier community Goldwater absorbed the traditions of manliness and independence typical of the western frontier. In those early days the East, that area of civilization and culture between the Atlantic Ocean and the Mississippi River, was separated from the West by more than distance. The East had tradition and class and financial power; the West was identified with the vulgar necessity of survival in a hostile environment. No one said it publicly, but it was there all the same, an inescapable acceptance of inferiority.

Goldwater went east to prep school, then came back to Arizona for one year of college before entering the family business. In 1929 people in Arizona did not yet feel that a university education was essential. But as a member of the United States Senate, and particularly as his party's candidate for the Presidency, Goldwater was always painfully conscious of his limited formal education. His critics never let him or his public forget the fact that he left college at the end of his freshman year.

Goldwater made his first race for the Senate because he truly believed the policies of the New Deal and the Fair Deal threatened to destroy the freedom of the Republic and limit the opportunity of its citizens. He did not see himself as a leader of the cause but rather as an ally of those Americans who were attempting to halt the ever expanding activities of a dangerously powerful central government. When his work as a member of the Senate began to claim the attention of a widening public, as it did after his single-handed opposition brought about the passage of the Landrum-Griffin Act, he refused to claim credit.

Goldwater was amazed at his own popularity within the Republican party. All the while he was building a spectacular record as a raiser of funds, he insisted that the local organizations were truly responsible.

Where other men in Congress looked upon the occupant of the White House as an old comrade in the political wars, Goldwater exhibited a genuine, almost naïve attitude of worship and respect. He frequently criticized the action and decisions of Dwight Eisenhower, but his attitude toward the office of the President was something quite different.

When Goldwater followers began suggesting seriously that he should become a candidate for the highest office in the land, he disputed the wisdom of their choice. In the first place he came from a small, politically unimportant state. Because he was an Episcopalian the Jewish people regarded him as a deserter. Because his father had been a Jew, he suffered from all the animosities of anti-Semitic prejudice. Goldwater was instinctively aware that if he became a candidate for the Presidency, there would be some, both Jew and Gentile, who would spit on the hand he extended asking for support.

Goldwater has always admired intellectual capacity. The not-so-subtle snobbery which unites the holders of college degrees into a select fraternity would, he predicted, deny him their support.

Not long after his first election to the Senate, a friend of Goldwater's stated quite bluntly in my presence, "He's a great guy all right and I like him, but he won't get along well in Congress—he's never read a book." This criticism has been repeated many times by writers of think pieces and certain newspaper columnists.

Within a month after this observation was first voiced, I arranged an evening at my home with the Senator, his wife, and the man who had so blithely condemned Goldwater to the outer darkness of an activist world.

The Senator's critic was a professional writer, a man who prided himself on his acquaintance not only with the classics but with contemporary contributions to literature, both fact and fiction. In the course of the evening my guest mentioned a book he was reading at the time and had not finished. Goldwater picked up the conversation, discussed the book with understanding, quoted some of the more significant passages, and in the next thirty minutes demonstrated that he had read most of the books his critic considered worth remembering.

Goldwater, with a candor alien to most politicians, gave generous credit to Brent Bozell for his contribution to *The Conscience of a Conservative.* He never denied his dependence upon professional assistance with *Why Not Victory?* and in preparing his widely read newspaper column. In these efforts, which were favorably received by members of the intellectual establishment, Goldwater was the guiding participant and the major contributor. But he did not have a college degree. There was nothing he could say, nothing could be said for him which would alter the self-righteous, deprecating attitude instinctively adopted by his critics.

To some men the power and perquisites of the Presidency represent the summit of political achievement. To Goldwater, the thought of living in the White House held no particular charm. On those rare occasions when he would permit a discussion of his possible election, he invariably exhibited an instinctive distaste for that public office which strips its holder of all privacy and independence. "Do you think I want to live like that," he once asked me, "with reporters and Secret Service men and secretaries looking over my shoulder every minute of the day and night?"

During the presidential campaign Goldwater, and particularly some of his managers, were accused of being rude and arrogant in their attitude toward those who wanted to help. The charge cannot be denied; yet this attitude is a complete contradiction of the Goldwater I knew in the years from 1952 to 1962. During that period he displayed an amazing capacity to view himself and his critics objectively. His successful elections, his developing personal popularity, never kept him from seeing the other side. On one occasion Goldwater appeared on television with Secretary of Labor Arthur

Goldberg, later a Justice of the United States Supreme Court. Goldberg made repeated snide references to Goldwater's wealth and to the fact that he had inherited a department store. He insinuated that the Senator's western background prevented him from understanding the virtue of labor's position.

When the program was over, Goldwater called me from Washington. I was extremely incensed over the treatment he had received and offered an uncomplimentary opinion of his adversary. The Senator's response was typical of his attitude: "No, you'd really like this fellow," he told me; "of course he doesn't agree with us, but he's a very bright, competent man, and there is a lot in what he says."

In addition to the Senator's genuinely humble respect for the power and responsibilities of the Presidency, there was another factor which had a bearing on his reluctance to become an eager candidate for that office. He recognized how difficult it would be for any President to influence truly the great bureaucratic machinery of the federal government. During his years in the Senate he had encountered the built-in momentum of self-perpetuating habits and policies, and he recognized that any attempt to turn the tide would be met by fierce resistance on a thousand different fronts. The President and his Cabinet are theoretically in command of policy, but when such decisions must be translated into action, the second echelon of governmental employees assumes control, and here Parkinson's Law is supreme. Eisenhower had tried and failed to halt the gradual transfer of power from the people to the federal government. All the complexities of our industrialized society argue for an expansion of the federal power.

Goldwater, whose opposition to nationwide bargaining power for unions is well-known, is equally distressed over the expansion of big business which, in his view, must ultimately destroy the private entrepreneur, the independent, the man who wants to work for himself.

Goldwater did not want just to be President; he wanted to be President only if, by so doing, he could turn aside and slow down those forces which, in his opinion, are combining to diminish the significance and the responsibility of the individual.

The first meeting of the inner circle after the assassination was held on December 8th. Goldwater quietly reviewed the situation and outlined his reasons for wanting to abandon the project.

Running against the articulate, idealistic young President, a man whom he had known and learned to like when they both served in the Senate, had held some appeal. He could anticipate a campaign in which the issues would be honestly and sincerely debated. It could be a contest "not of personality but of principle." He believed Kennedy would have refrained from personal attacks or political smears. He could envision a Republican effort completely free of low-level innuendo. It would have been a productive discussion, one which would have appealed to the voters' understanding rather than to voter prejudice.

Since 1955 Goldwater had served in the Senate under the administration of Lyndon Johnson as Majority Leader. He respected the Texan's capacity for engineering political deals, but he despised the Johnson methods. Where Goldwater was direct, Johnson was devious; where Goldwater stuck to principle, Johnson bent with compromise. Where Kennedy was quick and witty, Johnson was ponderous and dull.

When he had finished, Senator Norris Cotton took the floor to argue that nothing had really changed. The issues were still the same. He compared Goldwater to DeGaulle and the American government to the Third Republic of France in its days of decline. He did not say that victory would be easy or even possible. But he did say it was Goldwater's duty to his country to lead the conservative forces. When he finished speaking, there were tears in the eyes of many of the men in that room.

It was the same, but it was also different. It would be different. Where the odds against victory had been formidable, they were now, in Goldwater's opinion, almost insurmountable.

In November, 1964, Lyndon Johnson would have been President barely one year. The sense of grief and guilt being exhibited by the American public might easily be transformed into an expression of loyalty for Johnson.

The men who were determined Goldwater should seek the nomination insisted there could be no turning back. If the Senator refused to become a candidate, what would happen to the conservative movement? If their leader refused to run, if their champion, their symbol of courage, their spokesman, were to appear timid and afraid, unwilling to lead the troops, this would be a desertion, a betrayal of the principles and the ideals which Goldwater had advanced.

There is an element of truth in the claim that Oswald's bullet struck down both the champion and the challenger. Burch, Grenier, Kleindienst, White—as well as those supporters who had been with Goldwater from the very beginning of his Senate career—all agree that after November, Goldwater changed. He was never quite the same. The Senator's heretofore unfailing good humor vanished. He no longer sought counsel and criticism in the old eager way.

He agreed to run because there was nothing else he could do.

Part Three

The Road to San Francisco

9

On January 3, 1964, Goldwater's entire foot was in a cast as a result of recent minor surgery, and he was forced to walk on crutches. Yet when the Senator hobbled before the microphones and cameras of national television installed on the patio of his hilltop Phoenix home to announce that he would be a candidate for the Presidency, the choice he offered to the Republic was a meaningful one.

Baroody, McCabe, Hess, and Kitchel had wanted the Senator to make his announcement from Washington, D. C., because the newspaper and television facilities in the nation's capital guarantee a maximum exposure. Goldwater flatly refused their suggestion. If he was going to run, he would make his announcement from Phoenix, Arizona, in familiar surroundings. He would officially become a candidate in the state where he had launched his earlier successful political campaigns.

The Senator's sentimental or, as his critics describe it, superstitious attachment to Arizona was demonstrated again and again throughout the presidential effort. He ended the primary and the general election campaigns by visiting Fredonia, Arizona, a tiny hamlet just south of the Utah border, where there are not enough potential voters to affect the outcome of a countywide race. But Goldwater had concluded his two successful campaigns for the Senate in Fredonia, and sentiment compelled him to return.

Because he had launched his drives for the Senate from the Court House steps in Yavapai county, he opened his general election campaign for the Presidency from the same Court House steps in Prescott, Arizona.

Those who wanted him to announce from Washington did not persist in their arguments. They had won the major victory when the Senator agreed to become a candidate. They were willing to let him have his own way in such a small matter as the locale of the public declaration.

The date January 3rd was chosen for a number of reasons. The Republican National Committee was scheduled to begin its midwinter meeting at the Mayflower Hotel in Washington, D. C., on January 8th. It was important the Senator appear before this gathering of Republican leadership as an announced candidate. The Christmas holidays would be a poor time for an announcement. Dean Burch said the problem of logistics was so monumental it was utterly impossible to bring the representatives of various news media to Arizona until after New Year's.

Goldwater said that he had decided to become a candidate for the Republican nomination in response to millions of Americans who wanted a choice. He said it would be a campaign of principle not personalities, and he suggested there would be a direct and decisive confrontation between two antagonistic political philosophies—the welfare state, represented by the Democrats, and a society of free, independent, responsible individuals to be represented by the Republicans.

When he had finished, the reporters asked questions. Had the Senator selected a campaign manager?

"I'm glad you asked that question," he responded, "Denison Kitchel will be the general director of this campaign; he will be the Head Honcho. Dean Burch of Tucson will be his assistant." Mrs. Emory Johnson would head the women's activities, and Richard Kleindienst would be in command as field director for the Goldwater for President Committee.

Mrs. Johnson, a long-time member of the Republican National Committee from Arizona, was well-known to party politicians. She had participated in numerous senatorial campaigns outside Arizona and had been a hard worker in Goldwater's successful 1958 effort.

Richard G. Kleindienst, forty, a graduate of Harvard Law School, had served one term in the Arizona state legislature in

1953 and 1954. He was elected state chairman of the Republican party in 1956 and re-elected in 1958. As the manager of Governor Paul Fannin's successful campaign for re-election to a second term, Kleindienst held a position of power in the Arizona Republican structure.

The campaign staff named by the Senator was soon nicknamed the "Arizona Mafia." At the time of the announcement some politicians in the party responded with an almost audible "Oh, no!"

Kitchel might have been able to run Goldwater's campaign for the Senate in friendly Arizona, but to let a neophyte run a presidential effort was, they felt, a pretty risky on-the-job training program. Dean Burch was well liked, but he had no history of national political service, and most Republicans had expected that Richard Kleindienst would run for governor in 1964.

The pointed omissions of that staff announcement produced even more reaction. Clif White, who had started the Draft Goldwater movement; Peter O'Donnell, the national chairman; Mrs. Ione Harrington, his co-chairman, were not given so much as a friendly pat on the back. It was obvious that Goldwater believed the Draft Goldwater movement should be liquidated.

Goldwater announced he was starting his active campaign as of that morning. He would enter the New Hampshire primary and a number of other preconvention contests. The next day, Saturday, Goldwater and his team—Kitchel, Burch, Johnson, Kleindienst, Hess, Baroody, and McCabe—departed for Washington, D. C.

Of all the men Goldwater had selected, only Kleindienst could be called an experienced politician, and his appointment had been settled just a scant twenty-four hours before the announcement.

On January 2nd, the former state chairman had been returning to Arizona by automobile from the Rose Bowl football game in Pasadena. When he reached home, he found a message calling him to Kitchel's law office.

"I was dirty and tired. I had on my slippers and my golf shirt," he says; "so I called Kitchel and asked what he wanted. He told me that Goldwater was going to run for President, that the Senator wanted me to join the effort. I went down to Kitchel's office. The only other person present was Bill Baroody. I was told that Kitchel would be the general director of the campaign, Burch his chief assistant. The Senator wanted me to serve as Director of Field Operations, whatever that meant."

Kleindienst suggested it would be wise to find someone from outside Arizona, a politician with more national acceptance, but Kitchel and Baroody insisted. Goldwater did not want anyone else; he wanted Kleindienst.

Before they left for Washington, Kleindienst asked Kitchel what role they proposed to assign to Clif White.

"That will be up to you," Kitchel told him. "We haven't said anything to Clif. You can keep him as your assistant if you want, or you can send him back to New York."

Kleindienst has described what followed as "the screwiest experience of my life." He arrived in Washington on the night of January 4th. The newly created Goldwater for President Committee had taken space at 1101 Connecticut Avenue; the volunteers of the Draft committee were busy trying to move furniture and typewriters, charts and files into this new upstairs office space.

The Republican state chairmen were scheduled to gather at the Mayflower Hotel on Wednesday, January 8th. Meanwhile Goldwater had flown to California on Monday the 6th to meet with his West Coast supporters headed by Senator Knowland and Sheriff Pete Pitchess of Los Angeles county.

"I believed," Kleindienst said, "there were two things of paramount importance. We had to get our office fixed up so that we had something to show the members of the National Committee, and then we had to work out a plan of approach.

"I very quickly concluded that this Draft Goldwater Committee was the real organization."

Unfortunately, Kitchel and the Senator had both made statements indicating the Draft organization was now to be superseded by the Goldwater for President Committee.

Most of the Goldwater followers among the Republican state chairmen arrived in Washington a day early for their meeting. Clif White, who was not invited to the Arizona announcement, had spent the holidays perfecting his plans for dealing with the members of the National Committee.

Kitchel called a meeting in Kleindienst's suite at the Mayflower for the purpose of hearing White's proposals and clarifying White's future role in the new organization.

The briefing took the better part of an hour. White says Kleindienst and Burch asked many questions about personalities involved, home-state connections, attitudes toward Goldwater in prior contacts made by the Draft committee.

Twenty minutes before the group was scheduled to adjourn, Kitchel said, "As you know, Clif, Barry has asked Dick to be Director of Field Operations for the Committee. He will report to me. I guess the best thing for you would be to serve as sort of an assistant to Dick."

For twenty-six months White had been the active commanding head of the Republicans who wanted Goldwater to be their candidate for President. He had traveled more than a hundred thousand miles. He was intimately acquainted with the peculiarities of each individual state. He knew the people in the party who were opposed to Goldwater as well as those who were in favor of the Senator. Of the four men in the room, White was the only one who had ever participated in a presidential campaign on any level. To be thus summarily demoted, offered a position under Kleindienst, was more than White could accept.

"I don't want to sound like a small man," he told Kitchel. "Titles aren't all that important to me either, but hundreds of people in this country have been working for me. When they find out you've made me somebody's assistant, I will lose their confidence, and I won't be any real help in this campaign. I can't take that job."

According to White, Kitchel responded by saying, "Well, it might be helpful if you would stay on with us until Friday."

It was Dick Kleindienst who stepped in to prevent what might have been a disastrous division of the Goldwater forces at the very start of the official campaign. "We need you," he told White, "I don't want a little thing like a job title to force you out after all the Draft movement has done for Goldwater. We can work it out, and you've earned a place in this organization."

After some further discussion, Dean Burch suggested that White be designated Coordinator of Field Operations; Kitchel appeared to agree.

By this time it was past nine o'clock. White escorted Kitchel upstairs to a public room where members of the National Committee who had been enlisted by the Draft Goldwater movement were waiting to greet the new campaign director. Kitchel introduced Burch as his assistant, mentioned Mrs. Johnson, then explained that Kleindienst was the man the Senator had appointed Director of Field Operations. He said White would be kept on to work with Kleindienst as an assistant.

All the earlier conversation, White's logical objection, the arguments of Burch and Kleindienst were wasted. It was now official—Clif White had been relieved of authority and responsibility. The next morning, according to both Kleindienst and White, Kitchel coldly informed Peter O'Donnell there would be no place for the Texas Republican leader on the Goldwater for President Committee staff. Although he was denied any official position by this decision, O'Donnell continued to work for Goldwater's nomination, and as the leader of the Senator's supporters in Texas he was an official member of the Committee's field staff.

To many observers the only consistent characteristic of the Goldwater campaign was the total lack of advance planning, and the committee's action, or rather lack of action, in planning for financial support illustrates this contention.

In politics there is a very pertinent paraphrase of St. John: "In the beginning was the word and the word was money." Certainly no political effort can be successful unless it is supported with adequate financial resources. When Goldwater announced in Phoenix and became an official candidate, he did not have a finance chairman or a finance committee. Kitchel and Baroody, who had been busy on other matters, apparently believed that once the Senator announced, the money would pour in.

Thirteen days later on January 16th, Goldwater telephoned Daniel C. Gainey of Owatana, Minnesota, and asked him to form a finance committee. Gainey, an early Eisenhower supporter, had served as treasurer of the national Republican party. He accepted the assignment with the stipulation that G. R. Herberger, who operates a chain of department stores in the upper Midwest and is also involved in real estate development in Arizona, be named his assistant.

Herberger had been the most successful fund raiser for the Republican party in Arizona, and these two men, assisted by Bill Middendorf, a New York investment broker; Roger Milliken of South Carolina, one of the principal owners of the Deering-Milliken Mills; Stets Coleman, a southern industrialist; and Jeremiah Milbank, a wealthy financier of Connecticut and New York City, took on the task of raising the Goldwater money. According to Clif White, they produced about three and a half million dollars before Goldwater was nominated in San Francisco, and in addition to this, Henry Salvatori of California raised almost one million dollars to support the primary effort in that state.

The awkward situation between White and Kleindienst was never completely resolved. White denies there was any bad blood or difficulty and maintains that he and Kleindienst divided responsibility and worked well together.

Under pressure, it is difficult to form correct, objective political judgments, and Kleindienst, who was regarded as a Johnny-come-lately by the early Draft Goldwater people, was forced to operate under extremely difficult conditions. Sometime in late February a letter attacking Kleindienst, his ability, and his personal conduct was delivered to Congressman John Rhodes of Arizona. Rhodes called Kleindienst to his office and let him read the contents.

Whatever the merit of the charges in that letter, Kleindienst confronted White and accused him of having inspired the complaint. White denied the charge, but as a result of this meeting, each man's area of operations was sharply defined—Kleindienst would take charge of the primary states and certain state conventions; White would be responsible for the other convention states. He would also have complete authority to make all arrangements for the operations at the convention itself and would command the Goldwater forces in San Francisco.

When Kleindienst reported the incident to Kitchel, Goldwater's campaign director believed the compromise was a mistake. In his opinion, the proper action would have been to fire White.

10

In the period prior to 1962, whenever Goldwater could be persuaded to discuss seriously the possibility of his candidacy for the Presidency, he repeatedly stated his opinion that the primaries were unimportant and, with the exception of California, a waste of time and effort.

The way to win the nomination, Goldwater believed, was to announce, then make six or eight major speeches in various sections of the country, and be represented at every state convention by a skillful, experienced politician. Do this, win the California primary, and the battle would be over.

An overwhelming majority of the delegates were to be chosen at state conventions by precinct committeemen, and country chairmen—working Republicans who had earned the right to speak for the party—and Goldwater had been effectively cultivating the affections of these Republicans for more than six years.

Primary campaigns divide the voters into warring camps. In the long run, nothing is gained from situations which invariably produce intemperance. It is difficult enough in a general election to answer the critics. In a primary, where the attackers are members of your own party, no candidate can escape injury.

A series of primary battles leaves the victor exhausted and bloody, requires the expenditure of campaign funds sorely needed for the general election, adversely affects state party organizations, and creates issues which an opponent in the general can exploit.

Overexposure in a primary can kill a candidate, and Goldwater knew it. The myth that Dwight Eisenhower had become the 1952 nominee because of his victory in New Hampshire was precisely that, a myth. Ike won because his team at the convention in Chicago outthought and outmaneuvered the Taft supporters.

In 1960 John Kennedy chalked up an impressive group of primary wins. But it was the Kennedy political machine, working adroitly in the convention states and then at Los Angeles, which earned the nomination for the Massachusetts senator.

Somehow, somewhere, all these understandings, all the long-range tactics Goldwater wanted to follow were lost in the shuffle. John Grenier insists that when he went on the payroll of the Goldwater group in November, 1963, California's was the only primary under consideration.

In December, 1963, Peter O'Donnell, with some of his lieutenants, went to New Hampshire to inspect the battlefield personally. He returned to Washington convinced that Kitchel was being misled by the New Hampshirites—notably Senator Norris Cotton; Speaker of the New Hampshire House Stuart Lamprey; and the gracious and charming widow of New Hampshire's longtime Republican chief, Senator Styles Bridges.

"There are serious weaknesses in organization, finance, public relations and advertising, and in my opinion, we stand a great chance of being clobbered," he reported to Kitchel.

O'Donnell was told that the people in New Hampshire knew what they were doing, that anyway "elections here weren't conducted in the same manner as elections in Texas or Arizona."

Dean Burch recalls a meeting held in Washington on December 19th or 20th at which Raymond Moley, the *Newsweek* political columnist, urged the Senator not to enter the New Hampshire primary. Moley's thesis was that Goldwater had most of the chips and the contest was meaningless.

Under New Hampshire law candidates run in what is referred to contemptuously by the local politicians as a beauty contest. The outcome of this preferential primary does not commit the state nor its delegates to support the winner. The delegates run on a separate ballot; they may be, but are not necessarily committed to a particular candidate. Moley argued that if for some unpredictable reason Goldwater lost in New Hampshire, it would be a serious defeat. If he won, it would be an insignificant victory.

In September and October, Kitchel and Baroody had sent their public opinion samplers into New Hampshire. Goldwater was then leading with 65 per cent of the votes. These two, who hoped to pattern the race after the Kennedy campaign, were confident the Senator would walk away with the nation's first primary.

Kitchel, Burch, and Kleindienst look back on New Hampshire, which Goldwater lost to a write-in candidate, Henry Cabot Lodge (who was then six thousand miles away in South Viet Nam), as a defeat with a silver lining. Burch says, "We all underrated the New Hampshire primary, but the one error which costs us the election comes back to the candidate himself. He was not psychologically attuned to a presidential primary. Most of his speeches were off-the-cuff. Tony Smith was in the hospital, and we didn't give Goldwater any press or public relations support."

Politics in New Hampshire were decidedly different from anything Goldwater had experienced in Arizona. The weather was cold, travel was difficult, and the crowds were small. Those in charge of the campaign schedule had Goldwater *making as many as eighteen appearances in one day.* The Senator would speak for ten or fifteen minutes, then answer questions. There would be twenty to fifty New Hampshirites and just as many reporters for newspaper and television. They would ask the same questions the Senator had been answering all day.

A part of Goldwater's difficulties in New Hampshire was the aftermath of the bitter contest between Doloris Bridges and Representative Perkins Bass for the right to succeed to Styles Bridges' seat in the Senate. Goldwater had publicly supported Mrs. Bridges out of deference to his friendship for her dead husband, and she lost to Bass in the primary.

Kleindienst says another problem was that the campaign was run by a committee. Stuart Lamprey had been designated as the campaign director, and Norris Cotton was the campaign chairman. "The two of them were absolutely incompatible in their personalities and their attitudes. On two occasions I had to make an emergency trip to New Hampshire to arbitrate a dispute between Lamprey and Cotton because the Senator was threatening to resign as chairman of the Goldwater campaign committee prior to March 10th.

"I'd get Cotton in one room," Kleindienst explains, "and tell him how Stuart Lamprey really thought he was a great guy. Then I'd go to Lamprey and tell him how much Cotton admired him. They were both devoted to Goldwater, and I've never met two finer gentlemen. But trying to win a primary under those conditions was no bed of roses."

It was in New Hampshire that Goldwater as a candidate for the Presidency first made his now famous controversial remark about the need to permit the commander of NATO discretion to use tactical nuclear weapons in the case of an enemy assault.

Goldwater says he used the word "commander." A number of reporters say he used the plural "commanders." Late in the general election campaign both *U.S. News* and *Time* magazine reported that what Goldwater had suggested was in fact United States policy under Eisenhower and Kennedy. But by that time the damage was beyond repair.

On November 3, 1964, it became apparent that millions of elderly Americans were convinced that if elected, Goldwater would abolish Social Security immediately and put an end to their governmental retirement checks. This shibboleth, which became the club Nelson Rockefeller used over and over again in his attempt to beat down Goldwater's lead, grew out of a curious event in the New Hampshire primary.

In Concord, Goldwater was asked by a reporter to elaborate and clarify his earlier attacks on the Social Security system.

In *The Conscience of a Conservative* and numerous early speeches Goldwater had criticized the Social Security system as (1) actuarially unsound; (2) a pseudoinsurance program totally unfunded; (3) a proposal originally intended to do no more than prevent stark privation—it had been sold to the American public as retirement insurance; and (4) an actual tax levied against the nation's payrolls but collected and spent outside the government's annual budget.

Goldwater responded to the reporter's inquiry by discussing in detail these four points. The story carried next day in a Concord paper was a fairly accurate account of the Senator's concern for the solvency of Social Security and his argument that steps must be taken to strengthen the program in order to prevent it from collapsing. But the headline said Goldwater wanted to destroy Social Security.

According to the Senator, the headline writer was discharged for his bad judgment, but the damage was done. Forty-eight hours later the Rockefeller people were busy distributing thousands and thousands of handbill reprints of that damaging headline.

The Goldwater supporters claim that Rockefeller somehow gained access to a list containing the names and addresses of New Hampshirites who were on Social Security. They say he mailed the damaging headline to every Social Security recipient in the state.

The missile flap, which became the genesis of a bitter running feud between Goldwater and the Pentagon, grew out of the Senator's remarks at a news conference in Portsmouth, New Hampshire. In response to a question, the Senator said: "The nation's long-range missiles are not reliable." Filtered through a press which never pretended to be friendly, the phrase was reported in some dispatches as "not accurate," in others as "not dependable." The commentators and the columnists were quick to attack this as unjust criticism of our scientists, the Department of Defense, and indeed the entire administration.

In 1960 John F. Kennedy had earned the applause of this same group when he said time after time that the Eisenhower administration was responsible for "a missile gap." Goldwater's remark may have been unfortunate—it was far from inaccurate. But like so many of the Senator's statements in New Hampshire, no foundation had been laid, no careful documentation had been offered to enable the listeners to understand correctly the intent of the candidate's remarks.

As a member of the Senate Armed Services Committee and a brigadier general in the Air Force Reserve, Goldwater seriously questioned the Pentagon's decision to phase out manned bombers and risk our ability to defend the North American Continent with the various missile systems from the *Atlas* to the *Minuteman.*

A great many nonpolitical military authorities supported Goldwater's position. No missile had ever been flown from a silo to a target. We have nothing more than the opinion of the engineers on which to rest a belief that the hardened bases will in fact resist the effect of a near atomic explosion. There have been no tests conducted under simulated wartime conditions to demonstrate whether or not the silo doors will open in the event an enemy were to explode a nuclear warhead in the near proximity of our missile complexes. Under test conditions the *Atlas,* the *Titan I* and *II,* and the *Minuteman* had not demonstrated anything resembling infallible reliability. On more than one occasion an attempt to fly the *Titans* from a test silo had ended in fiery failure.

In 1963 a number of scientists published the suggestion that the explosion of a high-yield atomic weapon creates its own radio pulse, that such a pulse could interfere with the magnetic guidance systems installed in the American missiles. They speculated that it might be possible to defend a target effectively against enemy ICBM's by producing a protective high-altitude nuclear explosion. The Russians, just before concluding the Test Ban Treaty, had exploded a high-yield atomic device.

But in New Hampshire Goldwater said none of these things. He just said the missiles were unreliable. And the damage was done. He assumed that his audience, being well-informed newsmen, would possess all the background facts which made the statement a fair conclusion.

By mid February the polls began to indicate an alarming drop in Senator Goldwater's popularity in New Hampshire. But Kitchel simply refused to believe the polls. He had been to New Hampshire. He had witnessed the crowd reactions, and, as Burch put it, "The Goldwater forces were extremely confident. They believed that all they had to do was to make Goldwater available and the customers would beat down the doors to accept him."

In New Hampshire, Goldwater may have been as unfairly treated by the press as his supporters claim. History supports the positions he took on NATO, on Cuba, and on the reliability of the United States missile system. But every observer agrees that his campaign and his organization were miserably inept.

It was here the Senator began to build his deep resentment against schedulers—eager supporters who committed him to sixteen and eighteen appearances in a fourteen- or sixteen-hour day.

The advertising agency Kitchel had employed, Fuller, Smith and Ross, was assigned to make a documentary of the Senator in New Hampshire. They photographed Goldwater at meetings and supermarkets. Technically their work was excellent, but the film, which was used in short segments on TV, revealed all the shortcomings of the campaign. Goldwater, carrying the burden of his painful heel, the unaccustomed cold, and the frantic schedule, appeared angry and belligerent. His off-the-cuff speeches may have satisfied live audiences; when they were replayed on TV they lacked unity and were almost monotonous.

Kitchel, who frequently accompanied Goldwater in New Hampshire, has said, "The Senator, becoming bored with the sound of his own voice saying the same things over and over again, tried desperately to make each speech just a little different. And the newspaper writers in his audience interpreted these variations as inconsistency."

It was really the lack of advance planning which lost New Hampshire—the failure of those responsible to provide an adequate staff to prepare the press releases, to maintain a continuity in the candidate's speeches, and, above all else, to protect an exhausted candidate from becoming his own worst enemy.

Rockefeller, the only opponent the Goldwater forces recognized, benefited from an excellent staff and adequate preparation. The governor of New York had gone to college in New Hampshire; he was at home with the people. He seemed to enjoy the supermarket handshaking display of personality which really did nothing at all to help the voters understand what kind of President he would make.

There were some bright moments, and both Kitchel and Goldwater were deceived by the enthusiastic, overflow crowds which gathered to hear the Senator in the final days of the campaign.

The stop-Goldwater forces, having concluded that regardless of what happened in New Hampshire the Republican party would never swallow Rockefeller's divorce and remarriage, were busily looking for a more acceptable candidate. Fifty-two per cent of the population of New Hampshire lives within sixty miles of Boston, and Henry Cabot Lodge was a Boston brahman. He had been Eisenhower's Ambassador to the United Nations; he was a fellow New Englander, and he was available—not in person of course, but in some ways this made him even more attractive. His name could be injected, his image could be built, without subjecting him to any of the dangers which always confront a candidate on the campaign trail. Being in Saigon, it was not necessary for Lodge to answer any questions or to take any specific stands on the issues which were rapidly dividing New Hampshire Republicans, making them either anti-Rockefeller or anti-Goldwater.

Robert Mullen, who organized the write-in campaign for General Eisenhower in New Hampshire in 1952, was quietly named chairman of the national Draft Lodge Committee. Insiders say his preparations for making Lodge an upset winner in the nation's first primary election were laid as early as November, 1963.

With Paul D. Grindle, a professional manager of political campaigns, and David Goldberg as the front men, the Lodge write-in effort blossomed in February. Six different mailings were sent to the voters of New Hampshire. George Lodge, the ambassador's son, gave his blessing to the effort. In the days just before March 10 the Lodge people saturated the New Hampshire television market with a five-minute program which had been made four years earlier when Dwight Eisenhower was introducing Lodge as the Republican candidate for Vice-President. A superimposed blast of trumpets at just the right moment obscured the word "Vice" in Ike's introduction. Unsuspecting viewers were led to believe the former President was advocating the nomination and election of Henry Cabot Lodge in 1964.

Clif White, who was not permitted to go into New Hampshire, and Kleindienst, who was there many times, both believe that Rockefeller and Goldwater suffered from overexposure. In their opinion, it was a case of "a plague on both your houses." Lodge beat Goldwater by more than twelve thousand votes. Nelson Rockefeller ran third, with Margaret Chase Smith in the number four spot.

The slate of Goldwater delegates, headed by Senator Norris Cotton, was defeated. This was a severe blow to the prestige of an incumbent Republican senator. In San Francisco, when Cotton was offered the chance to make one of the Goldwater seconding speeches, he refused.

The victory celebration which had been scheduled for a private suite in the Madison Hotel in Washington, D.C., turned into a wake. Goldwater told the press that he "goofed in New Hampshire," and a number of people said that his biggest mistake was leaving the state on the Saturday before the election after announcing that "he had it in the bag."

At least three members of the finance committee blamed Kitchel for the loss and suggested he should be replaced by a more experienced campaign manager, but Kleindienst says New Hampshire was the catalytic agent which drew the Goldwater team together and enabled it to function effectively, and Kitchel is quoted as having said, "In one way, New Hampshire was a good thing for we learned so much."

11

The importance of the Oregon presidential primary has been magnified out of all proportion. Only eighteen delegate votes were at stake. In calendar sequence there were a number of meaningful primaries between New Hampshire and Oregon—Illinois on April 14th, with fifty-eight delegates to be chosen; New Jersey on April 21st, with forty delegates; Massachusetts, April 28th, with thirty-four; Pennsylvania on the same day with fifty-four; Texas on May 2nd, with sixty-six votes at stake; Washington, D.C., on May 5th, nine votes; Indiana and Ohio on the same day, a total of ninety delegates; Nebraska and West Virginia on May 12th, with a total of thirty votes.

The Oregon preferential presidential primary is unique. It requires the Secretary of State to print a ballot containing the name of every potential candidate who has been "widely mentioned as a possibility in the national press." The candidate's consent is not required. The only way to get off the ballot is by filing what is known locally as a "Sherman Declaration." The General once said that if nominated, he wouldn't run; if elected, he wouldn't serve.

Sixteen states hold preferential primaries, but in eleven of these the outcome is not binding upon the delegates elected. In Oregon the winner receives all of the delegate votes for at least the first two ballots. In 1940 Thomas Dewey won the Oregon primary and went on to become the Republican nominee. In the minds of the Goldwater staff Oregon was important for two reasons: the date, May 15th, would come just two weeks and three days ahead of the California primary, and, because of the peculiar Oregon law, it was probable that all candidates would be on the official ballot. When the campaign opened Kitchel and Burch were confident Goldwater would defeat Rockefeller in New Hampshire. A second victory in Oregon would, they believed, cinch the nomination.

On Sunday, January 19th, Kleindienst flew to Portland expecting to announce the appointment of Sigfreid Unander, former Oregon state treasurer, former member of the Federal Maritime Commission, and wealthy scion of a pioneer lumber family, as state chairman of the Goldwater for President effort. As chairman of the Senatorial Campaign Committee, Goldwater had helped Unander in 1962. It was taken for granted that this influential Oregon Republican would make himself available to Goldwater in 1964. But no one had thought to consult Unander in advance. After two days of careful consideration, Unander told Kleindienst that certain business and personal reasons made it impossible for him to accept the offered post. And Secretary of State Howell Appling, who had earlier indicated he wanted to help Goldwater, gave Kleindienst a bleak appraisal of the situation.

William E. Walsh, a respected lawyer from Coos Bay, had resigned a position as president of the State Board of Higher Education in order to devote his full time to managing the Rockefeller campaign. It was imperative, Appling said, that someone be named immediately to head the Goldwater forces. "And whoever takes this job will need the help of an experienced political manager."

Oregon, once a safe Republican state, has in recent years demonstrated considerable independence. Appling and Governor Mark Hatfield are Republicans, but the state's two United States senators, Wayne Morse and Maurine Neuberger, are both liberal Democrats.

Appling suggested the names of a number of Republicans who might be persuaded to take on the Goldwater assignment. When Kleindienst returned to Washington on January 21st, he gave Kitchel and Burch a full report and then recommended that they ask me to take charge of the Oregon primary as a representative of the Goldwater for President Committee staff.

On Sunday morning, January 26th, Senator Goldwater called

from Washington, D.C. He asked me to come east for a briefing and then go to Oregon.

On Wednesday, January 29th, I met with Kitchel, Kleindienst, White, and Burch at the committee headquarters at 1101 Connecticut Avenue. Kitchel promised his full support, authorized an immediate allocation of campaign funds to Oregon, and agreed with Kleindienst that it would be an uphill battle. One week later I said goodbye to my wife and four children in Phoenix and moved to Portland for the duration. It was an experience I will never forget.

For more than ten years I had been looking forward to the possibility of a Goldwater for President campaign. I had accepted Goldwater's decision to change campaign managers in 1963 with a great sense of personal disappointment. I had not been invited to be present when the Senator made his opening announcement on January 3rd in Phoenix. And now I was extremely pleased at the prospect of being able to help, of having some small part in the Goldwater for President effort. I believed then and I believe now that his election would have served the best interests of the Republic.

During my term as state chairman of the Republican party in Arizona I had helped to organize an association of western state Republican chairmen and as a result had formed many friendships with the political leaders in the Northwest. Because of my brief connection with the Unander campaign in 1962 I was acquainted with some of the problems of Oregon, and I felt at home in my new assignment. If issues mean anything in a political campaign, Goldwater should have carried that Oregon primary easily. A public opinion poll taken in early February indicated the state's voters were in favor of a tougher stand against Cuba and Russia. Seventy-five per cent wanted a national policy of victory over communism, and 92 per cent said that government spending should be kept within the limits of government income. These were the very issues which I believed had motivated Goldwater to seek the Presidency.

Howell Appling had asked Kleindienst to consider Dr. Edwin

Durno, a prominent retired Medford, Oregon, physician, who had served one term in Congress from the Fourth District, as a possibility to head the Oregon for Goldwater Committee. When they tried to contact Durno, they discovered the good doctor was on the high seas, returning from an extended tour of Europe and Africa. Durno landed in New York City on January 28th. He cut short his vacation, came to Washington, agreed to accept the post, and then flew home while his baggage went on around through the Panama Canal.

Despite the fact that he had been out of the country for six months and had lost contact with the current political trends, Durno proved to be an excellent choice. His enthusiasm and devotion to Goldwater more than compensated for the fact that as a resident of southern Oregon he did not have any close political ties with the Republican leaders in the heavily populated Portland area. And by the time I arrived in Oregon on February 6th, Durno had recruited a number of capable volunteer assistants, including Mrs. Harry Pallady, a very gracious former president of the Women's State Federation, to serve as co-chairman of the state. Mrs. Pallady is one of the most effective women I have ever met in politics.

Kleindienst had not overemphasized the potential power of the Rockefeller organization. F. F. Montgomery of Eugene, a three-term member of the House of Representatives and Republican minority leader, had been named by Walsh as field executive. Clay Myers, Jr., a Portland insurance man and former chairman of the state Young Republicans, had been employed full time. William Moshofsky, assistant to the president of the Georgia-Pacific Corporation, was on the job as tricounty field executive in Multnomah, Washington, and Clackamas counties, an area containing about 40 per cent of the state's population.

The Rockefeller headquarters, located in an expensive downtown store, was in full operation and was well supplied with photographs, literature, and buttons.

Rockefeller made his first visit to Oregon on February 6th, 7th and 8th. Goldwater came to Portland on February 12th to speak at a Lincoln Day dinner. The affair was completely sold out, and two thousand more Republicans paid to sit in the galleries to hear the Senator.

Before the end of the third week in February we had a downtown Portland Goldwater headquarters (rent free), fully staffed with eager volunteers working under the capable direction of Mrs. Marian Wright, who had served as secretary of the now defunct Draft Goldwater movement. Durno was busy naming chairmen in the various counties, and Mrs. Pallady was on the road building a women's organization.

My immediate concern was to find a finance chairman. Ernest W. Swigert, respected head of the Hyster Company, was the logical man for the job. He was a committed conservative, an experienced fund raiser, and he enjoyed the affection of the business community. But Swigert was unacceptable to the national Goldwater committee because he had been a founding member of the John Birch Society. One of Swigert's close personal friends urged me to ignore the injunction, "I don't see how you can refuse Ernie the job on the ground that he's a member of the Birch Society when I happen to know that Denison Kitchel was an early Bircher."

My response was something light and noncommittal, and then I turned the conversation to other matters. Later I checked the story through contacts in Belmont, Massachusetts. It was true. Kitchel had been a home chapter member in 1960-61. He had been persuaded to join the society by his longtime friend and associate, Frank Brophy of Phoenix, and had subsequently resigned long before Goldwater appointed him to manage his campaign because Welch charged Eisenhower with being a Communist.

Some months after the general election was over I told Dick Kleindienst what I had learned about Kitchel and the Birch Society. I have never seen a man so completely flabbergasted. His reaction convinced me that he had no prior knowledge of Kitchel's association with the Birch Society—a fact which must be considered the best-kept secret of a campaign which was to be distinguished by a lack of security.

Fortunately for our Oregon operation, Swigert was not offended at all by the national policy. He told me he would go down into his basement and shut off the lights and work in the dark if that is what it took to help Barry Goldwater become President. And he did.

I had to leave Oregon on February 16th, to attend the first and only national meeting of the Goldwater for President Committee. We met at the O'Hare Inn in Chicago. Kitchel presided over the program, designed, as Kleindienst put it, "to prove we weren't a bunch of amateurs." It was an impressive, and I think productive, session. Certainly it was well attended, and the reports were encouraging.

The nation had been divided into regions, following the pattern established by the Draft Goldwater group. Volunteer state chairmen were functioning in thirty-nine states. Mrs. Johnson reported that the women's division was organized and operating in more than twenty states. John Grenier, director of Region II, promised at least two hundred and fifty delegate votes out of the eleven southern states. Wayne Hood, director of the Great Lakes region, was confident Goldwater would get a majority of the delegates in Illinois and Indiana. Michigan was expected to support favorite son George Romney; Minnesota was split; Wisconsin would commit to favorite son John Byrnes. In the Plains states, Dick Herman was counting on Oklahoma's twenty-two votes. He expected Goldwater to win the Nebraska primary, attract support in Iowa, Kansas, Missouri, and the Dakotas. In Region VII, which eventually became mine, Arizona, Idaho, Montana, New Mexico, Wyoming, and Washington would, according to the state chairmen in Chicago, go for Goldwater. New England and the Middle Atlantic states were not counted in anyone's column. But with only 655 votes required for victory, the future looked bright.

Kitchel announced the New York advertising agency of Fuller, Smith and Ross, had been appointed to handle the Goldwater for President Committee account. As the newest official member of the Goldwater staff, assigned to emergency operation in a single state, I was in no position to ask questions. But a number of the people present whose political experience paralleled mine were disturbed by the selection when we were told that Fuller, Smith and Ross had never handled a political campaign or a political candidate. The effective use of radio, television, newspaper advertising, and billboards to persuade the voters to support a particular candidate calls for a special talent—the task is quite different from that of persuading consumers to buy a particular brand of canned beans or to use the Yellow Pages. But the choice had been made, and it was too late for change. The second bit of information which we found so disturbing was not made in any public announcement. We discovered it almost by accident. The details of the contract signed with Fuller, Smith and Ross committed the Goldwater for President Committee to pay the agency a retainer of forty-five thousand dollars per month. This fee would be in addition to all earned commissions and all costs of production and preparation. Peter O'Donnell, who had dealt with agencies handling political accounts, was particularly incensed. "Anyone of a half-dozen big outfits would be tickled to death to get this account," he said, "just for the commissions." Before the contract was finally broken at O'Donnell's insistence, the agency was paid $135,000 in fees—money which, again to quote O'Donnell, "had to come from the contributed dollars of people who believed in Goldwater."

Despite my uneasiness over this demonstrated lack of experience, I left the Chicago meeting confident that the Goldwater organization was capable of winning the nomination. Kitchel, Kleindienst, Burch, and especially Clif White, had created a national organization which was truly impressive. And all this had been accomplished within six weeks after the candidate's official announcement.

I returned to Portland full of confidence and enthusiasm. The volunteers were working, Mrs. Pallady and Dr. Durno had filled most of the county chairmen spots on our organization chart, and Ernie Swigert had been busy in his basement. Through his good offices we were able to put together a local finance committee of responsible Oregon leaders. A local advertising agency, Showalter Lynch, had contracted for adequate billboard space. Television and radio time had been spoken for. We were on the move.

When Goldwater lost in New Hampshire on March 10th, his

Oregon supporters took it in stride and vowed to work harder. We were supremely confident that the Goldwater we had known in 1960 and 1962 would overpower his opponents. We blamed a hostile press and the liberals of the East for the New Hampshire debacle. Even the arrival of David Goldberg on March 12th to set up Lodge headquarters, and the fact that the mails were soon overloaded with appeals for Lodge patterned after the New Hampshire write-in approach failed to dampen our optimism.

Dean Burch had scheduled Goldwater into Oregon for appearances on April 6th, 7th and 8th. His itinerary called for one day in the Portland area, one day in Eugene and Corvallis, and one day in southern Oregon.

The Senator arrived by commercial airline shortly after noon on Sunday, April 5th. The flight had been delayed in San Francisco by mechanical difficulty, and it was more than an hour late. But a crowd of more than five hundred enthusiastic supporters had waited patiently at the airport to greet him. I had been told in advance that the Senator would make no speeches on Sunday and that he did not like airport demonstrations, and I had done everything I could to discourage the demonstration.

Goldwater came down the ramp from the plane accompanied by Vern Stevens, Karl Hess, and Ed Nellor, who had been appointed press secretary after Tony Smith's illness. The Senator marched through the crowd, pausing just long enough to speak to two eight-year-olds who wanted his autograph, climbed into a waiting automobile, and drove to the Hilton Hotel. The effect on the men and women who had waited patiently with banners and hats and badges to greet their hero was disastrous.

In the presidential suite at the Hilton we went over the prepared text of the television speech the Senator was to make on Monday evening and discussed the rest of the April itinerary, which was to include a return trip at the end of the month.

Goldwater, remembering the tremendous crowds which had turned out to see him in 1960 and 1962, found it very difficult to believe the Oregon voters were not completely familiar with his positions on Social Security, national defense, and foreign policy.

But he agreed to bear down hard on these three points while he was in the state.

The wounds of New Hampshire were still open. When it was suggested that we film his Monday morning press conference and then release the film on television, the idea pleased him.

"Most of the reporters have been very honest and fair," he said, "but we can't afford any more stories like the Concord piece with its headline about Social Security."

Goldwater had a quiet dinner in the hotel and retired early. The next morning, because of the dispatches which had been written out of New Hampshire, I paid particular attention to the Senator's statements at his press conference. His answers to the questions were precise and informative, and there was no equivocation. I had announced at the opening our intention to film the whole proceedings and use the film on television. No one objected, and it seemed to me that with the cameras watching and the microphones listening, the newsmen reacted by framing their questions in specific language. We released the film for early viewers that evening.

It was a new departure, and on Tuesday morning the papers devoted considerable space to what they called a revolutionary technique. Zan Stark of UPI in a by-line piece claimed the reporters strongly resented being made to perform on a Goldwater political television program. They had not, he said, enjoyed their role of nonpaid actors.

Stark's comments made me realize I had erred in releasing the film so quickly. It would have been better to wait a day, until after the reporters' stories had been published. We had, unfortunately, scooped the morning papers and the men who represented them.

At noon on Monday the Senator spoke to an overflow luncheon crowd at the Sheraton Hotel, and if audience reaction is significant, he made a lot of votes. Monday night about three hundred people representing most of the counties in Oregon assembled in the Hilton Hotel ballroom to participate as a live audience in the Goldwater television show. Some of them had driven more than two hundred miles, and as the camera panned the room, the banners and signs suggested that Dr. Durno and Mrs. Pallady had done an excellent job.

The Senator's speech dealt with foreign policy and the American errors in Cuba and Southeast Asia. He used maps and charts to illustrate his points and to emphasize the steady retreat of freedom before the advance of Communist imperialism.

By prearrangement the Senator did not come to the podium until just before airtime. We wanted to broadcast the full effect of an enthusiastic audience greeting the candidate. When the thirty-minute period ended, the Senator left the rostrum, paused only briefly to speak to one person at the edge of the crowd, then entered the elevator and went up to his suite on the fifteenth floor. His sudden departure had not been prearranged. In his 1958 campaign for the Senate in Arizona, where we had used the same type of television presentation, Goldwater had always stayed around and visited with the audience afterwards. And I fully expected he would spend at least half an hour with these Oregon people who had come so far to see him and meet him.

Dr. Durno and Mrs. Pallady did their best to fill the vacuum. But the disappointed Goldwater supporters were angry and bewildered.

When I went upstairs in response to the Senator's summons, relayed by Vern Stevens, I told him I thought the speech was good but that his abrupt, almost rude departure had been a mistake. He said it had been a long day, and it had been. He was tired, and I could believe it. Moreover, he wanted to call Mrs. Goldwater in Washington, where it was now past midnight. He also told me that he must leave for Washington after lunch the next day, which meant canceling the afternoon's schedule in Eugene and the appearances in Medford.

The next morning we drove to the campus of the University of Oregon at Corvallis, where the Senator spoke in Gill Coliseum. This time he was relaxed, friendly, and extremely patient. The university official who handles the Coliseum estimated the crowd at between 5,500 and 6,000. The reporters in their stories said we had between 4,000 and 4,500, mostly students.

From Corvallis the Senator went on to Eugene for a luncheon meeting and then departed in a chartered airplane for San Francisco and a connection to Washington. It has been erroneously reported elsewhere that Goldwater, while in Portland on April 6th, decided to scrub the rest of his appearances in that state. If he reached that decision then, he did not tell me about it. When he left, I expected him to return, pick up the dates we had missed, campaign in the Portland area on May 4th and 5th, and then come back to Oregon on May 14th.

On April 20th, after all our plans had been made and announced for Goldwater's return visit, Dean Burch called from Washington to tell me the Senator had decided to cancel the rest of the Oregon schedule. Burch said that he and Kitchel approved the decision and offered a number of reasons—the difficulty of reaching Oregon on a commercial airline, the awkward situation with Nixon, Lodge, and Senator Smith running in absentia, a desire to concentrate on California.

Burch told me I was to stay on the job and do what I thought best, that the official press release would give "the debate on civil rights" as the reason for the cancellation. Then he said, "How do you like standing up in a hammock, Steve?"

That is what we did for the rest of the Oregon campaign. The newspaper reporters, the television representatives, the Rockefeller, Lodge, and Nixon people all said we had written off Oregon. There were numerous monotonous variations—Goldwater, realizing he could not win the Oregon primary had given up hope for the nomination and was quitting, Goldwater did not like campaigning, the Washington staff did not approve of what the Goldwater people were doing in Oregon. In one version I was blamed for the Senator's decision to withdraw.

In retrospect, I think the cancellation was wise. But at the time all it did was increase my determination to continue the battle. Now it was a different ball game. We could not win, but I thought we could prevent Lodge from adding Oregon to New Hampshire. The volunteer workers were wonderful. Mrs. Mildred Sundeleaf, our tricounty chairman; Bob Gunderson, our Portland city man; Peter Buck, an Oregon lumberman who had abandoned his business to devote full time to the Goldwater cause; Mrs. Barbara Crouch, who ran our telephone campaign; Swigert; Prescott Cookingham; Mrs. Dorothy Leland; our agency people; and Mrs. Wright just were not about to concede anything. We decided that while we probably could not persuade any undecided voters to support Goldwater after his withdrawal, we could make sure that everyone presently committed to the Senator voted.

On May 4th, supporters of Richard Nixon opened a headquarters and started a fancy boiler-room telephone vote solicitation directed by an extremely competent professional, George Kent. Nixon had carried the state in 1960 and was extremely popular. This new activity added additional weight to the heavy burden we were trying to carry. I was particularly incensed because this situation could have been avoided.

One week before the official deadline Nixon had seriously considered taking his name off the Oregon ballot. Sig Unander suggested to one of the former Vice-President's close advisers that a Nixon withdrawal would be beneficial to all concerned. Unander argued that Nixon's only chance for the 1964 nomination would come as a compromise choice if Goldwater failed to win on the first two or three ballots. If Nixon stayed in the Oregon primary and won, he would have only eighteen votes. If Lodge or Rockefeller won the primary, Nixon could be blamed by the Goldwater people for splitting votes away from the Senator. In return for taking his name off the ballot he could be promised that if Goldwater was not nominated in San Francisco, the Oregon delegation would swing to Nixon.

The plan had many advantages—both to Goldwater and to Nixon. It was reasonable to believe the Nixon supporters in Oregon would swing to Goldwater rather than to Rockefeller or Lodge for a number of reasons. Ideologically, Nixon and Goldwater were close together; they were both from the West; and if Nixon did withdraw, we were certain to make a net gain.

The negotiations were carried on through an intermediary who was friendly to both sides. But the former Vice-President wanted to be reassured by someone on the Oregon delegation that if a deadlock did develop after the second ballot, he could be reasonably confident the votes would come his way.

This information came to me on a Sunday, and when I called our Washington office the only person I could reach was Clif White. I asked Clif to call Nixon's office in New York City and leave a message requesting the former Vice-President to make a particular telephone call on Monday morning. I explained the situation in detail, and White agreed to follow through.

The call was not made on Monday. When I demanded an explanation, White told me that Kitchel had come into the office and vetoed the operation because he did not think it would be proper for anyone on the Goldwater committee to approach Nixon with any kind of offer. Of course, I had not asked White to make an offer; I had only requested that he relay a message. But the call was not made, Nixon did not withdraw, and now we had an active contender who might be expected to attract a sizable block of Goldwater votes. Rockefeller and Lodge would divide the liberal Republicans; Nixon and Goldwater would split the conservatives.

The pollsters were all predicting a Lodge victory. The state's most important newspaper, the *Oregonian,* endorsed the ambassador editorially. Rockefeller, Scranton, and Margaret Chase Smith were all dismissed as minor contenders. But when Goldwater abandoned his personal campaign in Oregon, the governor of New York recognized an opportunity. He more than doubled his schedule of appearances, and he found a new slogan: "I'm the only man who cares enough about your votes to come to Oregon."

Among politicians there is a generous skepticism of the accuracy of the pollsters. This can be explained in part by examining the type of questions asked and the persons interviewed. In Oregon, the Lou Harris pollsters took a very small sampling and asked questions such as: "Do you agree with Senator Goldwater that we should get out of the United Nations?" A negative response was considered a vote against Goldwater, and the fact that the Senator had never seriously proposed withdrawal from the United Nations invalidated the interpretation of the response.

On the same day Burch told me Goldwater had canceled Oregon, Kleindienst informed me that I had been promoted to the position of regional director and would thereafter be responsible for all the western states with the exception of California. On May 2nd we held a regional meeting in Portland. Luke Williams, the

Goldwater chairman for the state of Washington, promised that no matter what happened in Oregon, Goldwater would get twenty-two of his state's twenty-four votes. Alaska was conceded to Rockefeller as the result of some bad management on our part. But Jerry Neils and Helen Johnson of Montana promised the solid support of their delegation. Bill Wright of Nevada said we would get six votes at San Francisco, and we got six. Jim McClary of Idaho promised and delivered fourteen. Fred Finlinson of Utah said they would elect a slate pledged to Goldwater, and they did. Herb Baus, president of a political public relations firm in charge of the campaign in California, contributed the only gloomy note—it would be touch and go in the Golden State, he said.

We might lose Oregon, but in the rest of the states in my region where the delegates would be chosen at state conventions the prospects were bright. All I had to do was derail the Lodge bandwagon.

Many of the Oregon Republicans remembered the lackadaisical campaign Lodge had put on as a candidate for Vice-President in 1960. The situation in South Viet Nam had not improved after the overthrow of the Diem government, and Lodge was continuing to behave like a reluctant guest at the wedding feast.

Through two hastily organized committees, we sponsored some newspaper ads designed to remind the Oregon voters of the Lodge deficiencies. I learned that Goldberg was planning to use the same four-year-old TV program which had been so helpful in New Hampshire. So I sent a telegram to Dwight Eisenhower at Palm Springs asking him either to authorize or condemn the use of that particular five-minute film. Twenty-four hours later I had the answer:

> Repeatedly I have expressed publicly my high esteem for each of the individuals prominently mentioned as possible nominees for the presidency in 1964. I respect each and oppose none.
>
> The film in question I have never seen, nor have I been contacted in any fashion in respect to its use prior to your communication. If it expresses my high respect for Cabot

Lodge, it is accurate and I do not object to that esteem being reaffirmed in any place in America. If it suggests that I have given any public indication of a preference for any person over any other in the current contest, then it is a definite misrepresentation.

(Signed) Dwight D. Eisenhower

When I released the contents of the wire to the newspapers, the Lodge managers canceled the television presentation scheduled to start the next day. They did edit the film and use it later, but the cutting was obvious, and the news stories had exposed what appeared to be a shabby attempt to make Oregon voters think that Eisenhower was supporting Lodge in 1964.

On May 15th the Oregon voters rewarded the man who "cared enough to come." Lodge ran second, Goldwater third, and Nixon fourth. Henry Cabot Lodge was never again a factor in the contest for the nomination. The pollsters who had predicted his victory were suddenly busy attempting to rationalize that error.

12

The California primary was actually won for Barry Goldwater at the Los Altos, a rococo stucco apartment house on Wilshire Boulevard in Los Angeles. Here in a three-bedroom suite on the second floor, which the ancient night clerk proudly said had been built to order for screen star Greta Garbo, the Goldwater team directed by Burch and Kleindienst produced a miracle.

The men who reversed the trend of a steady decline in Goldwater popularity were Lee Edwards, public information director for the Goldwater for President Committee; Ed Nellor, the Senator's acting press secretary; Eugene Hooker, an artist attached to Fuller, Smith and Ross; Karl Giegerich; Eunice Latham and George Lyon of that agency; Vern Stevens of Oregon, the Senator's first official advance man; Charlie Justice of New Hampshire, who was Goldwater's security man and constant companion during the campaign; Chuck Lichenstein, who had come over to the committee from Baroody's American Enterprise Institute; Rus Walton, executive secretary of United Republicans of California (UROC), a new and militantly conservative group; Ron Crawford, a thirty-four-year-old Los Angeles stock broker who volunteered his service; Richard Herman of Omaha, Nebraska; and a host of script writers and advertising men.

No one planned the Los Altos operation. For those of us who were directly involved it was eighteen days of unbelievable pressure punctuated by moments of despair and frustration.

The candidate who emerges victorious in the California primary wins a slate of delegates pledged to his nomination. In 1952, then Governor Earl Warren went to Chicago with the votes of the California delegation in his pocket and wound up with an appointment as Chief Justice of the United States Supreme Court.

By May 15th our private and confidential tally sheets showed more than four hundred delegate votes for Goldwater. Grenier and White were counting six hundred and forty-two, but not all of these had been elected. A disastrous loss in California coming on top of Oregon and New Hampshire might radically affect the eventual outcome. Earlier, the candidate himself had said that if he lost in California, it would be impossible to win the nomination.

Kleindienst moved his base of operations from Washington, D.C., to Los Angeles on May 1st. He spent the next two weeks touring the state, visiting with the Republicans who were working for the Senator and those who had not been invited to join the Goldwater team. He inspected headquarters from San Diego to Sacramento. Everywhere he went it was the same story. The California Republican party had never recovered from 1958.

Lieutenant Governor Goodwin Knight moved up to become chief executive when Warren was appointed to the Supreme Court. In 1954 he won re-election by more than a million vote plurality. It had been expected that he would again seek that post in 1958, but William Knowland, then in the United States Senate, decided to return to California and seek the governorship. It was claimed that he had his eye on the presidential nomination and believed that as governor of politically important California his chances would be enhanced. Knight, under severe pressure from party leaders, reluctantly stepped aside and became a candidate for Knowland's seat in the Senate. Knowland lost to Democrat Pat Brown, and Knight was defeated by Democrat Clare Engle. The political wounds from that game of musical chairs were still bleeding.

Richard Nixon added further complication to the situation when he returned to Los Angeles after his defeat in 1960 and became active in state politics. Assemblyman Joe Shell announced he was running for governor in 1962, believing the former Vice-President had no aspirations for that office. At the last minute Nixon entered the contest, won a bitter primary fight, and then lost in the general election.

There were at least three Republican parties in California—the Knowland faction, the Nixon supporters, and the Shell backers. The California Republican Assembly, a long-established, semi-official advisory group, was in competition with the regular state party organization, and the United Republicans of California was challenging both.

In the early spring of 1964, Knowland, chairman of the California Committee for Goldwater, and Pete Pitchess, sheriff of Los Angeles county, who was in charge of the southern portion of the state, had been remarkably successful in building a Goldwater organization. On the first day for filing these workers secured fifty thousand valid signatures to fill the petitions for Goldwater in one eight-hour blitz. Rockefeller did not file until just before the deadline, and Stassen never could meet the qualifications.

Kleindienst discovered the California Committee for Goldwater was as loaded with emotion and temperament as a Grade B movie script. All the players were devoted to the Senator's cause, but some of them were equally committed to advancing their own position.

The Nixon people were suspicious of the Shell group. The die-hard Knowland supporters were nursing a grudge over their hero's defeat six years earlier.

The first showdown between the Rockefeller and Goldwater forces came at the Young Republican convention held in San Francisco on July 27 and 28, 1963. A Goldwater man was elected national president, and the California YR's amended their by-laws to permit an official endorsement of the Senator.

The United Republicans of California meeting in state convention gleefully endorsed Goldwater. This action had been anticipated. When the California Republican Assembly met and gave its blessing to the Senator, the Rockefeller people cried foul, charged rigging, and some of them walked out of the meeting.

In Los Angeles such leading figures in the Republican Associates, a finance group, as Charles Ducommun, Leonard Firestone, and Justin Dart adopted a policy of "let's wait and see." Northern California, with its tradition of liberalism, was almost violently anti-Goldwater. In southern California, San Diego and Orange counties were equally violently anti-Rockefeller.

George Hinman and John Wells, the New York governor's political lieutenants, had hired the firm of Spencer–Roberts & Associates, the most successful managers in California politics. Long before the snows melted in New Hampshire the unfavorable press reports from that primary had started to erode Goldwater's popularity in the Golden State. Republican National Committeeman Joe Martin, Jr., resigned his office to work full time for Nelson Rockefeller. State Chairman Caspar Weinberger and a number of members of the California legislature openly opposed Goldwater.

In January, Knowland had named Bernard Brennan, a Los Angeles attorney, to direct the southern California Goldwater effort. He also employed the firm of Baus and Ross to handle public relations and advertising. Baus had successfully directed more than seventy campaigns, and Brennan had managed the Nixon effort which carried California in 1960. Unfortunately, a smoldering feud developed between them, and their failure to work well together affected the entire organization.

Goldwater and Burch flew out from Washington on the morning of April 15th for a conference at the International Inn adjacent to the airport. Herb Baus had arranged an itinerary which included an appearance on the Steve Allen CBS nighttime TV program and a Sunday afternoon guest spot on an NBC show to be released only in California; he planned to use the Senator's remaining time to film TV spots for use in the final weeks of the campaign. Baus says the schedule had been cleared and approved by Dean Burch. Goldwater claimed that he had not been told about the appearances and ordered them all canceled. After a stormy argument the Steve Allen show was reinstated, but Knowland was sent to pinch-hit for Goldwater on NBC.

On the afternoon Nelson Rockefeller was defeating both Goldwater and Lodge in Oregon, Dick Kleindienst reported his negative findings on the California organization.

"I told Goldwater and Burch that if the election were being held that day, we would lose California by at least two hundred thousand votes," Kleindienst says. "The organization was narrow and limited in its concepts. Good Republicans had been excluded. Our billboards, radio, TV, newspaper advertising just didn't match the smooth professional job the Rockefeller people were doing."

Kleindienst was the most controversial man on the Senator's staff, and by all accounts the only member of the inner circle who ever questioned the group's political decisions.

After New Hampshire Kleindienst had gone to Illinois. His conversations with rank-and-file voters convinced him that Goldwater must do something to contradict the charge that he intended to abolish Social Security. At a strategy session attended by Baroody, McCabe, Kitchel, George Humphrey, Arthur Summerfield, and the Senator, Kleindienst suggested that when Goldwater made his only scheduled appearance in Illinois he should give full attention to the Social Security problem. The suggestion was rejected. After the meeting, Baroody and McCabe took Kleindienst into a private office and accused him of being disloyal. As Kleindienst remembers it, Baroody said: "Don't you know what it is to have team work? We've decided what Goldwater is going to do in Illinois. You knew about the decision, and yet you brought up this Social Security business in front of all the other people."

"I have just one loyalty, and that's to Goldwater," Kleindienst replied. "If disagreeing with you is being disloyal, then I don't understand your definition. What I said in that meeting is true. The Senator must contradict the stories now being spread by his political enemies, and so long as I'm a part of this effort I'm going to say what I believe."

Goldwater went to Illinois on April 14th, delivered the speech Karl Hess had written at the direction of Baroody, McCabe, and Kitchel, and barely mentioned Social Security. Kleindienst was not invited to any more strategy sessions.

But Baroody, McCabe, and Kitchel were not present in Los Angeles. Now Dean Burch was running the campaign. Kitchel and the Baroody group were still dictating the content of the speeches, but the politicians who always had difficulty contacting Kitchel found it easier to talk to Burch.

Kleindienst's prescription for averting defeat in California was to bring the Senator's political team from Washington and to put Dean Burch in charge for an all-out last-minute effort. The effect of such a proposal would be to take authority from Knowland and Pitchess and the rest of the California group. Volunteers in a political effort receive very little in the way of tangible reward beyond the bolstering of their own egos. The old frictions in California had produced a dangerous situation—Knowland, Pitchess, Brennan, and Baus would certainly interpret the act as an indication that Goldwater had lost confidence in their ability and their leadership.

Kleindienst pointed out that his suggestion was dangerous. If Knowland reacted with resentment, the move could destroy the entire Goldwater organization. He was equally positive that unless the change was made, Rockefeller would win the primary.

Goldwater discussed the situation frankly with Knowland and Pitchess. To their everlasting credit, they eagerly accepted the proposal and worked with Burch in complete harmony during the final days. Burch stayed on in California, and the men who made up the Los Altos team flew in to join him.

I left Portland on Saturday, May 16th, for Phoenix, intending to spend a day or two at home and then go on to the political conventions in Washington, Idaho, Montana, and Utah. On Sunday morning Goldwater called me from Los Angeles and asked me to come to California at once.

On Monday morning, May 18th, we held our first meeting at the Los Altos. Goldwater had gone to Washington, but Burch, Kleindienst, Nellor, Edwards, and Lichenstein gathered with Brennan, Baus, Henry Salvatori (California finance chairman), and Dudley Thompson, Brennan's administrative assistant.

Our first concern was radio and TV spots. Thompson and Baus assured us that adequate time had been purchased, but when we asked what messages they intended to use, their response was shocking. First Thompson said they had made some. Then he said they were in the process of making them. Then he said they were having the scripts prepared. Baus maintained he had submitted a number of concepts to Brennan for final approval and had been told that Neal Reagan of the McCann, Erickson agency was handling production.

It all added up to exactly nothing. We were two weeks and one day away from the primary which would spell success or failure.

The local TV was saturated with arguments on behalf of the New York governor—and we had nothing.

In Oregon we had used radio spots voiced by five different Republican congressmen. They were effective, hard-sell arguments in support of Goldwater. I gave Thompson a master recording, and he promised to have duplicates made for immediate release. Burch, Salvatori, and Brennan started to work on a budget for the final days. Gene Hooker of the Fuller, Smith and Ross agency was designated to lay out newspaper ads. Mrs. Latham was instructed to telephone New York and order all the Goldwater film which the agency had made between New Hampshire and Oregon. We sent Dud Thompson to gather up samples of the California material which might be available for radio or TV.

Fuller, Smith and Ross had a thirty-minute TV film entitled *The Goldwater Story* and a fifteen-minute panel discussion on the Goldwater candidacy, featuring Senators Curtis, Mundt, and other Republican leaders. But the twenty-, forty- and sixty-second spots consisted almost entirely of excerpts from Goldwater campaign speeches in New Hampshire. Kitchel, Baroody, and McCabe, convinced that the Senator was his own best advocate, had decided to concentrate their TV efforts on Goldwater selling Goldwater. The Senator can be extremely persuasive, but in twenty or forty seconds a third person can say things about a candidate which the candidate cannot say about himself, and there was little we could salvage from the early material.

Thompson returned to the Los Altos at two o'clock that afternoon. He told us he had been unable to find the scripts. For an hour we listened to his complaints about the inefficiency of Baus and Ross. Finally Ed Nellor brought in teams of writers to prepare more effective TV spots. Everyone at the Los Altos wrote short messages for radio, concepts for TV, and contributed to the planning of the newspaper campaign.

Baus and Ross had purchased three half-hours on the best stations in California to be used the final week of the campaign. But no thought had been given to program content. Toward the end of that first week the Los Altos crew completed its first assignment. Radio spots were on the air; the TV spots were being made;

newspaper advertisements were plated and ready for distribution. Things were looking up.

In the meantime the Rockefeller people were concentrating almost entirely on personal attacks against Goldwater. They repeated the distortions which had come out of New Hampshire and then assaulted the distortions. One mass-produced, widely distributed Rockefeller brochure asked: "Do you want a leader or a loner?" and then went on to suggest that Lodge, Scranton, and Nixon were all supporting the wing of the party represented by the New York governor, while Goldwater, the "loner," advocated policies and remedies long since rejected by the party.

In the precincts thousands of Goldwater supporters started asking "Do you want a leader or a lover?"

The Senator was scheduled to arrive in Los Angeles for a week end of appearances on May 22nd. At the Los Altos we believed he should bring with him a strong statement contradicting the Rockefeller misrepresentation.

Burch called Washington and told Kitchel that we had such a statement and would like to have the Senator release it. At first Kitchel said, "No, Goldwater is not going to challenge any other Republican"; then he had us read the statement to a stenographer in Washington, and when the Senator arrived he did issue a radically watered down release questioning some of the Rockefeller claims.

At a conference Saturday night in the Ambassador Hotel I suggested that for his final TV presentation Goldwater follow the pattern established in his early Arizona victories, with the Senator and his family in a living-room setting, the dialogue to be a serious discussion of why Goldwater felt it was necessary to seek the Presidency—his vision for the country, what he hoped to accomplish, his concern for the errors of the present administration, and a specific presentation of what he would do in the event he should become President of the United States.

Kitchel and Hess opposed the concept, but the Senator brushed aside their objections, saying, "Steve and I have done this a number of times, and it has always been effective."

Chuck Lichenstein proposed that we send camera crews into the southern California streets to interview citizens and record the questions they would like to have the Senator answer. We decided that both concepts would be scripted and made ready for production when the Senator returned to California on May 28th.

In that final ten-day period the grass-roots organizations covering vast areas were busy distributing literature, soliciting support, and perfecting a get-out-the-vote system. In northern California, where Rockefeller was much stronger, an unauthorized strategy was employed. The Phyllis Schlafly book, *A Choice Not an Echo,* was available in quantities at an extremely low price. Volunteers took it upon themselves to deliver these books in the precincts to voters who indicated a preference for Rockefeller. After the election a survey made of the "book precincts" indicated this technique was extremely effective. Rus Walton of UROC, who made the analysis, told me that in comparing residential areas composed of voters with the same economic, educational, and occupational backgrounds, the Goldwater vote was more than 20 per cent stronger in the "book precincts."

After San Francisco the Senator and his managers were severely criticized by those who objected to the contents of the Schlafly book, *None Dare Call It Treason,* and *A Texan Looks at Lyndon.* (These will be discussed in detail in another chapter.)

The Los Altos crew pumped new blood into the California operation and by Sunday, May 24th, the feeling of despair had been replaced by a note of cautious optimism; then the bomb was dropped.

Howard K. Smith, moderator of the ABC-TV program "Issues and Answers," had invited Goldwater to appear for a pretaped interview to be released on Sunday afternoon. In the course of the discussion Smith said he understood the Senator had recommended interdicting the supply route from Red China which the Communists were using to feed their war machine in South Viet Nam. "How," he asked, "could this be done?" Goldwater had replied, "Well, it is not as easy as it sounds, because these are not trails that are out in the open. There have been several suggestions made; I don't think we would use any of them. But defoliation of the forest by low-yield atomic weapons could well be done. When you remove the foliage, you remove the covering."

Kitchel and Hess were present in the studio when the program was taped. They failed to recognize the possibility of misinterpretation. And before the program was released on nationwide TV, the wire services, under a Washington dateline, quoted Goldwater as advocating the use of atomic weapons in Viet Nam. UPI apologized for its error later and ultimately issued a retraction, but the denial never caught up with the news story, and Goldwater was branded as a militarist who would provoke an atomic war.

No one has ever satisfactorily explained just why or how the story was released. From Goldwater's standpoint the reporting was unforgivable. At the convention and throughout the election campaign the Senator was bitterly criticized for "a hostility" toward the press. Perhaps it would have been more politic to forgive and forget, but the gross distortion in the New Hampshire headline about Social Security, the totally false UPI dispatch, and a dozen other equally egregious errors all suggest that perhaps the press itself must accept some of the blame.

At the Los Altos we were greatly concerned over the policy which prohibited any reference in the Goldwater campaign to Governor Rockefeller's divorce and remarriage. Many of us felt the issue must be exploited.

In the week of May 25th-30th, Rockefeller was scheduled to address the convention of a fraternal order in Long Beach, and had been invited to speak to the students of Loyola University. The fraternal order canceled its invitation, and Cardinal McIntyre of the Diocese of Los Angeles moved to block the Rockefeller appearance at Loyola University. The Cardinal explained to the press that he did not want anyone to get a false impression that the Roman Catholic Church was giving its official blessing to the candidacy of a man who had been divorced and then remarried.

On Thursday, May 28th, sixteen Protestant ministers, representing a wide segment of the Christian community, met in Los Angeles and issued a statement suggesting that Nelson Rockefeller should withdraw from the race because of his demonstrated inability to handle his own domestic affairs.

The one issue which both Goldwater and Rockefeller had ignored was now out in the open. The Cardinal's words and the statement by the Protestant ministers echoed from church pulpits on Sunday, May 31st. On June 1st, Mrs. Margaretta Fitler Murphy Rockefeller presented her new husband with a son.

Goldwater returned to Los Angeles on May 27th. Preparations had been made to film the family script at a Hollywood studio the following morning, and John Wayne was on hand at eight o'clock to do the narration. Burch, who was with the Senator at the Ambassador Hotel, called the Los Altos at ten minutes of eight to tell us that Goldwater had canceled the film upon his arrival in Los Angeles the night before. No one had bothered to inform Wayne. A number of excuses were offered—the Senator was too fatigued, the production would be too complicated, there was not time. Ultimately, I learned that Kitchel and Hess vetoed the family show.

Goldwater did go to the studio to film the question-and-answer program prepared by Lichenstein.

Dean Burch now says that Goldwater was more like a candidate during those final days of the California primary than at any other period between January and November. His appearances, culminating in a tremendous rally at Knott's Berry Farm, brought out the faithful. On June 2nd he beat Rockefeller by a few more than sixty thousand votes.

Much has been written about the violent, intemperate, partisanship of Goldwater supporters. The Senator's adversaries were cloaked with a halo of sweet reason, but at the Knott's Berry Farm rally a threat to assassinate the Senator and bomb the gathering was taken seriously by agents of the FBI. The G-Men could not officially act as Goldwater protectors, but their investigation of the incident prompted them to delay the Senator's appearance for more than thirty minutes, and they advised canceling the meeting. They told the Goldwater managers it was impossible to guard the Senator from what they believed was some crackpot in the crowd, capable of murder.

Between June 2nd and the opening of the Republican National Convention on July 13th, a series of weak and poorly planned maneuvers were instituted in an effort to undo the effect of the California primary. At the Governors' Conference in Cleveland, Scranton, Rockefeller, Romney, and Nixon all tried and failed. They wanted to stop Goldwater, but not a single one of the four would declare himself ready to lead the battle.

Scranton visited Ike at Gettysburg on June 6th, and this was widely accepted by the press as evidence that the former Republican President was ready to support the governor of Pennsylvania.

Clif White, Dick Kleindienst, and I had gone to the Governors' Conference to resist if we could any further division in the Republican party. When word of the Scranton-Eisenhower meeting reached us, White called George Humphrey and asked his help.

Scranton was scheduled to appear on a nationwide TV program Sunday morning from Cleveland. It was predicted that he would announce his candidacy and claim Eisenhower's support. Ike himself was scheduled to arrive in Cleveland to address the conference on Monday night. He was to be the house guest of George Humphrey.

According to Clif White, Humphrey called Eisenhower Saturday evening and told the former President, who had named him Secretary of the Treasury, in blunt words that if the rumors were true, if Ike intended to support Scranton, it would be very embarrassing for Goldwater-supporter Humphrey to have the former President as his house guest.

Eisenhower is reported to have called Scranton on Sunday morning to tell him the friendly visit in Gettysburg was just that. Ike was not supporting any candidate for the nomination. The Scranton bubble collapsed.

When Ike arrived in Cleveland, Humphrey met him and never left his side while the two were in the Sheraton-Cleveland Hotel. Eisenhower made a speech which Goldwater himself might have written, hammering away at the evils of big government.

Nixon did not arrive until Tuesday. At a press conference he said it would be a tragedy if Senator Goldwater's views as previously stated were not challenged and repudiated. But Governor Mark Hatfield of Oregon bluntly told the conferees; "The war is over. Now," he said, "it is time to start thinking about November."

It was over, but Scranton did not get the message. On Friday, June 12th, speaking to the Maryland state convention, he became an active candidate. This last-ditch effort to derail the Goldwater bandwagon merely solidified the Senator's strength in the remaining convention states.

In Tacoma, Washington, Goldwater forces threatened to rewrite the party by-laws which gave a seat on the delegation to the statutory officers—chairman, vice-chairman, and finance chairman—because John Hauberg, the finance man, was not a Goldwater supporter. I stayed up all night at that convention and finally convinced the instigators of this revolt that Goldwater had the nomination and that we should be looking to November and not disturbing the harmony of the party.

I found a similar situation brewing in Idaho Falls, where the Republicans were meeting in state convention to name their delegates. Governor Robert Smylie was not a Goldwater supporter, and the Senator's partisans were determined to keep him off the delegation. I spent a second sleepless night pointing out that one vote would make no difference, but that to deny an incumbent governor official status in San Francisco would seriously injure our chances for victory in November.

In Montana, Governor Tim Babcock had earlier recommended an uninstructed delegation. But under the threat of the Scranton candidacy the Goldwater people were determined to seek passage of a resolution committing Montana to vote for Goldwater. Babcock, who had been an early supporter of the Senator, finally agreed to change his position, and Montana's fourteen delegates were pledged to the Senator.

Between the day Scranton announced and the day the convention opened in San Francisco, not a single delegate we had counted for Goldwater switched to the Pennsylvania governor. Our private polls indicated that for all his efforts, this Johnny-come-lately in the race failed to gain as many as ten votes.

Part Four

San Francisco

13

The Mark Hopkins Hotel stands arrogantly on the crest of San Francisco's Nob Hill. An undersized automobile courtyard guards the entrance to a magnificent high-ceilinged lobby. The rear of the building descends two full stories to meet the sloping ground and thus provides space for an inside hotel garage. Such an arrangement is convenient for guests. It was especially convenient for the leading contender for the presidential nomination and for the men on the Goldwater team who could depart for the Cow Palace in their special vehicles unhindered by the thronging partisans in the courtyard and lobby.

Directly across California Street from the Mark, the Fairmont Hotel extends a spacious and gracious invitation. Cater-cornered, the ancient red sandstone mass of the Pacific Union Club serves as a monument to the wealth of San Francisco's social leaders. A block south, the spires and stained-glass windows of uncompleted Grace Cathedral bestow a blessing in granite and marble upon the city of hills and history.

In other seasons the Mark and the Fairmont have served as rendezvous for the traveler and the native, the securely rich, and the climbers on their way up. But in July of 1964 these gracious hostelries had cast aside all pretense and abandoned themselves to the politicians of the Republican party.

The Goldwater forces dominated the Mark. There were a hospitality suite in the Room of the Dons, a finance committee headquarters in the Regency Room, and a press headquarters equipped with typewriters and mimeograph machines in the Argonaut Room.

Political headquarters had been established on the fifteenth floor, and a strategy command post in the presidential suite on the seventeenth floor was occupied by William Joseph Baroody, Sr., chairman of the American Enterprise Institute.

Baroody, who avoided any contact with the political figures coming to the Mark to pay their respects to Senator Goldwater, had been authorized by Denison Kitchel to assemble a brain trust, a corps of intellectuals who would contribute from their special knowledge to Goldwater's public statements, speeches, and policy positions.

Both Kitchel and Goldwater had great confidence in Baroody. The brain trust was composed of Dr. Warren Nutter, Professor of Economics at the University of Virginia; Harry Jaffa, Professor of Political Science at Claremont Men's College in California; Professor Glen Campbell of the Hoover Institution; Washington lawyer Ed McCabe, who was publicly identified as Head of Research for the Goldwater for President Committee; and Chuck Lichenstein, another protégé of Baroody and Karl Hess.

There is nothing in American politics quite like a nominating convention. Destiny walks the streets of the convention city. Delegates come for fun and games, to meet in secret session, to aspire, connive, and to confirm.

To be a delegate to a national political convention, to be a participant in the making of history, to wear an official badge and display the colors of your leader is raw meat rich enough to compensate for all the tedious meetings back home, the neighborhood canvass, the labors in the precincts. But only the naïve among the delegates and the deliberate pretenders among the commentators and columnists hold to the notion that the delegate's task is to consider the candidates and then exercise personal judgment as to the fitness and the acceptability of the contenders.

Contrary to the arguments advanced by some newspaper writers and television oracles, the business of the convention is in reality to finalize the decisions which have been made weeks and months earlier at state primaries and in state conventions. The delegates were in San Francisco as representatives of the nationwide Republican constituency to ratify a judgment already expressed.

Millions of American citizens in recent years have found exciting entertainment in the television broadcasts of political conventions. The pontifications of the commentators are avidly received. The whole affair has taken on the aspect of a new spectator sport. Regrettably, this new audience response is not based upon an understanding of either the mechanics or the purpose of these quadrennial exercises in selfgovernment.

There is no constitutional provision for political parties in the United States, and there is no federal statutory authority for the nominating convention. Both are essential to the success of our present representative form of government.

The first successful candidate to be nominated by a party convention was Andrew Jackson in 1831, who was then running for a second term of office. But the first seven Presidents were elected and eleven presidential elections were held, before the convention nominating system was adopted.

National political parties are loose confederations of state party organizations. In most states the party is subject to statutory regulations, and is held together by the cement of patronage and political heritage.

It might be argued that recent developments in electronic communications—television, radio, high-speed newspaper printers, and the transportation speed of the jet age—have lessened the importance and the need for national nominating conventions.

Delegates to a national convention are selected in a variety of ways. Both political parties follow the same general rule in allocating the number of delegate votes to a particular state. Election of delegates may be at large or by congressional districts in a statewide primary. Some states name their delegates at a state convention. Some states combine these methods.

In those states which by statute select their delegates at conventions, the decision to instruct or not to instruct is at the discretion of the qualified voters in the state convention.

The delegates assembled at San Francisco were charged with the responsibility of adopting a national platform, nominating candidates for President and Vice-President, officially electing a new Republican National Committee to serve from 1964 to 1968, and adopting the rules of the convention. Hopefully the party would emerge united behind the platform and candidate and in position to attract a majority of the votes to be cast in November.

Party continuity is maintained by the National Committee whose members are elected to serve for four years, continuing in office until their successors have been elected at the next national convention. In practice, the national committeeman and committeewoman from each state is chosen either by a state convention or by a statewide election. But those so elected do not in fact become members of the National Committee until the convention places its official stamp of approval on the state's selection.

The system frequently creates lame ducks. Mrs. C. Douglass Buck, the charming official who would read the roll call of votes at the Cow Palace, had not been a candidate for re-election as national committeewoman from Delaware and would cease to be a member of the National Committee at the end of the 1964 convention. San Francisco was officially chosen as the site of the 1964 convention on June 22, 1963, over Atlantic City, Chicago, Dallas, Detroit, Miami Beach, and Philadelphia by a committee headed by Jean Tool. In July of 1964, Mr. Tool, former Republican state chairman of Colorado, was no longer a member of the National Committee.

Only once before had the Republican party held a convention in a West Coast city, and there were some observers who argued that the return to San Francisco in 1964 was a reflection of the increasing vigor of the Republican party in the western half of the United States.

The 1,308 official delegates were housed in twenty-eight different hotels. A corresponding number of accredited alternates were scattered about the city, some of them separated from their official state delegation.

There were three power centers—the St. Francis Hotel overlooking Union Square, where the Platform committee held its meetings in the week prior to the convention opening; the Mark Hopkins which housed both Goldwater and Scranton headquarters; and the new San Francisco Hilton whose main ballroom was divided into press conference rooms, a public relations office for the distribution of press releases, and work rooms for the wire services and other reporters.

The committee on arrangements had attempted to accommodate the convention to eastern and midwestern television audiences. Partisans frequently complain of the treatment their cause receives from the "big eye." But no wise politician can ignore the tremendous impact this exciting new communications medium exerts on American life. Few candidates ever achieve the great audience which is theirs at the hour of nomination and during the acceptance speech.

The deliberations and pronouncements of the Platform committee are the natural prelude to the convention itself. Political realists insist that the Party Platform is a meaningless collection of promises which no one intends to keep. Recent history would support this contention. The Platform is written and adopted before a candidate is nominated, but contests within the Platform committee are frequently a key to the relative strength of the contenders for the nomination.

In Chicago in 1960 the nomination of Richard Nixon was a "no contest" affair. The Platform committee wrote and rewrote, rejected and adopted in response to a clash of wills beween the governor of New York and the then Vice-President. Mr. Nixon, with the nomination assured, was able to exert influence on the Platform's statements through the committee's chairman, Chuck Percy of Illinois.

It has been suggested that the 1964 committee on Platform was subservient to the desires of Goldwater and fashioned its statement to express the philosophical position of the man who ultimately received the nomination. The critics are only partially correct. Goldwater, through his supporters, did influence the language of the Platform, but this is true only because a majority of the members of the Platform committee shared the convictions of the Senator from Arizona. The oft repeated charge that the Goldwater team ran over the Platform committee with a steamroller will not hold up if the makeup of the committee is reviewed.

Under party rules each state is permitted to name one man and one woman delegate to participate as a member of the Committee on Resolutions (Platform). These members are usually selected by the Republican state chairman, and unless it is suggested that Goldwater forces also controlled fifty independent Republican state chairmen, it is ridiculous to claim they controlled the makeup or the conclusions of the Platform committee.

Congressman Mel Laird, chairman of the 1964 committee, and Congressman John Rhodes of Arizona represented the Goldwater thinking during the deliberations. The truly influential connection between Goldwater and the Platform committee was completely overlooked by the news media. William Baroody, Jr., served as Mel Laird's administrative assistant; his father, in the presidential suite of the Mark Hopkins, was in command of the Goldwater brain trust.

The Mark Hopkins is an admirable hotel and provided suitable personal headquarters for a presidential candidate, but the difficulty of access, the constant flow of visitors and supporters, created problems for the working staff. During the convention the elevators reserved for the public were always crowded and always late. It was frequently necessary for the Goldwater staff men to travel to the fifteenth floor in a freight elevator normally used by room-service waiters, but the Mark was in keeping with the status required of a major contender, and the Goldwater advance men began preparing their base of operations there the second week in April when Jim Day of Washington, D.C., took residence at the Mark.

The bedrooms and hallways on the fifteenth floor were carefully mapped. Space in the center was allocated to Dean Burch and the administration. At one end a parlor suite was converted into headquarters for the field operation; at the opposite end of the hallway a press room was established. The television studio was installed adjacent to the press headquarters, and provision was made to originate both TV and radio broadcasts. One full-size bedroom was given over to a special telephone switchboard. Mother Bell was queen of the fifteenth floor. There was a private telephone for each Goldwater regional director. Additional private telephones served the press section, radio and television, the administration, and the strategy group on the seventeenth floor.

Jim Day reserved a room or a suite in each of thirty-six different hotels where the official delegates were to stay. Twenty-nine private lines with a direct connection to the Goldwater switchboard in the Mark were installed in these delegate hotels, and there were direct lines leading from the Senator's quarters to the Cow Palace.

Traffic-choked streets physically separated the Republican delegates from the Goldwater men on the fifteenth floor of the Mark. The telephone system brought them all together, made them instantly available. A Goldwater regional director or a Goldwater state chairman could communicate with any member of the Goldwater staff independent of the clogged hotel switchboard, and the communication was private.

Commencing July 5th the regional telephones were manned from eight o'clock in the morning until long after midnight. Each regional director had at least two volunteer assistants. Most of the traffic was routine, but Mother Bell helped to cement all the Goldwater delegates into a solid army of strength for the Arizona Senator.

All the newspapers commented on the efficiency of the Goldwater operation, but not a single reporter remarked on the fact that Governor Scranton, who did not become an official candidate until June 12, 1964, and occupied the twelfth floor at the Mark, had a communications trailer similar to Goldwater's (though not so elaborate) and had a floor telephone system and short-wave radio. This remarkable display of efficient advance planning could have caused some lifted eyebrows. Actually all of these facilities were provided to the Scranton organization by Nelson Rockefeller.

Dean Burch moved into his administration post on the fifteenth floor of the Mark on July 1st. White and Kleindienst were there ahead of him. The political men, the regional directors, came in on July 5th.

In the Fletcher Knebel novel *Convention* the author conjures up a computer loaded with derogatory personal data on the delegates. In the novel this information is used in an attempt to coerce a vote favorable to one of the contenders, but the device ultimately reacts against his sponsor.

In the regional directors' room at the Mark were a dozen big, black, looseleaf notebooks indexed and cross-filed. They contained detailed information about each delegate—length of service in the party, how the delegate was chosen, business connections, profession, clubs, schools, place of prior residence, wife's name, children's names, information which could offer some key to the delegate's probable attitude toward Goldwater, personal history useful in establishing a closer personal relationship. But in the total collection there was not one item of derogatory information.

Convention officials, officers and staff of the National Committee, and delegates assigned to the Platform committee, all arrived in San Francisco in that week before the convention. The assignment from White and Kleindienst to the regional directors was: "Keep track of the delegates in your region." To carry out this command was a monumental task.

The newspapers and the television and radio reporters focused attention on the Platform committee and on the contenders. The regional directors on the Goldwater team looked after each delegate with loving solicitude.

Was the state delegation coming in a body? By train, plane, or car? What date did the delegation plan to leave its home state? When were they scheduled to arrive in San Francisco? Where were they to be housed?

The answers to these questions—gathered long in advance—made it possible for the regional directors to make contact the minute a delegate checked into his or her hotel.

Some delegations were met by Goldwater representatives when they arrived in San Francisco. The Goldwater hospitality room at the airport was staffed by volunteers and operated twenty-four hours a day. On Friday, Saturday, and Sunday, as the majority of the delegations arrived, each individual was recorded by name, hotel, room number, and telephone number.

Preliminary organization of the state delegations had been first projected early in February, long before the delegates were actually chosen. In most states there was a designated Goldwater leader, an inside man who would be a member of the delegation. He would receive the signals and pass them on to the Goldwater delegates in his state. In addition, there was an outside man who was not a member of the delegation. The inside men would attend every caucus; the outside men would observe and report and keep track of the delegates' whereabouts.

Kleindienst was responsible for the "buddy system." In every delegation there were those whose loyalty was not of the "signed in blood" variety. Goldwater delegates were assigned to keep tab, to eat and drink and live with a "buddy" who might be susceptible to pressure from the stop-Goldwater movement.

To keep track of the southern region, Peter O'Donnell and John Grenier established a headquarters occupying most of the second-floor public-meeting space in the Jack Tar Motel. Locator boards bearing the names of the southern delegates, their room numbers, and telephone numbers in two-inch letters, stood ten feet tall around the room. Over the boards were plastic sheets. Delegates do not spend a great deal of time in their own hotel rooms. The plastic covering permitted the staff to follow each delegate almost hour by hour by writing his new location with a grease pencil.

If a delegate went to dinner at one of the wonderful restaurants in the city which is famous for its food, the inside man or the outside man assigned to that state would advise the locator board where the delegate could be reached by telephone.

It was true that most of the southerners were committed to the Senator from Arizona, but delegates can be stampeded, persuaded, given misinformation. In the event the opposition was able to mount a real threat to Goldwater, it was imperative that the men in the Mark be able to reach the delegates immediately.

On the fifteenth floor at the Mark smaller locator boards scanned by closed-circuit TV cameras enabled White, Kleindienst, Burch, and Kitchel to determine at a glance where each of their lieutenants might be found at a particular moment.

If Wayne Hood went out to dinner at Fisherman's Wharf, the name of the restaurant and the telephone number where he could be reached was on the locator board. If Dick Herman was supervising activities in Region Five headquarters at the Del Webb Townhouse Motel, the locator board carried that information.

Most of the delegates would travel to the Cow Palace in chartered buses or taxicabs. A fleet of automobiles equipped with two-way shortwave radio was at the disposal of the Goldwater staff and regional directors. Under the rules established by White and Kleindienst, the regional men went out in separate automobiles.

"If there is to be an accident or an incident," White explained, "we don't want to lose more than one of you. We can't predict the accidents, but we must be prepared for the incidents."

To communicate with all the delegates, California supporters of the Senator had purchased time for commercial announcements on one of the San Francisco radio stations. The Goldwater delegates monitored these broadcasts on portable radios.

The Senator from Arizona arrived in San Francisco on Monday, July 6th. He was given a welcome usually reserved for conquering heroes and modestly admitted that he thought he had enough delegates to win the nomination.

The fifteenth floor was overcrowded with Goldwater staff. A constant stream of well-wishers—Republicans from every corner of the nation—fought their way through the lobby. Denison Kitchel had arranged with the hotel management to have the elevators by-pass the fifteenth floor. Those seeking admission were required to walk up from the fourteenth floor where the elevators stopped. The stairway was guarded by a Pinkerton man, who admitted only authorized personnel, identified by a gilt American eagle lapel pin. Wearers of the pin could bring visitors past the guard. Others seeking admission were detained until some staff member would vouch for them.

In the regional headquarters our count was 770 votes for sure, with the possibility of a favorable break in the Ohio delegation adding more. White and Kleindienst had kept their part of the bargain. The field organization had carried out its assignment. Unless something happened, the stop-Goldwater movement was doomed to defeat.

But until the votes would be counted sometimes on the evening of Wednesday, July 15th, the Goldwater team was taking nothing for granted.

14

At twenty-six minutes past nine on the morning of Saturday, July 11th, an unmarked chartered bus turned right off the Bay Shore freeway at the exit marked "Cow Palace." In the next five days thousands of delegates and alternates, spectators, reporters, columnists, and commentators would travel this same route. They would come to criticize, to speculate, some of them to picket, others to participate in the ritual of selecting the Republican party's candidate for President in 1964.

The passengers on this particular bus were a part of the convention, yet apart from it. They comprised the Goldwater team, experienced, practical politicians, enlisted from every corner of the nation to secure the nomination for the Senator from Arizona. For some, this short trip from the Hotel Mark Hopkins to the Cow Palace was the prelude to the end of a journey which had commenced four years and one hundred thousand miles ago. They were confident but not cocky.

Under the leadership of Richard G. Kleindienst and Clif White, these men had carried the flag of their hero into every state of the union. They enjoyed a carefully cultivated first-name acquaintance with most of the delegates. They had learned to share responsibility.

In the days and weeks following the convention these men would be described in scandal magazines as Barry's Bully Boys, would be accused of railroading the convention, would be catalogued as members of some sinister right-wing extremist group.

Early in February at a point in the preconvention campaign when no one really believed Goldwater might win the nomination, the task of organizing the convention communications had been delegated to Clif White.

Looking more like a college professor, which he had been, than a hard-nosed political expert which he was, White stood in the stepwell at the front of the bus holding a walkie-talkie radio in his right hand. Now, speaking over the public address system normally used by sightseeing guides, White repeated the message he had received by shortwave radio: "I have just been told a group of reporters who came out early to inspect the interior of the building are still inside. We will proceed to a side street and wait until we've been notified of their departure. Please avoid attracting attention when we are parked."

White could remember 1952 in Chicago when the preconvention favorite, Senator Robert Taft of Ohio, had lost the nomination to the popular war hero Dwight Eisenhower. Clif had been a soldier in the ranks at the convention. He had seen the Lodge and Dewey lieutenants first confuse and then stampede delegates. He could remember the hour when Lodge had skillfully challenged the credentials of the Taft delegates and then raised his sign with its sanctimonious admonition: "Thou shalt not steal." Lodge had gone on to successfully question the integrity of the Senator from Ohio whose entire political life had been a symbol of integrity. That nomination had been lost because at the crucial point in the convention the Taft forces had not known their exact strength. A motion which might have been defeated was allowed to pass.

As a result of his long background in the jungle of eastern seaboard politics, White understood and respected the power centers committed to the stop-Goldwater movement. He knew how delegates could be threatened, coaxed, controlled, and he had laid his plans accordingly.

In 1952 the opponents of Taft had united behind Eisenhower. Outnumbered at the start of the convention, they had been able to prevent some Taft delegates from being seated, had persuaded others to join the General's cause. This year it was different. The opposition had not been able to coalesce around a single candidate. After the unexpected Lodge victory in New Hampshire the anti-Goldwater voices had attempted to make the 1960 vice-presidential candidate a popular hero. But Henry Cabot Lodge was in Viet Nam. He had accepted an appointment in the diplomatic service from the man who defeated Nixon and dashed Republican hopes of continuing in power.

As Richard Nixon's running mate in 1960, Lodge had campaigned in such a leisurely fashion as to offend the dedicated party workers. Now four years later it had been difficult, if not impossible, to arouse any enthusiasm for Lodge in the hearts and minds of Republican chairmen who had gone through the 1960 defeat.

The Rockefeller victory in Oregon, where Lodge ran second, had compelled the stop-Goldwater forces, momentarily at least, to focus their attention on the governor of New York. After the Arizona Senator confounded the pollsters and squeaked by in California, the stop-Goldwater movement should have collapsed like a burst balloon. It did not. The die-hards moved in behind Pennsylvania's Governor William Scranton, and that affable latecomer was now optimistically predicting Goldwater would fail the nomination on the first ballot and ultimately be rejected by the convention.

Spokesmen for the stop-Goldwater movement hopefully recited details of the Philadelphia convention which had resulted in the unexpected nomination of Wendell Willkie. They found comfort in the 1952 defeat of Taft by Eisenhower and suggested that the Old Guard, captained by Henry Lodge, would yet produce a miracle in San Francisco. Clif White was planning to disappoint them.

Kleindienst and White had divided the nation into six territories or regions. To head the regions they had recruited an elite corps of practical, knowledgeable political pros. These men, with their assistants and some, but not all, of the state lieutenants, were on the bus, ready for a preview and a briefing on the communications system.

White believed it was necessary to maintain constant contact with the Goldwater people in each state delegation. With the able technical assistance of telephone company executive Nick Volcheff, direct telephone lines had been installed to seventeen key positions on the convention floor.

At forty-two minutes past ten White was advised by short-wave radio that the Cow Palace was clear of reporters. Seven minutes later the bus pulled into a private parking area at the southeast corner of that ungainly structure which had been built for the glorification of pure-bred beef animals and a display of the no longer needed open-range cowboy skills.

The plan developed by White and Kleindienst at the outset of the drive for the nomination was based upon two requirements—know the delegates who will vote for you; maintain contact with the delegates so that they will know how to vote in accordance with Goldwater's wishes on every issue.

To be successful the plan required instant and constant communication between the command post and the floor of the convention. The nerve center had been established in an oversized house trailer parked near the southeast door of the convention hall. The delegates would vote on the floor, but the victory would be won in this ungainly contraption, built for mobility but now resting on a foundation of concrete blocks.

A uniformed Pinkerton guard responded to White's knock and admitted the team to the trailer. The 10-×-55-foot interior floor space was divided into three areas. At the far end a full partition was installed to provide privacy for the operators of a powerful shortwave radio transmitter and receiver. The five feet in front of the partition had been given over to White's command post. A wood and plexiglass barrier reached almost to the ceiling. Stretching along one side were the six positions assigned to the regional directors—two men in cubbyholes separated from their neighbors by a sheet of plexiglass. Above each position was a portable television set to permit the regional directors a view of the proceedings inside the Cow Palace.

In each cubbyhole were two telephones. Each phone was marked by region; each button on the phone was identified by the name of a state.

In other conventions radio systems had experienced unexplained failures. To prevent any jamming of the transmitter, Nick Volcheff installed an antenna in the ceiling of the Cow Palace where it was concealed by the shadowy steel of the roof's supports. If any radio transmission was to be overpowered, the Goldwater communications would be dominant. The receiver, using this same antenna, might be employed to listen in on all other short-wave communications systems. A regulatory agency of the federal government had assigned a special frequency to the Goldwater radio system. But conversations on shortwave radio can be monitored. Frequencies can be discovered. And White, in planning the facilities, had decided to put his major dependence upon the telephones. True, they could be tapped, but it is far more difficult to locate and tap telephone lines than it is to discover and monitor a radio conversation.

When the team had completed its inspection of the physical facilities, White took up his position at the command post and, using a public address system which had been installed in the trailer, explained how the telephones would be used. "The field directors," he said, "will find each telephone identified by region. There is a direct line from your telephone here in the trailer to the instrument installed in your delegations on the floor of the Cow Palace. To reach a state, all you need do is depress the state button. This will ring a bell and flash a light on the instrument inside. The men on the floor will wear headsets at all times. When their lights flash they will throw a switch and be ready for a two-way conversation.

"From this switchboard," White said, "I can talk on a direct line to any regional director's station or to all regional directors and to all telephones on the floor.

"We have two direct lines to the Mark Hopkins Hotel. The Senator will be watching the proceedings on television. He can communicate his desires directly to me and I will relay them to the appropriate regional director or to all stations on the system."

White explained that a general order would be preceded by the announcement that this was an "all-call." He went on, "I will repeat the 'all-call' announcement three times and then give the instructions."

White explained that, in addition to the seventeen direct lines, thirty walkie-talkie sets would be used to communicate with state delegations where there were no telephones. As a further precaution, each regional director would be provided with the necessary number of pages who would maintain positions near that director's floor telephones in readiness to carry confidential messages from the delegations served with a telephone to Goldwater groups where there were no telephones.

Each regional director was instructed to keep in contact with his delegation. The phones were to be checked at fifteen-minute intervals. "When we come out here Monday," White said, "I want a report from each director. We must know that our delegates are in their seats and ready to vote, and I want from each one of you an estimate of the number of delegate votes your region can be expected to give in support of Senator Goldwater's wishes. The first vote of any importance will come on the acceptance of the Platform. The inside man on each delegation will poll his people and report the number of sure votes. If you're not sure of a delegate vote, don't count it. If we decide to support a measure or defeat a measure, we must know in advance that we have the votes to achieve victory."

White explained that each regional director would have a permanent floor pass, plus a press badge, and a page ribbon. "Something may come up which will make it necessary for you to go on the floor, but this phone at your station must be covered at all times during the convention. The six chairs behind you against the opposite wall of the trailer are for the stand-by men who will take your place if you leave the trailer for any reason."

At the Chicago convention the ushers had led the Goldwater demonstrators who were on the floor when the Senator was nominated down one of the aisles and outside the arena. Many of these demonstrators had difficulty in re-entering the hall. Kleindienst and White were determined this would not occur in San Francisco. They had made a trade with the representatives of the other contenders, and the doorkeepers assigned to the southeast door were all Goldwater people.

When he had finished explaining the mechanical setup inside the trailer, White passed out the headsets and volume controls which were to be connected to the permanently installed boxes on the convention floor. Then he announced the team would take the headsets to the floor and check out each telephone to be sure it was functioning.

"One thing more—it's our belief that no one at this moment has any idea of what we've done to establish communications. When the convention opens they will see our telephones on the floor, but the Rockefeller and Scranton people also have telephones. By Monday it will be too late for anyone to try to duplicate what we have here. In the event a reporter or a representative of any of the other contenders should come into the hall while we are conducting this test, you will all return to the trailer as quickly and quietly as possible and wait until the hall is clear."

The flat floor of the arena had been allocated two-thirds to delegate and alternate seating, one-third to an elevated platform where on center stage the dignitaries would sit. Here the chairman would preside before an ample podium. Here the speeches would be made. Flanking the center platform were two elevated, railed-off areas for the press, outfitted with tables and telephones.

Television booths had been located high above the arena floor. Multiple cameras had been installed to scan the delegates, the alternates, the podium, and the spectators.

With a camera stand in the middle of the center aisle, the makeshift auditorium was relatively free and clear of obstruction. Seating on the floor was divided with the front half allocated to the official delegates and a corresponding area behind a passageway for the alternates. The portable chairs were fixed in position; telephone cables beneath a temporary flooring terminated in little boxes securely fastened to the arm of the aisle chair in most delegations. We discovered that both Rockefeller and Scranton had a telephone communication system terminating in a trailer outside the Cow Palace.

Compared to the arrangements provided for the 1960 convention in Chicago, the seating in San Francisco was spacious and comfortable; the aisles were wider and more numerous, and the platform was clearly visible to everyone in the hall.

Spectators would be confined to the seats in the gallery. Because the podium was near the rear of the hall, at least two-thirds of the visitors would be able to see the speakers' faces. And for those holder of tickets in the stands behind the podium there would be some compensation. Confined to a view of the speaker's back, they would have an unobstructed view of the antics and the actions of the delegates on the floor who faced the podium.

With the empty seats and the half-draped bunting and the preoccupied workmen as their only witnesses, the Goldwater men checked out their telephones and discovered the first error. The phones had been installed on the first aisle seat in the delegation, a space usually allocated to the ranking party member in that state, the national committeeman, the state chairman, or the elected chairman of the delegation.

Dick Herman, the alert and experienced commander of Region V, the Plains states, spotted the difficulty. "We'll have to move these instruments to the second aisle seat," he told White, "because not all of our people are chairmen of their delegation, and I doubt if the elected chairman will want to give up his seat."

White made a note on his clipboard. "We'll have them moved this afternoon," he said.

The regional directors returned to the trailer, called each of their floor stations where an assistant with a headset was waiting, and then reported to White on their direct console lines if their stations were functioning.

At the master control White manipulated his keys, spoke to the trailer over the intercom, checked his direct wire to each regional director's station, then instituted the "all-call" which permitted him to speak directly to every telephone on the convention floor.

The men in the trailer, who were to wear their headsets almost constantly during the first three days of the convention, went through the dry run with the same dedication which had enabled them to assemble a majority of the delegates on behalf of their candidate.

Lloyd Waring, middle-aged investment banker and former state chairman of Massachusetts, had the responsibility for Region I, comprising Connecticut, Maine, Massachusetts, New York, Rhode Island, and Vermont.

Waring was on the receiving end of some good-natured kidding over the New York assignment, a state which could be expected to give its ninety-two votes to Governor Rockefeller. But he faced his tormentors good-naturedly and promised that Goldwater would get some votes from every state in Region I with the exception of Maine. And he was right.

Ed Failor, director of Region II, a probate judge from Iowa, had been an early participant in the Draft Goldwater movement. He and Clif White enjoyed a friendship which extended back to the days when both were active in national Young Republican efforts. The Middle Atlantic states were Delaware, the District of Columbia, Kentucky, Maryland, New Jersey, Pennsylvania, and West Virginia.

Wayne Hood, director of Region III, was an old political hand who had been executive director of the Republican party in the successful Eisenhower campaign of 1952. He had taken a leave of absence from his job as executive vice-president of the Trane Refrigeration Company of Wisconsin to labor in the Draft Goldwater effort. Now it was his responsibility to keep track of the delegates and the voting in Illinois, Indiana, Michigan, Minnesota, Ohio, and Wisconsin. This was the heartland of Goldwater strength. The Illinois delegation, led by Chuck Percy and Senator Dirksen, was almost solid Goldwater. Indiana's thirty-two delegates were committed as the result of a primary. Michigan, with strong sentiment for favorite son George Romney, was an unknown quantity. Minnesota was divided. Wisconsin was solid. Ohio was busily getting on the bandwagon as evidenced by Governor Jim Rhodes' announcement that morning that he would not be a favorite-son candidate.

The once solidly Democrat South, Region IV, was represented in the trailer by John Grenier, a tough-minded lawyer who had put together the Goldwater organization in eleven states. Although not an original member of the Draft Goldwater team, Grenier had been spending his full time on the Goldwater candidacy for more than a year, and now the South was solid Goldwater country.

Contenders for delegate berths in Florida had gone through a spirited election contest, but their disagreement was over which group was the most committed to the Arizona Senator. Alabama was instructed, Lousiana was committed, North Carolina was all for Goldwater. In Tennessee, Sam Claiborne, chairman of the Goldwater committee, had managed to see to it that all twenty-eight delegates elected to San Francisco from that state were die-hard Goldwater supporters. In Virginia and Georgia there were at least fifty-two Goldwater votes. Arkansas, where Nelson Rockefeller's brother Winthrop had given the Republican party new leadership, hope, and lavish financial support, was expected to cast some of its votes for the New York Governor. But there were also Goldwater supporters in the Arkansas delegation.

Wirt Yerger, Mississippi's Republican chairman, had been a Goldwater supporter at the convention in 1960. Chairman J. Drake Edens of South Carolina was carrying out a commitment first made by the state committee in 1960. The Texas delegation was legally pledged to the Arizona Senator.

In Region V, Dick Herman was responsible for Iowa, Kansas, Missouri, Nebraska, Colorado, North and South Dakota, and Oklahoma. Herman was an original member of the Draft Goldwater movement, and he had been a participant at the historic meeting in Washington in 1960 which marked the commencement of the campaign of Goldwater for President. Oklahoma had been the first state in the nation to commit to Goldwater. Nebraska was ours as the result of a primary. In Colorado we had all but two delegates, North and South Dakota were solid, and in the other three states there were only minor defections.

Region VI was mine. The delegates from Idaho and Montana were instructed to vote for Goldwater. Anderson Carter headed a solid contingent of Goldwater strength from New Mexico. Our flag was flying at full staff in Wyoming and Utah. Alaska had gone to Rockefeller. Hawaii's delegates were confused. Washington had elected twenty-two Goldwater delegates out of twenty-four, and in Oregon four of the delegates threatened to vote for Goldwater despite the peculiar primary law which committed the state to the winner of that May 15th trial heat.

California was considered the host state. Arizona was called the home state. But these 102 votes were legally, morally, and sentimentally committed to Goldwater—California's as the result of the June 2nd primary; Arizona out of pride for its native son.

When the testing had been completed and the headsets were safely secured in the trailer protected by the Pinkerton guard, the Goldwater men climbed back into the bus for their return trip. There would be briefings every morning on the fifteenth floor of the Mark Hopkins; detailed mimeographed instructions to the Goldwater chairmen in the several states; and for the regional directors, hours and hours and hours in the trailer, chained to a headset, responding to the commands of Clif White who in turn would be in direct communication with the Senator's suite at the Mark.

If the Goldwater effort failed, it would not founder on the reef of faulty communications.

15

By Sunday evening, July 12th, all the minor discontents had been quieted. The fifteenth floor was relatively calm, and the connecting door between the Goldwater and Kitchel suites was open. The Senator and his campaign director would soon begin dressing for the formal Republican Gala. This major fund-raising event of the convention was expected to produce about a half-million dollars for Senate and House candidates.

At forty-seven minutes past six, the Scranton letter exploded in this peaceful atmosphere with the violence of an atomic bomb. Twelve hundred words, each selected to carry a barb:

> Dear Senator:
>
> As we move rapidly towards the climax of this convention the Republican Party faces a continuing struggle on two counts.
>
> The first involves of course, selection of a candidate.
>
> Here the issue is extremely clear. It is simply this; will the convention choose a candidate overwhelmingly favored by the Republican voters, or will it choose you?
>
> Your organization does not even argue the merits of the question. They admit that you are a minority candidate, but they feel they have bought, beaten and compromised enough delegate support to make the result a foregone conclusion.
>
> With open contempt for the dignity, integrity and common sense of the convention, your managers say in effect that *the delegates are little more than a flock of chickens whose necks will be wrung at will.*
>
> I have doublechecked the arithmetic of my staff, and I am convinced that a true count at this minute puts your first ballot strength at only some 620 votes.

Our count differs from that of your managers because we have calculated an important element which you are incapable of comprehending. That is the element of respect for the men and women who make up the delegations to this convention.

We are not taking them for granted. We are not insulting their intelligence or their integrity.

We're not counting noses, we're counting hearts.

We're not issuing orders, we're providing a rallying point for responsibility in the Republican Party.

You will be stopped on the first ballot because a sufficient number of your nominal supporters have already indicated to us that they will not vote for you.

They are not breaking commitments to you; you have broken commitments to them.

You have too often casually prescribed nuclear war as a solution to a troubled world.

You have too often allowed the radical extremists to use you.

You have too often stood for irresponsibility in the serious question of racial holocaust.

You have too often read Taft and Eisenhower and Lincoln out of the Republican Party.

And that brings me to the second count on which the Republican Party is fighting for its soul.

In the last few days the ill-advised efforts to make us stand for Goldwaterism instead of Republicanism has set off ripples of public opinion across the nation.

All of us in San Francisco are so close to the hour-by-hour story unfolding here, that there is a danger we may overlook the overall impression being created in the minds of the American people.

Goldwaterism has come to stand for nuclear irresponsibility.

Goldwaterism has come to stand for keeping the name of Eisenhower out of our platform.

Goldwaterism has come to stand for being afraid to forthrightly condemn right-wing extremists.

Goldwaterism has come to stand for refusing to stand for law and order in maintaining racial peace.

In short, Goldwaterism has come to stand for a whole crazy-quilt collection of absurd and dangerous positions that would be soundly repudiated by the American people in November.

Meanwhile, we have tried as best we can in the rigged situation engineered by your organization to articulate another point of view.

These are not surface differences between you and the vast majority of Republicans. *These are soul-deep differences over what the Republican Party stands for.*

We cannot lightly ignore the deep convictions of 60 per cent of the Republican Party that Goldwaterism is wrong. Circumstances have given me the responsibility of speaking up for their position. Inclination has given you the task of defending far different opinions.

Neither of us can ignore our responsibilities.

I feel that I have nothing to fear from the convention or from the millions of Americans watching it because my position is a right one.

Certainly you should not fear a convention you claim to control, and I would hope that we have not reached the point where you fear to face the nation.

Therefore, I am asking that you join me in a request to allow both of us to appear before the convention on Wednesday prior to the nominating speeches.

Each of us should be permitted to speak on the issues.

Then we ought to have the opportunity to question each other.

Frankly, few people expect that you will accept my invitation.

If that is true, the implication will be quite clear: You have taken comfort in the inflated claims of your managers and you no longer have any regard for the opinions of uncommitted delegates or of the American public.

So, it is up to you. You must decide whether the Goldwater philosophy can stand public examination—before the convention and before the nation.

Sincerely yours,
William W. Scranton

The message did more than question Goldwater's credentials as a leader of the Republican party. It categorized Goldwater delegates as either violent extremists or stupid dupes taken prisoner by the Goldwater machine, and it repeated the charges that Rockefeller had used in all of the primaries and which were to become the theme song of the Democrats and Lyndon Johnson.

More than any other event in San Francisco, the intemperate message from the governor of Pennsylvania influenced the atmosphere of the convention. The epistle shattered the customary icy calm of Denison Kitchel. For Goldwater it was the final insult in the weary pilgrimage. Since the day of his official announcement in January, the Senator from Arizona had endured the shafts of distortion devised by Rockefeller, Lodge, and the eastern liberals. He had steadfastly refused to respond in kind. He had accepted an adverse press which seemed to find sadistic pleasure in singing a chorus of Goldwater mistakes.

Kitchel, who throughout the preconvention campaign had closed his eyes and ears to much of the criticism, was now required for almost the first time to recognize the hysterical violence of those who opposed the Goldwater nomination.

The Senator and his chief lieutenant went up to the seventeenth floor where the brain trust reviewed the letter. It was Harry Jaffa who suggested that Goldwater's response should be conciliatory, carrying the clear implication that the Senator did not believe the letter expressed the personal views of Governor Scranton. Jaffa, with his sensitive awareness of political history and his devotion to Abraham Lincoln, was more objective in his viewpoint than the others. Kitchel and Baroody argued that the letter should be returned without comment as an easy to understand expression of Goldwater's contempt for the charges and for the writer.

Goldwater recognized the possible political value in Scranton's attack. In his first campaign for the United States Senate a supporter of incumbent Ernest McFarland, the man Goldwater was challenging, had authored a last-minute smear, suggesting in newspaper copy and on the radio that Goldwater had a miserable war record, was actually more a resident of California than of Arizona, and had attempted to use political influence to advance his military career. On that occasion, Goldwater in a final election-eve TV appearance, had acknowledged the charges and responded by saying, "I can't understand what this man has done. I've never shown him anything but kindness."

That personal attack at the opening of Goldwater's career had been made public by its author. If the Scranton letter were returned, it might disappear. There was no way of knowing whether or not the governor of Pennsylvania had provided copies of his communication to the press. It was decided to return the letter as promptly as possible, but Kitchel proposed that copies be made and distributed to every delegate in San Francisco.

The regional directors were summoned to an emergency meeting on the fifteenth floor. The duplicating machines in the press rooms started turning, and Ed Nellor announced receipt of the letter, its return, and Senator Goldwater's disappointment that Bill Scranton would make such an attack upon the integrity of the Republican delegates. To underscore his displeasure, Goldwater announced that he was canceling his plans to attend the Gala. Mrs. Goldwater and Mrs. Kitchel would go, but the Senator would remain in the Mark.

By nine-thirty Sunday evening copies were being distributed to the delegates' hotel rooms throughout the city. Whatever his other shortcomings might be, William Scranton was a successful and experienced political warrior. Such a man never moves without reason. Could Scranton have thought that Goldwater would accept his challenge for a debate before the convention? Did he think Goldwater would be naïve enough to attempt a defense of the false charges he had ignored for six months? The letter was a challenge to a debate which the challenger must have known would be rejected.

What possible benefit could come to Scranton as the result of the letter? The language would alienate any Goldwater delegates. And concerned Republicans would resent the divisive effect of the challenge at a time when the party must unite if it was to have any hope of winning in November.

One immediate certainty was the elimination of Scranton as a possible vice-presidential candidate in 1964. Throughout the spring and summer months, even after the Pennsylvania governor officially became a contender, Goldwater had believed that with Scranton on the ticket the chasm between the eastern establishment and the conservative wing of the party might be bridged.

Many men have publicly rejected the notion of accepting second place on a national ticket but it is questionable if any politician given the opportunity to run for the Vice-Presidency would refuse.

The assassination of Kennedy and the elevation of Lyndon Johnson in 1963 made it even less likely that a man in Scranton's position would choose such a method to slam the door on the vice-presidential nomination. Who then could benefit from such an implausible act of deliberate disunity at the start of the presidential campaign?

If Goldwater won in November, it would effectively close the door on the hopes of every other 1968 Republican contender, for history suggests that the man elected for his first term in 1964 would be re-elected in 1968, and by 1972 the passing of the years would require a new and younger candidate. On the other hand, if Goldwater lost in 1964, the nomination would be wide open in 1968. Of course, if the Goldwater ticket made a respectable showing against the incumbent Johnson, either Goldwater or his running mate would be high on the list for nomination in 1968.

But someone who had failed to capture the brass ring in 1964 and who was willing to see the party go down to defeat in order to preserve his own chances for a try at the crown in 1968 might have been delighted by both the timing and the content of that angry epistle. If Scranton were eliminated from Goldwater's thinking, he would not have any preferential position in 1968. One certain result would be a widening of the divisions within the party and a lessening of the chances for a Goldwater victory in 1964.

The men on the seventeenth floor all responded emotionally. No one asked why; no one suggested the situation should be thoroughly analyzed before any action was taken. An experienced politician might have asked these questions, but with the exception of the candidate, who certainly had a right to be angry, there were no politicians on the seventeenth floor.

Goldwater followed Jaffa's advice and released a note to the press, expressing the belief that his old friend Bill Scranton had probably not framed the letter or intended the language to be so violent.

The practical politicians who comprised the field staff were appalled at the Scranton letter. It was no threat to their champion; indeed it virtually guaranteed Goldwater's nomination, but we could see the ultimate effect on the party. Dick Herman and

Wayne Hood both advanced the notion that the purpose of the letter had been to prevent Goldwater from selecting Scranton. Romney and Rockefeller were both unacceptable—Romney because of the serious Constitutional question about his being able to qualify (the governor of Michigan was born in Mexico, and in the view of most experts does not meet the natural-born citizen requirement); Rockefeller, because of his defection in 1960, his spending record in the state of New York, and his ideological alliance with the Democrat position, had never been seriously considered as Goldwater's running mate.

To some of the regional directors the letter appeared additional proof of the close cooperation between Rockefeller and Scranton. The New York governor had turned over his trailer space, his communications system, and his campaign staff to Scranton. There seemed a strong probability that Rockefeller's people had influenced the language and the dispatch of that angry challenge.

Monday morning newspapers, finding little in the way of excitement in the programed convention meetings, focused attention on the Scranton attack. When the governor made public his claim that he had not seen the letter and had not signed the letter but had authorized its transmission, his pathetic position overshadowed all other news.

The first day in any political convention is given over to the tedious preliminaries, formal ratification of decisions reached long before the delegates meet. There had been a spirited contest over the naming of the temporary chairman and keynoter, and in San Francisco these two assignments were consolidated and given to Mark Hatfield, the young, effective chief executive of Oregon.

In the very early stages it had been thought that Bill Miller, the national chairman, would deliver the keynote speech. When he declined, there was pressure to assign the honor to Bob Forsythe of Minnesota. This suggestion was opposed by the Goldwater forces on the grounds that the Minnesotan was a confirmed liberal. The same charge might have been made against Hatfield, but his field marshals, particularly Travis Cross, outmaneuvered the objectors. At the planning session in advance of the actual decision Cross was able to solicit from James Wood, Republican national committeeman from Arizona, a denial that Wood would oppose Hatfield. This was accepted as a Goldwater endorsement.

Hatfield's speech was the big event of Monday, but advance copies had been distributed, the delegates listened politely, registered their distaste when the governor chose to discuss extremism, applauded properly, and greeted adjournment eagerly.

The first day of the convention provided an opportunity to test and retest the effectiveness of the Goldwater command post and its elaborate system of communications. The short-wave radio transmitter could reach a Goldwater walkie-talkie anywhere in the hall, but we discovered the Scranton radio system was blocked out in certain locations by structural steel and by the pyramid erected for television cameras.

Sometime between five and five-fifteen on Monday, the Goldwater telephone system in three states was disturbed; whether by accident or design, cables were broken. The problem was remedied after the convention adjourned Monday night.

Long before the delegates arrived in San Francisco, the Goldwater men had received repeated warnings that forces opposed to the Senator might provoke unfavorable incidents. Certain national organizations had pickets in front of the Cow Palace. From time to time there was sporadic agitation which might have led to serious trouble. To guard against this, the Goldwater men had enlisted a corps of volunteer observers assigned to a fleet of patrol cars. This security detail covered every area of approach to the Cow Palace—the parking lot, the main entrance, the roadways, and the trailers in the rear. The teams were equipped with short-wave radio, polaroid cameras, and miniature tape recorders. Their assignment was to make certain that if any incident developed, we would have photographs of the participants and, wherever possible, a record of their remarks to the crowd. These men working under the direction of Charles Barr of Illinois were highly respected business and professional leaders. Their credibility as witnesses would have been difficult to challenge.

This was purely a defensive effort, calculated to permit us to counteract any unfavorable publicity which might have been generated by a prejudiced report of an incident. There were no incidents, and their major service was bringing sandwiches to the trailer where a constant diet of hot dogs and soft drinks had lost all appeal by the time the convention adjourned Monday night.

16

Any lingering doubts about what the Republican delegates intended to do in San Francisco were dispelled on Tuesday night when the Rockefeller-Scranton-Romney people forced a roll-call vote on an amendment to the proposed Platform. They lost 897 to 409, but the split in the Republican party was further deepened and widened.

Governor Rockefeller came to the rostrum to urge the adoption of an amendment on extremism. His voice was drowned out by a chorus of boos from the audience, and the Goldwater forces were blamed for this rude and senseless interruption.

In the command trailer we were watching the proceedings on television. As the first boo echoed from the convention hall, the regional directors began to call their floor contacts. "Stop the booing," they pleaded. When the telephone calls were completed, a curious truth became evident. The vocal objection to Rockefeller's words was not coming from the strong pro-Goldwater delegations on the floor.

Messengers were sent into the galleries with orders to quiet the offenders. Rockefeller made capital out of the demonstration. He thrust out his chin and went on with his speech, indicating that this, indeed, was what he meant by the extremism he deplored. To some of us, it seemed that he was enjoying the interruption.

With frequent pauses for emphasis he told the delegates how extremists in California had authored a hundred threats to bomb his headquarters in the final days of that primary, how his workers had been frightened away. The charge was not new. When it was first made I had contacted Pete Pitchess, the sheriff of Los Angeles county, who queried other law-enforcement agencies. He told me not a single police station or sheriff's substation had ever received any report of bomb threats from the Rockefeller campaign managers.

The reports by short-wave radio from the men in the galleries added a bizarre note. The boos were coming from the spectators, and many of the leaders were indeed wearing Goldwater buttons, but they were strangers. In planning the convention, Jim Day and Clif White had carefully arranged to have dependable Goldwater people at specific locations in the audience. Day and the men working with him knew most of these Goldwater partisans by sight. Some known Goldwater people had taken up the chant, "We want Barry," both in the gallery and on the floor, but the boos and the raspberries had not come from our supporters or our sections. The press made much of the incident, and Rockefeller's attempt to attack the Platform thus received more sympathy than it deserved.

The amendments offered by Governor Romney were quite different. A number of the regional directors suggested it would be good politics to let the Romney amendment on extremism, which was actually an innocuous paraphrase of the Platform statement, pass. But Clif White was under orders; the Platform was to be adopted exactly as it had been written, and we were to follow White's instructions.

Wednesday afternoon was interminable. All the hopefuls who did not have a prayer were nominated. The demonstration for Goldwater had come off exactly as Clif White and Jim Day planned it, climaxed with a spectacular shower of gold foil. Many Scranton demonstrators, who apparently had been recruited on the streets of San Francisco, tried to enter the hall on bogus passes. The deception was discovered when an usher noted the seat numbers on the tickets were identical and the ink smeared on contact. After the nominations had been made, Scranton, who was in the VIP trailer at the rear of the hall, asked permission to make a unity speech before the vote was counted.

On that Wednesday the only contigency which had been suggested as a possible effective move to block Goldwater's nomination was the use of delaying tactics, endless nominations, overlong seconding speeches, extended demonstrations which might postpone the voting until Thursday and provide the stop-Goldwater people with an additional twelve hours to work on the delegates.

Redoubtable Carl Curtis recalled a Democrat convention where the expected loser's unity plea had persuaded the delegates to change their minds. Curtis vetoed the Scranton request, and finally Polly Buck called the roll. When the voting reached South Carolina, J. Drake Edens had the honor of making Goldwater's nomination a reality.

Greg Shorey and Roger Milliken had started the Goldwater bandwagon by insisting that the Senator's name be placed before the 1960 convention. It seemed to me particularly fitting that now, four years later, the chairman of South Carolina, by adding his state's sixteen votes, made Barry Goldwater the Republican nominee.

On the night Barry Goldwater won the presidential nomination there was champagne in the trailer and in headquarters at the Mark Hopkins. It was an exclusive party; only those on the official staff were welcome.

I was in the hallway with my wife when the Senator came out of his suite. His words of greeting were typical of the man I had known, admired, and worked for during the years of his climb up the political ladder, "Well, Steve, you're the one who got me started in all this, and look what you've done now."

The Senator was gay, relaxed, and I think possibly a little frightened at what he could see ahead. Goldwater never underestimated his enemies. Of all the people involved in the 1964 campaign, the candidate saw more clearly than anyone else the odds against victory. He knew whatever he said or did would be distorted. The attacks in the press would increase in intensity. The great ideological division within the Republican party was symptomatic of the national uncertainty. He had won the nomination, and no matter what happened in November, his life would never be the same again.

In January Goldwater had refused to make a flat declaration that if he were nominated for the Presidency, he would not at the same time run for the Senate from Arizona.

In 1960 Goldwater had been sharply critical of Lyndon Johnson, who while running for the Vice-Presidency had also been a candidate for the Senate from Texas, and from the very first he had known that it would be an indication of weakness and a desertion of principle to try to hold his place in the Senate while running for President.

The decision, however, had been delayed and postponed and deliberately swept under the rug until after the Governors' Conference in Cleveland. Then he met with Fannin, Kleindienst, and Kitchel at his home in Phoenix to face the inevitable. Goldwater really wanted Arizona's Governor Fannin to run for re-election. This would strengthen the ticket in Arizona, but Fannin had served six years in a post which bestows little real political power on its occupant and at the same time makes him the target of criticism for every failure in state government. Fannin did not want to seek re-election. Moreover, Kleindienst was determined to run for governor. At the meeting, after Goldwater had expressed his opinion, Kleindienst interrupted to say, "Well, Senator, I think we ought to ask Paul Fannin what he wants to do. It isn't fair to assume that he will carry out orders." Fannin was ready to retire from public life; he did not want to run again for re-election, but in a gesture of loyalty to Goldwater he offered to seek the senatorial position, and so it had been resolved on July 2nd. Kleindienst would leave the Goldwater team and seek the gubernatorial nomination in Arizona. Fannin would run for Goldwater's seat in the Senate. But even then there were complications. Evan Mecham, who had won the party's nomination for the Senate in 1962, had for two years been bitterly, almost violently, critical of Paul Fannin. Mecham had announced that if Fannin sought election to any political post, he would oppose him, and the prospect of a bitter primary struggle was not welcome. As things turned out, Mecham withdrew from the senatorial contest, ran for governor in the Republican primary, and turned his vitriol against Kleindienst, a circumstance which contributed materially to a Republican defeat and the election of a Democrat, Sam Goddard, in November.

On that Wednesday evening Goldwater told us Bill Miller of New York State would be his running mate. The decision had been reached that morning. Goldwater did not consult with Eisenhower,

Nixon, or any other party leader. The Scranton letter had blocked the man who would have been his first choice, and most of the men close to the Senator had preferred Miller from the very start.

Kleindienst says he was strong for Miller because he believed the national chairman could draw the party together and swing some of the Roman Catholic vote. Clif White visualized the general election campaign as operating in two separate spheres with the presidential candidate taking the high road, explaining to the people the benefits of his program, and the vice-presidential candidate doing the gut fighting—Miller was respected as a gut fighter.

Now only the formality of the acceptance speech and the official designation of Miller as the vice-presidential nominee were left. There was really no longer any need for the elaborate operations at the trailer, but we were all there in our seats when the session opened on Thursday.

We were advised by short-wave radio of Goldwater's departure for the Cow Palace. Most of us left our posts long enough to watch the Senator drive in at the rear entrance of the building. We chuckled when we noticed that he was at the wheel of the big black limousine. Mrs. Goldwater, Mr. and Mrs. Kitchel, and Karl Hess were in the first car.

I had tried unsuccessfully to secure an advance copy of the acceptance speech. I knew that Karl Hess had been working with Bill Baroody in secrecy on the seventeenth floor, and I assumed that he and Kitchel had been choosing the phrases which hopefully would start Goldwater on his road to the White House. Later I learned the acceptance speech was the work of a committee. The first draft, written by Karl Hess, was not acceptable. Baroody took charge and insisted on using a memorandum which Harry Jaffa had prepared for the Platform committee. The subject was extremism. The words which attracted national attention which added to the disunity in the party, and which were to be interpreted and explained in a dozen different ways—"Extremism in the defense of liberty is no vice, and moderation in the pursuit of justice is no virtue"—were never intended by their author to be part of the acceptance speech. The manner in which the acceptance speech was written became the pattern for the Goldwater statements during the campaign—ideas and phrases gathered together under Baroody's supervision, edited by McCabe, Kitchel, and Hess, until all unity of thought and style was completely destroyed.

The paragraphs on law and order and violence in the streets were included at the insistence of Eugene Pulliam, publisher of the Phoenix and Indianapolis newspapers, who had sent two of his editors to San Francisco to deliver a proposed script to Goldwater personally. The material was excellent, and "morality in high places" became one of Goldwater's major issues, but when these suggestions were compressed into the body of the acceptance speech they lost force and effectiveness.

I had seen an earlier memorandum prepared by Rus Walton, emphasizing what we all knew—that Goldwater would have his greatest nationwide TV audience on the night he accepted the nomination. Walton's memo outlined the opportunity and stressed the need for a statement which would unite the party in San Francisco and enlist the enthusiasm and support of the nationwide audience.

If, as so many have suggested, the acceptance speech had a disastrous effect on the national television audience, it struck the men in the trailer with an even greater impact. In the mind of every politican this was the time for a conciliatory statement, the moment when arms should have been thrown open to welcome all those who had opposed Goldwater's nomination. Instead he said, "Any who join us in all sincerity we welcome; those who do not care for our cause we do not expect to enter our ranks in any case."

This was the moment to capture the imagination of the country with a provocative outline of the benefits of Republican victory would bring to the nation. This was the time to suggest that, if elected, President Goldwater would take steps to correct those situations which he believed were adversely affecting the economic, moral, and international health of the Republic.

One knowledgeable politician suggested it was a time when Romney, Rockefeller, Scranton, Javits, Keating, Hatfield, and Lindsay should have been invited to the platform. Such an invitation, couched in the proper language, would have been most difficult for a Republican to reject.

Instead, Goldwater emphasized the dissension which his critics had been saying all along he meant to achieve. The phrase about extremism, which for any other candidate in any other context might have been greeted with loud approval, ripped open old wounds and erected barriers which were never broken.

In many ways Goldwater's speech was excellent. He dwelt on freedom and on the failures of recent Democrat administrations; he mentioned the lawlessness in our streets. But the two unfortunate passages and the harsh, almost belligerent delivery overshadowed the good points. He gave his enemies new ammunition to use against him. He provided his friends with nothing which could be used to persuade the undecided.

Had the speech been given a month earlier when Goldwater was seeking the nomination, or two months later when he was seeking the Presidency, it might have been acceptable, but not on this night of victory.

Dean Burch admits he saw portions of the speech in advance, but he says: "If Goldwater had recited the Lord's Prayer there were certain people at the convention who were going to object to it." In his view, the only disadvantage to the extremism statement was that it "gave the people who were determined to beat Goldwater over the head, a handle to beat him with."

When Barry Goldwater went before the National Committee to ask that Dean Burch be named chairman and to announce that he intended to run his campaign through the regular party machinery, it was almost January, 1964, all over again. The Goldwater for President Committee was completely ignored, just as the Draft committee had been unceremoniously dumped to make way for the Kitchel-Burch-Kleindienst-Ann Eve Johnson combine.

The finance men, who had raised more than three and a half million dollars to help Goldwater win the nomination, were each given a handsome presentation wrist watch and dismissed. The regional directors, with the exception of John Grenier, did not even rate this much attention. Clif White, Wayne Hood, Dick

Herman, Lloyd Waring, Ed Failor, and I were allowed to depart without being told our services had been appreciated or asked by Kitchel, Burch, or the Senator himself to participate in the general campaign.

On Friday night the members of that original Draft Goldwater group gathered in a public room at the Fairmont Hotel. What should have been a joyous occasion was a sad and shabby spectacle. White, Ty Gillespie, Stets Coleman, Charlie Barr, Pat Hutar, Gene Perin, Dick Herman, Bill Rusher, Peter O'Donnell, Tad Smith, Ione Harrington, and most of the others met to drink a stirrup cup, to nibble half-heartedly at the hors d'oeuvres, and to try to find some comfort in the fact that fortune had played no favorites. All these men whose brave and almost quixotic early efforts had been ratified by the action of the Republican convention on Wednesday night were now excluded from the inner circle of the candidate they had created.

The mood was one of bewilderment, rather than bitterness. We knew that Doctor Charles Wiggamore Kelley had planned to come to San Francisco and had been told to stay in the East by Denison Kitchel. We knew that Mike Bernstein had been eager to lend his talents but had been rejected. And what of Bill Buckley and Brent Bozell?

Of all the men on the fifteenth and seventeenth floors of the Mark Hopkins who were now advising the Senator, there was not a single one from that early group. Kitchel, Baroody, Hess, McCabe, and Lichenstein had taken possession of the candidate. Someone said that surely there must be a useful place for displaced persons, but at the moment no one could suggest where that place might be.

Part Five

What Happened to Goldwater?

17

The decision to name Dean Burch chairman of the Republican National Committee, which came as such a shock to all those who were not members of the inner circle of the Goldwater campaign, was reached officially on July 14th. But the pressures which produced this action commenced much earlier.

Everyone on the staff knew Clif White wanted the job. Because very little in a political campaign is truly regarded as confidential, White's efforts to enlist the support of members of the National Committee were reported to Goldwater and Kitchel in the early spring of 1964. The Senator, by naming Kleindienst director of field operations, had indicated a lack of confidence in White. Burch says he had no indication he would receive the appointment until the day it was made in San Francisco. But according to Grenier, he and O'Donnell first broached the subject in April. Kitchel, who disliked politics and politicians, was never regarded as a possibility. And both of the southerners were impressed with the ability Burch had demonstrated as Kitchel's deputy.

Kleindienst had been pushing for the selection of Ray Bliss, the Ohio state chairman, and some members of the staff believed he had offered Bliss the chairmanship in return for the votes of the Ohio delegation.

On Tuesday morning, July 14th, Baroody, McCabe, Hess, Burch, Kleindienst, Kitchel, and Clif White met in the Senator's suite on the fifteenth floor of the Mark. For the first time, Goldwater appeared confident he would win the nomination and was willing to discuss future plans based upon that assumption. The decision to ask Bill Miller to be his running mate had been made, and this forced consideration of a new man for the national chairmanship.

Goldwater, who prior to the receipt of the Scranton letter had intended to try to unite the two wings of the party by asking the governor of Pennsylvania to come on the ticket, had hoped that Miller, whom he regarded as an excellent chairman, would continue in the post until after November. He had been aware that Bliss, Burch, and White all had some support for the job. But now the events of the week end required a decision.

When Dean Burch's name was mentioned, Kleindienst, the only man in the Senator's entourage who was never intimidated or kept silent by the threat of opposition, responded with an argument which was to be repeated over and over again during the campaign.

"Dean Burch," he told the group, "is one of my dearest and closest friends. I have great admiration for his ability. I'm fond of him personally, but I don't think he has the national stature for this job. He isn't known to the party leadership; he has never served as a member of the National Committee, and, in my opinion, Ray Bliss is the only man who can appeal to the Scranton people, the Rockefeller people, the Lodge people, and unite the party. Bliss is known by all the members. He is respected by press and public."

Goldwater was deaf to Kleindienst's argument. He believed that Bliss had opposed his nomination and could not be trusted. In the world of politics where today's friend and supporter is tomorrow's enemy and opponent, Goldwater has always put loyalty above every other consideration. To many observers the Senator has appeared to be a friendly, outgoing, easily approached politician. His willingness to respond to almost any question, to give his opinion on almost any subject, and his genuine interest in people have strengthened this impression. A review of the men he has chosen to be his administrative assistants and political advisers suggests that Goldwater always sought people personally loyal to him and willing to serve him without question or contradiction.

Goldwater did not announce his choice to the group, saying only that he would not accept Bliss. When White left the meeting, he believed Kleindienst's logical arguments against the appointment of Burch would prevail. Since the Senator had announced he would not take Bliss, White, perhaps because he wanted the job so desperately, still believed the appointment might come to him.

Despite those early conversations with Grenier and O'Donnell, Burch had no solid advance indication of Goldwater's desire, and it is probable he had been aware of the Senator's preference for Scranton as a running mate. At any rate, Burch had not given any serious thought to what he would do as national chairman.

In one aspect the Goldwater campaign was thoroughly consistent—it was an impromptu effort, hampered from beginning to end by a lack of advance planning. It might be argued that circumstances conspired to produce confusion and disorder. The assassination of President Kennedy, the last-minute announcement, Tony Smith's illness, the sudden decision to go into New Hampshire—all these had affected the drive for nomination. But in review it becomes apparent that it was impossible for anyone to make plans in advance because of Goldwater's reluctance to seek the nomination. In contrast, John F. Kennedy became committed to his presidential effort at least three years before he announced. Many of the failures of the Goldwater campaign must be traced to an inability to develop any solid planning.

Proper planning would have prevented the naming of four relatively unknown Arizonans as directors of his campaign effort. The fact that he entered the campaign without having made arrangements in advance for competent individuals to head the finance effort is a further indication that until the moment when he announced his intention to the world, the Senator had been genuinely undecided.

Many of the changes Dean Burch made in the National Committee structure and personnel were deliberate, but in San Francisco the treatment accorded to Courtney Burton was something quite different. Burton, a wealthy Ohio industrialist, had served as finance chairman of the National Committee since 1961. He was dedicated to the party and had been an early supporter of Goldwater. His critics charge that he was not a particularly successful money raiser, but he came to San Francisco as a volunteer who had doggedly tried to discharge what is probably the most thankless job in politics.

When the National Committee met on Friday in the St. Francis Hotel to elect Burch, Burton was present. Goldwater outlined his plans for the coming campaign, announced that it would be conducted through the National Committee under the leadership of Burch, but not one word was said about or to the national finance chairman. Some of the officers and personnel were relieved of their responsibilities before that convention week ended. Burch announced his intended change in the executive committee, dismissing George Hinman of New York, Harley Markham of Idaho, George Edsel of Minnesota, and Fletcher Swan of Colorado, among others. Dr. William Prendergast, the long-time head of research for the National Committee, was told that Ed McCabe would be the new man in charge. They offered Prendergast a subordinate's post which he promptly rejected. William Sprague, director of public relations at the National Committee, was given the same treatment. But no one said "yes" or "no" to Courtney Burton, and he returned to Ohio, nominally the finance chairman. Burch did announce that John Grenier of Alabama would replace Ab Hermann, the extremely competent and experienced veteran politician who had served as Bill Miller's executive director.

On Saturday afternoon, July 18th, the Goldwater inner circle, Kitchel, Burch, Grenier, Nellor, Baroody, Governor Fannin, and the Senator, left San Francisco for Phoenix aboard a chartered airliner. Gladwin Hill, West Coast correspondent for the *New York Times,* had requested an interview in San Francisco. Goldwater suggested that Hill come to Phoenix where there would be an opportunity over the week end for an uninterrupted visit. Many of the Senator's supporters, particularly Dean Burch, have charged that the bias and prejudice of the working press made it impossible for Goldwater to win the November election. Without arguing the merit of that charge, it is worth reporting what happened to Hill.

He did come to Phoenix; he did not see Goldwater. The security guards turned him back at the gate. Goldwater was not seeing any newspapermen, they said.

However, on the same Sunday morning, Ralph Camping, a

photographer for the *Arizona Republic,* went out to the Senator's house, hoping to be able to slip past security and get some pictures. A nineteen-year-old cub reporter went with him. Goldwater recognized Camping at the gate and invited the two *Republic* men to come in. He chatted with the cub reporter for a full thirty minutes on a wide range of subjects and granted permission to be quoted.

The Senator may not have known that Hill had come from Los Angeles, and he may not have realized how the national reporters would react when this cub scooped them. But the men around a presidential nominee are supposed to have this knowledge.

Burch went from Phoenix to Tucson to "sit on the desert and think." Kitchel, McCabe, Baroody, and Hess remained with the Senator to discuss strategy and campaign plans.

On Sunday, July 26th, Burch and Grenier arrived in Washington. For many years the National Committee has occupied quarters on the second floor of the Cafritz Building at 1625 Eye Street. Grenier decided the working space should be remodeled and rearranged, and while Burch wrestled with the problems involving the personnel and function of the committee, Grenier took charge of providing the necessary working space. Ron Crawford, who had been so useful in the California primary and as assistant to Jim Day in San Francisco, was brought in as temporary office manager.

Grenier rented a suite of rooms on the third floor for Goldwater, Miller, Baroody, McCabe, Kitchel, and the research division. Finance was moved to the ninth floor, and veteran Frank Kovac, who had left the National Committee to go with the Goldwater for President effort, was now reinstalled as temporary custodian in the Cafritz Building. Space for bookkeeping and personnel was found on the ground floor.

Because the regional system developed by Clif White had been so effective in the preconvention drive, Burch and Grenier decided to adapt it to the general election campaign, with one major modification—before the nomination the regional directors had worked in the field, traveling through the states under their command.

Now Grenier wanted them to be in Washington where they could contribute advice and share their intimate knowledge of the regions with the strategy group on the third floor.

On the organizational chart which Grenier developed, the regional effort was to be commanded by a director of political operations. Serving directly under him would be seven regional directors. Grenier wanted Peter O'Donnell for the top spot, but O'Donnell was unacceptable to the Goldwater high command and a stalemate developed.

At this point, Lee Edwards was the acting director of public relations and press for the National Committee. Edwards says Burch gave him the appointment in San Francisco. Burch says this is not true. He wanted an older, more experienced man, and in his own words: "I was looking for a PR man right out of a novel, more than somebody who was alive. I kept thinking that a PR man knows everything, does everything. You don't have to ask him—it's always done in advance."

At the end of July, Ed Nellor accompanied Goldwater to the annual encampment at the Bohemian Grove in northern California, long recognized as the meeting place for Republican leaders. The grove is off limits to newspaper men. The discussions and hijinks are strictly private, and while widely advertised as being a nonpolitical period for rest and relaxation, the meeting at the Grove was considered a magnificent opportunity for Goldwater to see and visit with the captains of business and industry.

Somehow a reporter managed to contact Nellor, and on August 1st the *New York Times* carried a story with a Bohemian Grove dateline saying Lee Edwards would be named director of public relations for the National Committee, Wayne Hood would be appointed director of political activity, and F. Clifton White was to serve as chairman of the Citizens for Goldwater-Miller Committee.

Burch and Grenier were furious when they read the story. They knew Goldwater was considering White for the Citizens post, and they resisted the appointment, arguing that White was bitter in his disappointment over not being named national chairman and could not be expected to cooperate with Burch. Grenier was still pushing

O'Donnell for director of political activities, and Burch believed Lee Edwards was too young and too inexperienced to be entrusted with the responsibility of public relations for a presidential campaign.

Burch says the Edwards announcement was a "bit of one-upmanship on Lee's part." He and Grenier took the position that Nellor had released the story without authorization. Grenier wanted to fire the Senator's press secretary; Burch decided to demote him. On Baroody's recommendation, Paul Wagner, a Nebraskan, was named Goldwater's press aide.

Burch says that in his search for a competent public relations man he consulted Richard Nixon, Len Hall, and Bill Miller. All of them recommended L. Richard Guylay, who had held the post for the National Committee during the 1960 campaign. As a result of the Lee Edwards announcement, Burch wanted to move quickly, and without looking further he decided to offer the job to Guylay. But there were complications.

In early 1963 the National Committee had engaged the Leo Burnett advertising agency of Chicago, and this firm had been serving as consultants without fee, anticipating the commissions they would earn from money spent in the presidential effort.

After leaving the National Committee Guylay had joined a public relations firm, Tom Deegan, Inc., which was a part of Marion Harper's extensive advertising-PR empire. Guylay was in an awkward position because the National Committee job was a temporary assignment. He was anxious to help, and he appreciated the offer; it was comforting to know that Nixon and Hall and Miller had recommended him, but he could not very well ask for a leave of absence unless a Marion Harper agency was going to handle the advertising.

Burch, who based his judgment of advertising agencies on his brief experience with Fuller, Smith and Ross during the preconvention effort, did not believe the agency's function was vital to a campaign. In order to get Guylay, he agreed to break the contract with Leo Burnett of Chicago and hire Erwin Wasey, Ruthrauff & Ryan, a Marion Harper subsidiary. It was arranged that Erwin Wasey would rebate two hundred thousand dollars in commissions to Leo Burnett to compensate that firm for the time and effort already expended.

On August 11th, Guylay's appointment was announced. Edwards was demoted to the position of deputy director; Erwin Wasey, Ruthrauff & Ryan was named as the ad agency; and Ed Nellor was quietly pushed into a position in the newly created radio division. As a compromise, Burch and Grenier selected Wayne Hood of La Crosse, Wisconsin, to serve as director of campaign organization.

In this same period, Goldwater asked Ralph Cordiner, retired chairman of the board of General Electric, to serve as finance chairman. Cordiner agreed to come to Washington to discuss the matter. He says he anticipated a private conference with the Senator, and was somewhat disturbed when Goldwater insisted that Kitchel be present and participate in the discussion. Cordiner finally took the job on the condition that no money would be spent or obligated until it had first been collected. Kovac was kept on as finance director, and Milbank, Middendorf, and Coleman were named Cordiner's assistants to help raise a budget of thirteen million dollars.

Clif White, despite the opposition of Burch and Grenier, was named chairman of the Citizens operation, but those details must be dealt with in a separate chapter.

When Wayne Hood arrived in Washington on August 6th, the regional divisions had already been established. New York, California, Texas, Pennsylvania, and Ohio (Region I) were to be treated as special cases handled directly by Grenier, Burch, and Hood. Maryland, West Virginia, New Jersey, and Delaware were placed in Region II. Region III consisted of Vermont, Maine, New Hampshire, Massachusetts, Connecticut, and Rhode Island. The Great Lakes states—Illinois, Indiana, Michigan, Minnesota, and Wisconsin—were in Region IV which Hood had directed in the preconvention effort. Colorado, Kansas, Missouri, Nebraska, North Dakota, South Dakota, Oklahoma, and Iowa made up Region VI, the area which Dick Herman had directed in the preconvention drive. The southern states—Arkansas, Florida, Georgia, Louisiana, Mississippi, Kentucky, North Carolina, South Carolina,

Tennessee, and Virginia—were included in Region V. The Far West—Alaska, Hawaii, Arizona, Idaho, Montana, Nevada, New Mexico, Oregon, Utah, Washington, and Wyoming—were placed in Region VII.

Hood asked Sam Claiborne, who had been Goldwater's state chairman in Tennessee, to take over John Grenier's old position as director of the campaign effort in the southern states. Dick Herman was named to continue in his position as director of Region V and on August 7th Hood asked me to come to Washington to handle the western states in Region VII.

The remodelers and the furniture movers were in charge of the second floor when I arrived on Monday, August 10th. Dick Herman had come in the day before. Sam Claiborne arrived the same day. The other regional directors had not been named.

We were told that we would be based in Washington in order to be available to the strategy group on the third floor. Our immediate task was to enlist as many field men as we thought necessary to work with the Goldwater leaders in the various states.

I found it difficult to believe that a regional director in Washington, D.C., could contribute to a campaign in eleven states three thousand miles away, but I was underestimating the resources of Mother Bell.

Nick Volcheff, the telephone company executive assigned to the Goldwater campaign, had been brought in to headquarters by Burch and Grenier to handle communications. Volcheff says that when he arrived there were as many as six instruments on a single extension. Under his supervision, a crew of forty telephone installers worked days, nights, and Sundays. The old manual switchboard had to be retained, but almost everything else was new. Private-line extensions from the committee switchboard were installed in the hotels or apartments of the executive personnel. Claiborne, Herman, and I stayed at the Jefferson Hotel, and this simple switchboard extension made our task immeasurably easier.

Through the magic of WATS (wide area telephone service), it was possible for a regional director to communicate instantly with anyone anywhere in the United States. The WATS lines are leased from the telephone company to permit direct telephone dialing on a long-distance circuit. The renter can specify the area to be served—a state or region or the entire nation. The National Committee at one time had eight long lines covering the entire nation and eight short lines permitting communication to points east of the Mississippi River. Automatic dialing devices installed on our phones at headquarters saved even more time and effort.

Because of the time difference (four hours between the East and West during daylight savings time), I found it necessary to adjust myself to the time zones of my region. My day began about eleven o'clock Washington time, which was seven o'clock Pacific daylight, and continued until after midnight Washington time when it was only eight o'clock on the West Coast. Because my private extension at the Jefferson Hotel could be connected to a WATS line at the National Committee switchboard, I could talk to any field man or any state chairman anytime, day or night, and they could reach me through the National Committee board. Before the campaign was over I came to the conclusion that a command post in Washington, using the regional director plan, with the proper telephone circuits, provides the maximum of convenience in the conduct of a national election.

In the headquarters at 1625 Eye Street we maintained a locator board. When a regional director went out to dinner of left the office to go to his apartment or hotel, that information was noted for the convenience of the switchboard operator. In the whole, long, three-month period there was never a time we could not be reached by telephone. Our ears became perpetually tender from the pressure of the handset instruments.

In the midst of all this turmoil and uncertainty, Grenier had a solid plan for converting Goldwater sentiment into victory. His three-step program was: (1) Identify the Goldwater voters. (2) Make sure they go to the polls. (3) Guarantee an honest count.

Dr. Ray Humphreys, a respected long-time staffer on the National Committee, had developed a quota system based on prior elections. Grenier combined this with a voter-canvass operation which had been developed and used with great success in Texas by Peter O'Donnell.

Mrs. Rita Bass of Dallas was brought into Washington to direct the voter-canvass drive in conjunction with Ray Humphreys. It was a simple program—recruit volunteers; teach them how to make a canvass call at every home in the precinct and then report back names and addresses of those voters favorable to Goldwater; organize a get-out-the-vote group to take these friendly voters to the polls on election day. To make sure the votes were counted honestly, Grenier named Harlington Wood, an experienced one-time federal district attorney in Illinois, to head a "ballot security operation."

The largest single private room on the second floor at the National Committee was turned into political campaign headquarters. Outline maps of the nation drawn on rigid, clear plastic were mounted in a case on one wall. In use they could be displayed one at a time or with one map overlaying the other, and each map contained specific information. All of then indicated the regional divisions. On one we kept track of the Goldwater travel. On another the Miller appearances were noted. On a third the names of the key people in each state were lettered. A fourth was devoted to communications and on the other walls charts were erected on which to record the results of the voter-canvass effort. Each state was divided into subdivisions, and as the campaign moved forward the names of Goldwater precinct, district, county, and state chairmen working on the canvass were lettered on the board together with numerical reports of calls made, favorable responses, and the number of Goldwater votes anticipated.

From August 8th to 16th, the tide of public sentiment had been distinctly anti-Goldwater. Joseph Alsop's piece in the *Saturday Evening Post* suggested that opposition to Goldwater was "fear of an itchy finger on the nuclear trigger." And in the same issue, Charles Mohr described Goldwater in a subtitle as "impulsive, intuitive, indifferent to advice, and capable of both great charm and great rudeness." Mohr quoted Goldwater as saying, "It's up to the precinct workers to do the selling job and to explain misunderstandings about my positions." Mohr also claimed that former President Eisenhower had said his real worry about Goldwater was not his conservatism but that "he might take this country into war." It was a thorough and complete hatchet job with a repeat of the false charge that Goldwater had suffered two nervous breakdowns in the late 1930's.

Three labor-union Republicans, Morris Hutchinson of Carpenters, James A. Suffridge of Retail Clerks, and Lee W. Minton of the Glass Bottle Blowers, had announced their opposition to Goldwater. And in general, the interpretive accounts of the "unity session" at Hershey, Pennsylvania, gave Goldwater the worst of it.

On August 11th, the Senator, speaking to the National Association of Counties, struck back when he said: "I won't say that the papers misquote me, but I sometimes wonder where Christianity would be today if some of these reporters had been Matthew, Mark, Luke, and John."

In New York state Clare Booth Luce, who had been announced as co-chairman of the Citizens for Goldwater-Miller, was threatening to run as a Conservative party candidate against incumbent Republican Kenneth Keating. Rockefeller announced that he had asked Goldwater to use his influence with Mrs. Luce to keep her out of the race.

Columnists Evans and Novak on August 12th, quoted verbatim a confidential memorandum from John Grenier in which the executive director had suggested that the staff refrain from talking to members of the press either on or off the record. They called Grenier "Burch's razor-sharp second in command" and said the key word in the directive was "control."

In the *Washington Daily News* on August 13th, John Herling implied that Ralph Cordiner was responsible for the General Electric price-fixing episode and said: "Cordiner's lack of popularity in the large sections of the business community will hardly inspire voluntary gifts for the Goldwater campaign coffers."

David J. McDonald of the Steel Workers was even more violent. The *Washington Evening Star* quoted the union leader as saying that Goldwater "actually despises poor people and wants to destroy unions." Then, "If you want to be unemployed and live in filth and degradation, go out and support Goldwater."

The episode in the Tonkin Gulf, when our Navy responded to

an attack by Communist torpedo boats, had blown up another controversy. McNamara announced the naval commanders had been authorized to use whatever force necessary to protect themselves against the attacks in the international waters between Viet Nam and Red China. Goldwater suggested this was implicit authority to use low-yield, tactical, nuclear weapons. Arthur Sylvester from the Pentagon denied this claim and called Goldwater untruthful. In response the Senator said that what he meant was that Mr. Johnson used fuzzy language in describing his strike-back orders. All in all, it was quite a week.

Burch invited all of the Republican state chairmen to a meeting in Washington at the Mayflower Hotel on the week end of August 16th. A number of former Goldwater state chairmen were included, but unfortunately, the elected members of the National Committee were overlooked. Goldwater had said in San Francisco he would run the campaign through the National Committee; nevertheless this first official act of Burch's seemed to contradict the promise.

At the Mayflower meeting Burch introduced Rudy Etchen and Al Tilt of the Erwin Wasey advertising agency. He also unveiled a proposed billboard which had been developed by Leo Burnett carrying the slogan "In your heart you know he's right."

Burch, in a press interview at the Mayflower meeting, announced plans for a twelve million dollar campaign. But he said the meeting was for the purpose of discussing "the nuts and bolts of the campaign—door-to-door canvassing, fund raising, advertising and public relations, vote quotas, and ballot security—any grand-strategy talk is out of order."

Goldwater appeared and amused the state chairmen by announcing that the National Committee might put out a book of Bobby Baker nursery rhymes entitled *The Butcher, the Baker and the Stereo Taker*. And Denison Kitchel issued a press release saying Goldwater's general campaign would formally open on September 3rd, in Prescott, Arizona, a change from a previous announcement that the formal opening would be on September 4th.

The state chairmen exhibited a mixture of optimism and pessimism. To some of them it seemed that in the four weeks since San Francisco the Goldwater campaign had been standing still. Now the Senator was served by a press secretary who had not even known the candidate when he took the job, an advertising agency which had not even been thinking of politics at convention time, and a public relations man who had been away from the committee since shortly after his participation in the Republican defeat of 1960. Moreover, it appeared to the state chairmen that Goldwater had gone on the defensive. The Hershey meeting was being interpreted as a concession to the Scranton-Lodge-Rockefeller wing of the party; the Senator's letter to Richard Nixon attempting to explain the meaning of the sentence on extremism had not been received by the party as Goldwater and his strategy people intended. But there was hope. Burch promised the Senator's itinerary would soon be published in detail. He said there would be new and compelling campaign literature, and when Ray Humphries reviewed the vote-quota and canvass program, these experienced politicians applauded. At last they had something they could get their teeth into, and they were all eager to start.

18

There is mystery and excitement in every political contest. The spotlight is focused on the candidate—his personality, his speeches, his special talents for the job—but the organization and strategists behind the candidate are equally important. Successful political campaigns are the result of the most delicately balanced team work. A persuasive, plausible candidate attracts the voters' attention; the strategists select the issues and control timing. The organization gets out the vote on election day and makes sure the ballots are properly counted.

Every four years a mighty army is mobilized to march beneath the banners of our two great political parties. Because most of those who work in politics are volunteers and those who are paid for their time could make much more following other pursuits, the building of a successful political organization requires time, judgment, tact, and sensitivity.

F. Clifton White had hoped to be named party chairman in San Francisco. The job had gone to Burch, and White had been permitted to depart for Hawaii without knowing what role, if any, he might expect to play in the presidential campaign. When he returned to his home in Rye, New York, on July 27th, he found a letter from Goldwater. White says the Senator's communication was warm and friendly: "Barry gave me full credit for my help in winning the nomination. He said he wanted me to be a part of his campaign team and asked me to call him in Washington."

White did call, and it was in this telephone conversation that Goldwater first suggested the creation of a Citizens for Goldwater-Miller Committee to be headed by White. They agreed to meet in

Washington and discuss the subject, but Goldwater was leaving for the Bohemian Grove, and before the projected conference could take place, the *New York Times* carried the story of White's appointment as head of the Citizens group.

Burch and Grenier were furious because they were opposed to White in any capacity. The *Times* piece was equally upsetting for White. He had not agreed to accept the appointment; a more temperamental or less experienced politician might have taken offense at the newspaper announcement of a relationship which was not established.

In past campaigns these independent citizens groups have not been welcomed by regular party members. In 1952 the Citizens for Eisenhower virtually took over the campaign. They raised more money, spent more money, and had more influence in the subsequent allocation of patronage than did the regular party organization. When a repetition of the 1952 situation threatened in Eisenhower's second election, some regular Republicans moved in quickly to take control.

Citizens groups are created—perhaps tolerated would be a better word—on the theory that disenchanted Democrats and lukewarm Republicans who cannot be drawn into a party effort will give money and support to a personal organization for the presidential ticket. White argued he was known as a violently partisan Republican, but the Senator was insistent. He wanted White, and finally a compromise was reached. White would become executive director and General James A. Doolittle and Mrs. Clare Booth Luce would be named co-chairmen of the Citizens group. They would sit in the front seat; White would do the work.

The space at 1101 Connecticut Avenue was still available, but most of the personnel of the old Goldwater for President Committee had moved to 1625 Eye Street. When White and his administrative assistant, Kansas State Senator Tom Vansickle, commenced to build a Citizens organization, it was natural they should turn to those who had been state chairmen for Goldwater during the drive for nomination. Most of these people were Republicans, though some had alienated the regular party organization by their work for the Senator prior to the convention.

Immediately following the San Francisco convention there was great enthusiasm for Goldwater. Hundreds of state, county, and other Republican organizations were pleading for campaign brochures, pamphlets, bumper strips, buttons, etc., but the National Committee did not have anything. Lee Edwards, in the brief period he served as acting director of public relations, had started to prepare two or three small pieces. But these were nothing more than a rehash of the old Goldwater committee folders. It was impossible for Edwards to develop anything new until the strategy group on the third floor decided what issues were important and how the candidate would be presented in the general election effort, and these decisions had not been made.

Lou Guylay, in his first week as head of the public relations department, decreed the Republican National Committee would not prepare, print, or distribute any campaign literature. Guylay contended that under the law the National Committee was prohibited from selling campaign material. These things, he said, should be produced by the Citizens group and then sold to local state organizations. The committee was having difficulty raising money, and Guylay's proposal was received as a welcome way to reduce the strain on the budget. Moreover, the new PR man told Burch this same procedure had been followed with great success in 1960.

White chose Rus Walton to head the press and public relations section of Citizens. Walton had managed Joe Shell's unsuccessful campaign for the Republican gubernatorial nomination in California in 1962. Prior to that he had been a regional director for the NAM in thirteen western states. When United Republicans of California was organized in March of 1963, he was chosen executive secretary.

When Rus Walton moved into the Citizens operation on August 10th, he was confronted with the backlog of requests for literature. Some of the orders had not been acknowledged; others had received an equivocal response because no one knew where the literature was coming from or what it would be. It is possible to argue that campaign literature is of secondary importance and that grand strategy—the speeches, the appearances of the candidate—should receive the major emphasis, but no national campaign can hope to be successful without literature, and this long delay in providing the essential material had a depressing effect on the workers in the field.

The brochures and pamphlets issued by the Goldwater for President Committee had, perhaps unconsciously, used photographs of the Senator which seemed to give the impression of a stern, unrelenting, uncompromising candidate. One straight-on head shot showed Goldwater with his glasses on, his mouth open, talking. It was so unfriendly the staff dubbed it "the old snarly picture."

In the files at headquarters Walton found a series of ten photographs taken by the Karsh brothers of Ottawa, Canada. They captured the resolute integrity of Goldwater and at the same time projected a friendly, warm image. Walton was told the pictures had been turned down by Fuller, Smith and Ross and by Leo Burnett and would not be available. He contacted the photographers' agent in New York and made arrangements which ultimately resulted in the use of all ten poses. Before the campaign ended, Walton and his staff prepared and printed twenty-nine million pieces of literature. They provided the plates to state organizations which in turn duplicated at least another twenty million pamphlets, brochures, bumper stickers, and posters. Had these been available in mid July instead of mid September, the campaign might have turned out quite differently.

In many ways the organization developed by Clif White paralleled the National Committee setup. In other respects it was quite different. The party had nothing to compare with "Doctors for Goldwater-Miller," "Pilots for Goldwater-Miller," "Dentists for Goldwater-Miller," "Mothers for a Moral America," and a host of other special political-action groups. The critics derided these as "paper fronts." If so, the color of the paper was green, for each group operating in its particular field raised a substantial amount of money to support the over-all campaign effort.

At the National Committee headquarters the critical attitude of Burch and Grenier toward White and his Citizens organization was manifested in a dozen different ways—some subtle, some not so subtle. Before the campaign ended, the group at 1101 Connecticut

Avenue came to refer to themselves as "second-class Citizens." Wayne Hood had a different outlook. He instructed the regional directors to build their organizations through the party wherever possible but to consult with White and his people at every step. In most cases this was accomplished with a beneficial effect, but White was also trying to build his own organization and during the final two weeks in August the developing political structures became competitive. In the southern region certain individuals with Citizens struck out independently of state party chairmen. In other areas the party organizations bitterly resisted the formation of Citizens. Some of the difficulty can be traced to jealousy over the collection of campaign funds, but most of it was a struggle for recognition and authority. On August 20th the Evans-Novak column in the *New York Herald Tribune* reported that Moulton G. Frantz, Republican chairman of Lehigh county, Pennsylvania, "gave Wayne Hood hell because the Citizens had opened a stall at the Lehigh County Fair."

Much has been said about the reluctance of certain leaders in the Republican party to support the Goldwater candidacy. The name of Mark Hatfield, Oregon's Governor, is erroneously listed as one of the spoilers. At Walton's request, Hatfield detached his personal director of public relations, Travis Cross, and made him available to the Citizens committee. Cross, an experienced and extremely competent PR man, would have been an addition to any campaign staff. He was an invaluable aid to the Goldwater effort. It was Cross who always remembered that protocol must be observed—something frequently overlooked at the National Committee. On at least two occasions the Committee attempted to carry on some delicate negotiations with the Oregon governor's staff at Salem, three thousand miles away, and completely ignored the fact that Hatfield's man, Cross, was in Washington only three blocks away.

At the National Committee headquarters Burch and Grenier gradually surmounted the difficulties of a late start—numerous changes in personnel and the special difficulties created by trying to work around the remodelers and furniture movers and telephone installers. On the second floor there was a determined spirit of cooperation. The regional directors who were established in August and those who came later—Sam Hay for the Great Lakes region, Fred Scribner for Region III and Jim Smith for Region II—offered unmatched political experience. Smith had worked as an assistant on Capitol Hill for a congressman from his region. Fred Scribner was the long-time legal counsel of the Republican party, and Sam Hay, former chairman of Milwaukee county, Wisconsin, had been an original Goldwater organizer in the Midwest.

The particular virtue of the regional-director concept lies in the fact that these men were intimately acquainted with the political problems and the political figures in their respective regions. Most of them were veterans of many past elections. They were not theorists; they were practical politicians who had dealt and could deal with the problems, the idiosyncracies of the personalities involved.

Lee Edwards and Lou Guylay had divided the responsibility in the PR department, and Jim McKenna, an experienced newsman, was busily developing a competent staff to handle the daily, almost hourly, news releases. In the front corner of the second-floor space, Rudy Etchen and Al Tilt of the Erwin Wasey agency were available for quick consultation, although most of the production was scheduled for New York. On the third floor in an office reserved for the Senator and his brain trust, forty speech writers, stenographers, and clerks, all selected by Bill Baroody, were busily framing major policy statements, planning the content of television presentations, and developing the over-all strategy. On the ninth floor the finance group, under the direction of Ralph Cordiner, with the assistance of Bill Middendorf, Jeremy Milbank, and Frank Kovac, concentrated on raising the necessary campaign money.

Political campaigns speak to the voters in at least four different voices:—what the candidate says himself, what his supporters say about him, what the press and the commentators say about the candidate, and what all three of these voices say about the opposition. The television networks make it possible for any candidate with enough money to present his views to a vast majority of American voters. But tradition demands that contenders for a public office make personal appearances. Wayne Hood enlisted Douglas C. Whitlock, a Washington attorney, to head the "Tour Committee." Whitlock was probably the most experienced politician on the Goldwater staff. As a University student in Indiana he had organized the nation's first Young Republican club during the 1928 campaign for Herbert Hoover. He had participated in the Republican campaigns of 1932, 1940, 1944, 1948, and 1960.

Each individual appearance of a candidate requires days of advance planning. The schedule for each stop must be worked out in minute detail, and in the jet air age the complexities of three or four major appearances in as many states in one day creates problems which almost defy description.

In the 1964 campaign Goldwater visited forty-five states and made one hundred and sixty-two different appearances. The Tour Committee also had to schedule Congressman Miller, former Vice-President Nixon, former President Eisenhower, Mrs. Goldwater when she was not accompanying her husband, the Goldwater sons —Michael and Barry, Jr.—and the Miller family. Local protocol had to be observed, political VIP's invited, seating arrangements, motorcades, baggage transfers planned.

Some understanding of the problems of the Tour Committee can be gained by examining the detailed instructions for one stop at Winston-Salem, North Carolina, on September 15th, which took just one hour and ten minutes and was followed by similar appearances the same day at Atlanta, Georgia, and Orlando and St. Petersburg, Florida.

BMG SCHEDULE FIRM—September 13, 1964
September 15—First Stop—WINSTON-SALEM
VIPs on plane to Winston-Salem:
Herman Saxon, State Chairman of N.C.
Robert Gavin, Candidate for Governor

9:00 EDT Leave Dulles

9:00 EST Arrive Winston-Salem, Smith Reynolds Airport

9:05 Meet Reception committee at airport head by Mayor M. C. Benton, Jr.

1. Mayor M. C. Benton, Jr.
2. W. A. (Nab) Armfield, 5th District congressional candidate.
3. Mrs. Armfield
4. P. Huber Hanes, Jr., Chairman of N.C. State Citizens for Goldwater
5. Mrs. Thelma Rogers, RNC
6. Mr. J. E. Broyhill, Sr., RNC
7. Mr. John C. (Red) Clifford, State candidate for Commissioner of Insurance
8. Mrs. Lewis E. Ludlum, Vice Chairman, Forsyth County Republican Party
9. Mr. Clarence Sturzenbecker, Chairman, Citizens for Goldwater, Forsyth County

No speech at airport—just bare formalities

9:10 Load Cars

9:15 Depart for Winston-Salem

9:30-9:40 Jack Tar Hotel—Greeted by Dr. Eldon Nielson (Ph.D.) Chairman, Forsyth County Republican Party (who made arrangements for Winston-Salem visit).
Senator Goldwater will make brief remarks to 300 breakfast guest contributors in ballroom. At head table will be:

1. Dr. Eldon Nielson
2. Mrs. A. E. Verbelia, Vice Chairman, N.C. State Republican Party
3. Mrs. Floyd S. Burg, Jr., Vice Chairman of 5th Congressional District
4. Mrs. W. L. Brune, Regional Chairman for Goldwater campaign.
5. Mrs. Mercer S. Ubele, 1st V.P. for Forsyth Citizens for Goldwater
6. Mr. L. N. Bagnal, 2nd V.P., Citizens for Goldwater

9:40-9:50 After brief remarks to breakfast guests, the French doors opening to marquee will be opened. Crowd will be assembled in street below. Goldwater will not go out on marquee but will stand at open French doors and address crowd.

9:50-9:55 Load cars

9:55-10:05 Motorcade to airport

10:05-10:10 Load planes, wheels up.

Whitlock, a dedicated Republican, had first offered his services to Goldwater in the late fall of 1963. He made one trip to New Hampshire before the Senator became an official candidate, but Kitchel had been unable to find any specific assignment for Whitlock's talents. It was not until Hood came to Washington that this experienced campaigner was given an official title and assigned to the job he had done so many times before.

Whitlock enlisted a staff of over eighty individuals—advance men, schedulers, clerks, typists, etc.—and more than 75 per cent of these were volunteers. Each projected stop had to be "advanced" at least twice, usually a week ahead of the appearance and then a day or two ahead. This function required the full-time attention of thirty-six men for the Goldwater-Miller appearances, including three brothers by the name of Teetor; fifteen more worked on the Nixon tours. In the final days of the campaign Whitlock reminded me, "We never lost a candidate." In 1940, when he was handling the Willkie presidential train, it disappeared for a period of more than three hours. Mr. Willkie, tired of traveling, decided he wanted a nap. He ordered the engineer to run the train on a siding midway between two remote stations in the Far West, and the Republican presidential candidate was actually lost to the Tour Committee for three hours.

An entirely separate department called "Transportation" was created by the National Committee under the supervision of Garry Kidwell, a talented young man who had once operated his own airline. Transportation leased the various aircraft, and at one time Kidwell had under his jurisdiction two Boeing 727's, the Miller Lockheed Electra, a DC-3 for the "Truth Squad," and several smaller airplanes. Vice-President Nixon was provided with his own leased Convair from October 1st to October 31st, and Barry Goldwater, Jr. used a loaned Aero Commander.

As the first of September drew near we began to hear the grumbling of party leaders who felt they had been left out of the planning. Antagonistic columnists charged that the Goldwater organization was split, fractioned, and unsure. Actually, the organization was simple and direct. Kitchel, who was general campaign director, was in complete charge of the over-all Goldwater effort. The "think tank," presided over by Baroody, was responsible for the preparation of speeches and statements to be released through the PR department and on nationwide television. The regional directors, under Wayne Hood, were assigned to the task of coordinating the field efforts and implementing the strategy devised by Baroody and Kitchel. Whitlock was in charge of Tours. Burch, as chairman of the national Committee, was involved in implementing every aspect of the campaign. Grenier was the executive officer.

Everything Burch referred to as the "nuts and bolts" was in place, ready to go to work.

In late August it was announced that the Goldwater party would travel in an especially equipped 727 Boeing Jet leased from American Airlines. Miller was to be provided with the Lockheed Electra. In the 1960 campaign Nixon had been left holding the bag for nearly one hundred thousand dollars worth of transportation provided for members of the working press. Most of this money was ultimately collected, but for a time the deficiency was a serious problem. The Goldwater management decided that seats on the Senator's airplane would be sold and the money collected in advance. The fifty-four press seats at the rear of the airplane would be allocated on a first-come-first-served basis for a price of $3,400. This produced some grumbling from the reporters, but as a result, the operation of the Goldwater airplane cost the Republican National Committee only a little more than regular air fare would have cost for the official members of the Goldwater group.

The Senator's jet was modified in a specialty shop at Tulsa, Oklahoma, to specifications prescribed by Nick Volcheff. Twelve telephones were installed for the candidate and his staff. An airborne one hundred-word-a-minute teletype capable of two-way transmission with both "ground modes" and "air modes" was provided. A data set permitted the preparation of tape in advance which could then be transmitted to Washington when the aircraft landed. A "jones plug" in the baggage compartment of the aircraft provided quick connection with pre-established telephone cables wherever the aircraft stopped. Volcheff said that during the campaign it never took more than one minute to establish a cable connection after the aircraft was parked at the ramp. In one instance the telephones were hooked up and transmitting in ten seconds. Householders who have experienced some delay when new service is requested from a local telephone company will appreciate that to handle the Goldwater aircraft Volcheff had to arrange as many as sixty private telephone lines in four different cities each day. Numbers had to be assigned in advance, cable positions spotted, additional telephones provided for the press.

When the 727 was airborne, communication was maintained through the Bell System air-to-ground radio east of the Mississippi. In the western half of the United States the Republican Party operated four short-wave radio stations all properly licensed by the FCC and used whatever commercial facilities were available. These could all be interconnected with a nationwide Bell System to provide instant communications.

The official opening which had first been scheduled for Friday, September 4th, in Prescott, Arizona, was moved back to September 3rd, leaving sixty-seven days available for active campaigning. Kitchel and Baroody wanted the Senator to be in Washington every Sunday and Monday to attend strategy sessions and film the projected thirty-minute television shows. This left forty-two days for personal appearances. At the first scheduling conference—attended by Burch, Baroody, Kitchel, Whitlock, and Hood—the days available were allocated to regions of the country rather than to individual states. It was decided Goldwater would spend a total of two and a half days in the Northeast, five and a half days in the Atlantic and Pennsylvania areas, ten days in the South and Texas, ten days in the Great Lakes area, four days in the Plains states, four and a half days in the West (exclusive of California), and five days in that key state.

This preliminary division of the candidate's campaign time is significant. New England, New York, New Jersey, and Pennsylvania were not totally written off, but it was obvious that those in command expected the Senator to find his greatest support in the traditional Republican Midwest, the Far West, and the South.

Originally it was planned to have a "Goldwater day" include four stops. This was later reduced to three. Evenings were reserved for major meetings, and some latitude was to be allowed for private gatherings with finance groups. In theory at least the schedule was to be tentatively approved two weeks in advance. Regional directors would then be expected to confirm local appearances so that details could be arranged one week in advance of the candidate's arrival. In practice, the schedule was rarely firm more than four days in advance, and some appearances were "scrubbed" with less than twenty-four hours' notice.

On alternate Sundays, regional directors were to be briefed by the Public Opinion Research pollsters of Princeton, New Jersey. Strategy sessions would be held Sunday afternoons, with Wayne Hood representing the political organization. The Senator would appear at least twice each week on nationwide television, and these programs, we were told, would carry the Senator into the homes of America and focus public attention on the real issues of foreign policy, domestic economy, federal spending, and federal interference.

Space does not permit a detailed report on each regional operation. But Region VII, embracing Alaska, Washington, Oregon, Idaho, Montana, Utah, Arizona, Nevada, New Mexico, Wyoming and Hawaii is a typical example. In each of these states the Republican chairman was involved as the nominal head of the campaign effort. In addition, the two National Committee members were active participants, but these party officials had responsibilities to candidates other than the presidental ticket, and to help in coordinating the over-all effort we had nine Goldwater chairmen, some of whom also served as the local head of the Citizens for Goldwater-Miller group. To cover this vast geographical area, I recruited eight field men. Six of these were volunteers who received nothing more than expenses and were available whenever and wherever needed. We shared the services of one professional campaign manager with a senatorial candidate in Montana; the other man was my full-time assistant, Jim Sage of Tucson, Arizona.

The field men who moved about from state to state within the region were selected for their competence and experience. In my region, Thad Baker of Yuma was a former county chairman and had long been active in Republican circles. Wes Phillips of Oregon was an experienced and successful manager of campaigns. Bob Mardian had business and personal connections in most of the areas of the region. John Pritzlaff of Phoenix had been a county chairman in Milwaukee and a successful candidate for the legislature in Arizona. Peter Buck of Oregon had demonstrated great competence during the Goldwater primary in that state. Jack Swift of Phoenix had been a legislative district leader with business connections in New Mexico which made him particularly effective. Jim Sage of Tucson had helped me carry Pima county, quite an accomplishment when I was losing my bid for the Republican nomination for the United States Senate. And Ed Buck of Reno, Nevada, deserves special mention. Buck, a respected and highly successful lawyer, had lived for many years in the Hawaiian Islands. He volunteered to go back to Hawaii at his own expense to work with the people he knew could be helpful to Goldwater. Mr. Buck died of a heart attack ten days after his arrival.

To operate the southern region, Sam Claiborne had a similar field organization and three full-time assistants in Washington, D.C.—Fred Agnich of Dallas, a volunteer who paid his own expenses; Fred LaRue, the national committeeman from Mississippi, who gave his time and paid his own way; and Willis Johnson, a devoted conservative whose home was in Washington, D.C. Dick Herman in Region VI had one full-time assistant in Washington, Bill Morrow of Nebraska, and nine field men. Jim Smith managed Region II all by himself, and in IV, Sam Hay was assisted by Gerry Johnson of Missouri. Fred Scribner in Region III was assisted by Dick Cooper, a veteran Republican politician of New Hampshire, and a field staff sufficient to cover his area.

19

The question of what happened to Barry Goldwater pleads for a precise, definitive answer. Those who were involved as partisan supporters of the Senator and those who opposed him would be pleased to find that one particular action or single statement overbalanced the scale in favor of Lyndon Johnson. In truth no such simple explanation can be advanced. In less complicated contests hindsight can sometimes illuminate the particular play, the brilliant offensive move, or the error in defense responsible for the final decision. In a political race the spectators are themselves participants; their mood and their assumptions must be considered.

In the seven weeks between the nomination and the formal opening of the Goldwater campaign in Prescott, Arizona, there occurred a startling perhaps decisive change in the public attitude and regard for the two contenders. Lyndon Johnson recognized the change. He may not have been responsible for it, he may not have planned it, but his political antenna received the message, and the selection of Hubert Humphrey as the vice-presidential candidate on the Democrat ticket cannot be justified or interpreted on any other basis.

James Reston, writing in the *New York Times* on August 26th, recognized the result, if not the proportion of the change when he said, speaking of Johnson's own party members, "They are not so excited about Johnson as they are afraid of Goldwater, genuinely afraid that his policies are bad for the country."

In the minds of the American voters Lyndon Johnson and Barry Goldwater had changed places. The Republican candidate was now the dangerous radical, the advocate of drastic change, the proponent of policies which might take the nation into a nuclear war, alter the domestic economy, destroy Social Security, and bring an abrupt halt to the program of federal farm subsidy. Johnson had become the prophet of the *status quo,* the conservative who would preserve the present foreign policy, admittedly a policy with many failures but easily defended in the public mind by the somewhat inaccurate claim, "At least we aren't fighting." Johnson would do nothing to upset economic prosperity or change the pattern of federal employment or interfere with the wasteful program of agricultural subsidies which the farmers themselves condemned. After thirty years of the New Deal-Fair Deal inspired proliferations of federal government, subsidies, grants, expanded employment and foreign aid, the very system Goldwater opposed had become the *status quo.* And that instinctive conservatism which resists change was now available to support Johnson in the continuation of programs and policies which knowledgeable conservatives actively oppose and condemn.

The issues which might have contributed to a meaningful decision in November of 1964 were now completely obfuscated, and Johnson, recognizing the election would not turn on liberalism vis-à-vis conservatism, was free to select Humphrey and thereby cement his alliance with the financially and intellectually potent left-wing liberal establishment.

The entire blame for this turnabout cannot be placed on the liberal press and the liberal commentators, although their contribution was a major force. Charles Mohr, writing in the *Saturday Evening Post,* said that "Goldwater not only wants change, he wants drastic change." Walter Lippmann on August 13th, called Barry Goldwater a "war hawk."

Johnson, playing the cozy waiting game, speaking soft and empty words, avoiding controversy, became a saintly figure when compared to Goldwater, who mentioned painful subjects and focused attention on that future day when the piper must be paid for present follies.

When Goldwater met with the Republican members of the House to discuss the NATO issue, he repeated his earlier suggestion that the commander of our first line of defense in Europe should be permitted use of tactical nuclear weapons in the event of an enemy attack. The Pentagon rushed into print with the frightening statement that the average nuclear weapon was now five times as powerful as the bombs dropped on Hiroshima, and this tortured logic was never challenged. Goldwater was speaking of very small weapons at the low end of the scale, not the average; but since that day in August, 1944, the American public has been fed a steady diet of horror stories until the word nuclear is associated with doomsday.

In his final week in the Congress, Goldwater offered a written statement in support of Senator Ribicoff's resolution condemning the treatment of Jews in the Soviet Union. This item deserves special attention. The resolution, which lists Goldwater as one of the original sponsors, passed the Senate by an almost unanimous vote. But the Johnson State Department objected strenuously on the grounds that the words might "offend the Soviet Union." At Johnson's insistence the Joint Committee of House and Senate conferees accepted a watered-down State Department version devoid of any reference to the Soviets.

When Goldwater, during the campaign, charged the Johnson administration with being soft on communism, the press tore into him for repeating an unsubstantiated hackneyed charge. Mike Bernstein points out the Senator could easily have proven his point by reciting the history of the Ribicoff resolution.

To many observers it seemed that Goldwater had been consistently on the defensive since San Francisco. The widely advertised unity meeting at Hershey, Pennsylvania, and the flow of news stories attempting to explain Goldwater's stand on nuclear weapons, Social Security, and TVA had all given the initiative to our opponents. We were told this would change when the campaign started officially.

Goldwater stopped in Cleveland long enough to lecture the VFW on the virtues of using low-yield nuclear weapons in the defense of Europe and then went on to a projected five-day vacation on the yacht "Sundance" off the coast of southern California.

By August the 26th, when John Grenier was ready to take his three-step, win-the-election program to the country, more than five hundred competent political experts covering the entire nation were at the disposal of the second-floor political organization.

Flying in a chartered F-27, Grenier's team went into the field to brief the local leaders. The first meeting was held in Sacramento, California, the second in Boise, Idaho, the third in Denver, Colorado, the fourth in Omaha, Nebraska; the group then swung into the South, moved up the Atlantic Coast into New England and concluded in the Midwest.

Each conference was attended by representatives from the adjacent states. At the Boise meeting we had people from Washington, Oregon, Idaho, Montana, Alaska, Arizona, and Nevada. In Denver the leaders of Wyoming, Colorado, New Mexico, and Utah were represented.

Ray Humphreys and Rita Bass explained the voter-canvass operation. Harlington Wood outlined the ballot-security program, and Grenier spoke on the over-all campaign plan—identify the friendly voters, get the votes to the polls, count the ballots. This aspect of the Goldwater effort had been thoroughly advanced; each state leader had received material covering all of his precincts with suggested attainable vote quotas.

At the Boise meeting which I attended only one thing had been overlooked—no one remembered to advise or invite the governor of Idaho, and when I went to see him the temperature in his office was about minus ten degrees Centigrade.

The voter-canvass program was probably the most meticulous and potentially effective plan ever developed for a national campaign. We estimated that in the period of its operation 75 per cent of the voters in the United States were called upon in their own homes. Literature was distributed, and the voter attitude was determined. On Election Day those who had indicated a preference for Goldwater either went to the polls or were taken to cast their ballot. Only one essential ingredient was lacking—an appealing candidate whose campaign was persuading the voters to join his team. On November 3rd there were just not enough Goldwater votes in the country to win, but the mechanics were all in order.

On September 1st, Kitchel was questioned by reporters in Newport Beach, California, about his conference with Goldwater on the yacht. He said they had talked about campaign strategy and "the problems we will have to meet when he [Goldwater] assumes the office of the Presidency. Among them," Kitchel said, "were appointments to Cabinet posts," but he refused to elaborate. There is an old fable about what happened to the man who sold the tiger's skin before he had killed the tiger.

The change of dates for the opening in Prescott created some minor problems. A crew of advance men had been sent to Phoenix to work out details with state chairman Keith Brown and executive director Bill Worthington of the Republican organization. Special space for a press room was leased at the Hotel Westward Ho in downtown Phoenix, and thirty private telephone wires were installed. The out-of-state press promptly complained about the downtown location; they preferred the Valley Ho, a resort-type hotel, in Scottsdale, much closer to Goldwater's hilltop home. An order was given to move the installed telephone lines; then the order was countermanded. There was some question about the ability of the Prescott airport to accommodate Goldwater's 727, and for a time it was not known whether the Senator would fly or drive. So Brown and Worthington had to plan for both contingencies.

In Prescott, Yavapai County Chairman Dick Smith made plans to accommodate an expected crowd of twenty thousand visitors. Early in the morning of September 2nd, a decision was made to move the time of the opening speech from the scheduled four o'clock to two o'clock. No one seems to know precisely why. One explanation is that this was done in order to give the eastern reporters an opportunity to make their first editions. Whatever the reason, the change was not announced until after lunch, when it was too late for release in the afternoon newspapers of Arizona.

Those partisans who were planning to leave their homes in time to be present for a four o'clock kick-off arrived in Prescott about the time Goldwater was leaving the Court House steps. Insead of the anticipated overflow crowd, the audience consisted primarily of local residents. No provision had been made for national radio or television coverage, although at least one major station in Phoenix had offered public service time. Richard Smith accepted the changed timetable without any audible complaint, but to move a big meeting from four o'clock to two o'clock requires a tremendous amount of extra effort. It is easy to postpone or delay; it is almost impossible to advance.

Goldwater security chief Hugh MacDonald and the Senator's personal aide Charles Justice had ruled against any parade from the airport to the Court House. But Goldwater was the first native Arizonan ever to be nominated to the Presidency on any ticket, and a political rally without a parade is about as exciting as a hot dog without mustard. The Prescott people held a parade anyway without the candidate.

At two o'clock the introductions commenced. The Yavapai County Court House, a magnificent marble and granite structure in the tradition of fifty years ago, dominates a square block in the center of town. A formidable flight of stone steps guards the front of the building, and here, standing before an improvised podium, Barry Goldwater opened his campaign for the highest office in the nation.

The speech which Karl Hess had written was in actuality a summary of the oft repeated Goldwater positions. It did include one new suggestion, a promise by the candidate that his administration would end the draft. He said:

> Republicans will end the draft altogether and as soon as possible, I promise you.
>
> Republicans understand that the military forces need trained volunteers who make the military service a career.
>
> Republicans understand that the purpose of the military forces is not social or political. It is to help keep the peace of the world. To use military services for political and social schemes as this administration does, is to drift closer to war on the ebbing tide of military strength.

Whatever else Goldwater had to say was lost. The reporters focused their attention on this new suggestion. The Senator, they said, was attempting to capture the votes of parents without offering any alternative which would maintain the military strength of the nation. It was, they said, a "political promise." And at about the same time Goldwater was speaking, the Pentagon released a statement to the effect that a committee appointed by President Johnson had been considering ways to end the draft for four months. This remarkable "coincidence" went almost unnoticed.

The origin and development of this first new declaration from the Goldwater campaign is worth tracing. In mid August Rus Walton sent a four-page memorandum on, "The Fear Syndrome and Selective Service" to the third floor "think tank." He said:

> A. One of our major campaign problems is that people are afraid that Senator Goldwater will get us into war. That he is "triggerhappy" or that he "will push the button."
>
> B. We must take some steps to remove this albatross within the national posture of "peace through strength."
>
> C. One suggestion is that the Senator call for the elimination, (except in times of extreme national emergency) of the selective service system.

Walton's memorandum called for a carefully worded statement which would emphasize the wasteful inefficiency of the draft under which some four thousand draft boards, with their clerks, office rent, and other overhead, were being used to induct an average of eight men per month per draft board. Prior to the Viet Nam crisis the monthly quota had fallen as low as twenty-one hundred, about one-half draftee per draft board. Eliminating this wasteful operation would permit a considerable savings of taxpayer's money. The paper also developed the accepted theory that wars of the future will probably be of two types which do not require hoards of men, brushfire wars such as Viet Nam or global conflicts which will depend not on national manpower, but on technology. Under the present system we are, according to Walton's information, spending ten thousand dollars to give a draftee two years of training only to have him seek discharge at the earliest possible moment.

Everything in the position paper was documented. Technological advances in the art of war deny the old argument that two or three years of training create a stand-by reserve of any value. Moreover the proposal was compatible with Goldwater's long-time position on the subject. The Senator, in and out of Congress, had argued in favor of a pay scale which would permit the armed services to attract and retain the technicians they needed.

Walton's suggestion contained considerable merit, both as a political move and as a step which would serve the long-range interest of the public. But the skimpy treatment given the proposal in the opening speech was almost a certain guarantee that misunderstandings would follow.

One minor incident in Prescott provides insight into what became a standard pattern of the campaign. While the crowd gathered in the square, the Goldwater party was in one of the county offices on the first floor. Mrs. Richard Smith, wife of the county chairman, was in the room in her official capacity as hostess. This was Goldwater's home state. Val and Dick Smith have enjoyed a personal relationship with the Senator extending back to his first campaign. She had been checked by security. When Goldwater made some inquiry about the order of seating on the platform, Val Smith came across the room intending to tell the Senator that the list was on the podium for ready reference. One of Goldwater's security men rudely blocked her progress and ordered her not to bother the Senator. "He's thinking," the man said.

Most of the newspapers said the Prescott crowd was "disappointing," only a very few explained that the sudden shift in plans was responsible. But the press dealt kindly with the error. They were far less critical than the advance men and the local party officials whose days of preparation were suddenly rendered meaningless and ineffectual.

Goldwater returned to Phoenix, rested on Friday, flew to Lockport to be with the Millers when the vice-presidential candidate opened his campaign, then returned to Phoenix to rest on Sunday before commencing a tour which would take him into California, Oregon, Washington, Idaho, Montana, and Minnesota.

The men on the second floor in Washington found the opening speech disappointing. They had hoped the Senator would enumerate the benefits he planned to secure for the Republic and its citizens and then spell out in very specific terms how these benefits could be achieved. They were particularly disturbed by a one-sentence paragraph in the advance copy. Goldwater said: "A major concern of ours has been the military security of this nation. Some distort this proper concern to make it appear that we are preoccupied with war. *'There is no greater political lie.'* [Italics mine]"

Lie is a harsh and violent word. In using the charge against his critics, Goldwater was adding to his own growing image as a harsh and violent man.

However, the real Goldwater, the Goldwater we knew, the man we wanted to see in the White House was accurately reflected and totally revealed in three paragraphs on the middle of page seven. Here, he said:

> Prudence requires that we proceed slowly and steadily in withdrawing the central government from its many unwarranted interventions in our private economic lives. Only so can the private economy adjust smoothly to its properly broadened tasks without the extra burden of sharp and erratic shifts in policy.
>
> Much as we may wish it were otherwise we shall only gradually be able to alter many policies of the central government. We shall be able to do so as we develop solutions permitting a smooth transition to new and better arrangements.
>
> But there are some things that we can do at once. We can start at once to slow down the expansion in federal spending. We can start at once to foster an economy that will provide jobs for our growing population. We can and will see to it that the jobmaking sector of the economy—the private sector—flourishes and absorbs the unemployed particularly among our youth.

Here was the promise of gradual reform to be instituted with great restraint—a slow healing of the wounds, a cautious transition. Of all the accounts I read of the speech only Charles Mohr, of the *New York Times,* said that Goldwater "vowed gradual change, if elected." James Reston, of the same newspaper, described the opening speech as an exercise in moral philosophy and then chided the Senator for his remarks about Johnson. Evans and Novak, in the *Herald Tribune,* claimed there was a bitter split in the Goldwater camp, and for the first time in any newspaper Baroody was named as the man in charge of Goldwater's strategy.

On Monday morning, September 8th, Goldwater took his campaign to San Diego. He met with local Republican leaders in the Crystal Room of the U.S. Grant Hotel. At twelve noon he made a public address in the Norton Plaza, and at one o'clock he spoke to thirty-five hundred people on a closed circuit TV system at the El Cortez Hotel. Then he flew on to Los Angeles, where fifty-five thousand people gathered in the Dodger Stadium at Chavez Ravine to hear and applaud the man the Republicans had nominated for President.

Julius Duscha of the *Washington Post* said there was a "religious revivalistic fervor about the crowd at Dodger Stadium." The Senator opened with a prediction of victory and an attack on Johnson. He mentioned the cloud over the White House and condemned Adlai Stevenson's advice to Colby College students. The American Ambassador to the United Nations, in discussing the civil rights problem, had said: "In the great struggle to advance human rights even a jail sentence is no longer a dishonor but a proud achievement." Stevenson, perhaps facetiously, suggested that one day a man might run for office on his record of arrests.

The candidate then promised: "As one of my first actions in the White House I shall ask the Congress to enact a regular and considered program of tax reduction of five per cent per year in all income taxes, both individual and corporate." This proposal was first advanced by the economist, Milton Friedman of the University of Chicago, and Goldwater said the cut would be possible without drastically reducing federal expenditures. As the economy grew and expanded, the programed tax decrease would prevent the government's share from increasing as private incomes increased. The proposal was offered to impose a reasonable restraint on federal spending.

Instead of debating the merits of the suggestion the press charged Goldwater with inconsistency because he had voted against the Kennedy-Johnson tax cut. How, they asked, could Goldwater seriously propose to cut taxes and at the same time promise to maintain and increase our military strength? They ignored or failed to comprehend the fact that if the national growth rate continued, the federal government's income even after the tax reduction would hold at about the 1964 level.

Goldwater went on to Sacramento, California, on the ninth and from there to Klamath Falls and Eugene, Oregon, with a night rally in Seattle, Washington.

Shakespeare observed that the evil men do lives after them, the good is oft interred with their bones. So it is with political campaigns. The unnecessary mistakes are never forgotten or forgiven. In Seattle, the Senator, obviously referring to the Boeing workers and the award of the TFX contract to General Dynamics in Texas, said that the plants in the Seattle area had produced thousands of excellent fighter planes which had destroyed our enemies in combat and he was sure they would do it again. His critics pounced on this as proof that Goldwater contemplated war.

In Klamath Falls, Oregon, reporters representing the *Portland Oregonian,* the *Portland Journal* and the *Portland Reporter* were scheduled to ride the Senator's plane from this southern Oregon town to Eugene, but there were only two seats. This was my region, and I had been assured in advance that the newspaper men would have space. To solve the problem Paul Wagner suggested that the three reporters match coins for the two seats; the *Oregonian* man was eliminated. *The Reporter,* a tabloid, is a venture of organized labor in the publishing business, and was the outgrowth of a prolonged and violent strike against the *Oregonian.* It was pro-Johnson all the way, while the *Oregonian* had in the past supported Republican candidates. A twist of fate?

Goldwater went on from Seattle to Boise, Idaho, Great Falls, Montana, and Minneapolis, Minnesota. One of our problems in Idaho was the interparty fight between Goldwater supporters and Governor Bob Smylie. At the state convention, Harley Markham, a long-time member of the National Committee and a Smylie supporter, had been opposed by Marion Wilbur, a Goldwater man. Wilbur lost. But after the convention Burch removed Markham from the executive committee and named Mrs. Steele Barnett of Idaho to take his place. Mrs. Barnett then sponsored Wilbur for state chairman of the Citizens for Goldwater-Miller group. I was aware of this internal conflict, and I prevailed upon Frank Whetstone, the Citizens' regional director, to name a noncontroversial Idahoan, Dave Little, to head the Citizens' effort.

When Goldwater's airplane flew into the Boise airport at ten minutes of ten on the morning of Tuesday, September 10th, Governor Smylie and Harley Markham led the official welcoming committee. The first man off the plane was Marion Wilbur. Every newspaper writer in Idaho gave more space to the peculiar circumstances of Wilbur's being on the Goldwater plane after he had opposed Markham and Smylie, than they did to the Senator's appearance in Boise. The Governor, who was just recovering from what he regarded as a deliberate slight—Grenier's failure to invite him to the Boise training session—did a slow burn which rivaled the magnificence of the Idaho sunset.

20

On September 13th, Julius Duscha of the *Washington Post* (writing out of Chicago) said: "The first week of the Goldwater campaign was a success. All of his major speeches drew large crowds and he said things that made news—the crowds seem to have been a tonic for Goldwater. The Senator is evolving a sharper and stronger campaign style; he is using more humor—and it is a cutting, telling, partisan humor that crowds love."

Lyndon Johnson had officially opened his campaign on September 8th at a Labor Day rally in Detroit attended by an estimated one hundred thousand people. The reporters said that "Johnson, with a tremor in his voice, told the crowd that 'for nineteen peril-filled years no nation has loosed the atom against another. To do so now is a political decision of the highest order. It would lead us down an uncertain path of blows and counterblows whose outcome none may know.' "

Johnson did not mention Goldwater by name. It was unnecessary. The implication was clear and devastating. The *New York Times,* under the by-line of Damon Stetson, quoted a retired teamster in Cleveland as saying: "In my position I am naturally strong for Social Security so I am against Goldwater." A steelworker in Homestead, Pennsylvania, said that he was "getting along to the age of retiring before long. They say Goldwater is against Social Security so you can bet that doesn't set well with me."

The *Chicago Sun Times,* the *Chicago Daily News,* the *Houston Post, the Oregon Journal, and the Medford Mail Tribune* endorsed the Johnson-Humphrey ticket. And Negro leader Roy Wilkins said: "If Barry Goldwater is President, it could lead to a police state."

Donald Janson in the *New York Times* told the nation Goldwater was in trouble, deep trouble because of the misunderstandings over his position on nuclear weapons and his failure to deal in depth with the agricultural problem. Janson said: "Kenneth Kassel, a lean, young corn and livestock farmer, paused near a hog shoot in Ayrshire, Iowa, to explain why he expected to switch his vote to President Johnson this fall. 'If the Republicans had somebody a little more level-headed, I'd vote for him,' he said. 'I'm afraid of Goldwater,' he continued, 'I don't know what he'd do if he got hold of the nuclear trigger, and Goldwater wants to get out of the farm programs. I hate inefficiency and waste in a growing federal government, but I don't see how we can get along without production controls for the present.' " Janson said, "Mr. Kassel's reasoning corresponded to that of many other Republican farmers questioned in a Corn Belt survey of views about the presidential candidates.

There was frustration on the second floor as the result of a decision reached in the "think tank." Kitchel and Baroody had decreed that Goldwater would not lower himself by making a direct appeal for votes with speeches focused on local problems or local interest. He would, they said, be a national candidate, an "honest politician." When this was first announced, most of us on the second floor believed the practical necessity of enlisting additional support for Goldwater would modify the ukase from the "think tank." But the results of the first western tour shattered our illusion.

In California the *bracero* problem was a red-hot issue. For many years the farmers there have imported Mexican nationals to perform stoop labor in the fields and to help with the harvest. These aliens came in under a special permit and earned wages about four times the going rate in their native land. They also acquired on-the-job training, and a number of the more successful farmers in the Mexican states adjacent to the American border are graduates of the *bracero* program. However, organized labor has been campaigning to prevent the use of these field workers, and in 1964 Willard Wirtz, Secretary of Labor, issued orders to terminate the program at the end of the calendar year.

George Murphy, who was successful in his campaign against Pierre Salinger for the Senate seat in California, mentioned the *bracero* program in almost every speech. Goldwater did not even give the problem a nod when he appeared at Chavez Ravine in Los Angeles.

Lumber and fishing support the economy in Oregon. The West Coast lumber industry is suffering from Canadian imports and, particularly, from a federal ruling which prohibits the shipment of domestic lumber between American ports in foreign bottoms. The Maritime and Longshoreman's Unions have steadily increased their wage demands until it is impossible for American flag lines to compete with foreign vessels. And the lumbermen pay the difference. Goldwater did not mention lumber or fishing in Oregon.

In Idaho a bitter controversy has been raging between the public and private power interests since it was first proposed to dam the Snake River. Eisenhower supported the investor-owned private-power producers and carried Idaho. The Kennedy-Johnson administration—and particularly Secretary of the Interior Stewart Udall—was aligned with the public-power advocates. It was expected that Goldwater, whose opposition to the expansion of government in competition with a legitimate private enterprise was well-known, would have something to say to the people of Idaho about this problem. It was not mentioned.

The eastern half of Washington and Oregon are wheat-producing areas. All of the states and communities touched on this first western tour—particularly Idaho, Montana, and Minnesota—are vitally concerned with the farmers' problems. Goldwater said nothing about agriculture, and Dick Herman, who was responsible for the Plains states, had been unable to get any spark out of the "think tank" when he mentioned the subject.

On September 11th, Goldwater appeared in Chicago before a convention of the American Political Science Association. He delivered an excellent, carefully documented, logically developed speech which had been written by Harry Jaffa on the roles assigned by the Constitution to the legislative, judicial, and executive branches of the government.

Jaffa was by far the most competent student of political science in the "think tank." Moreover, he is recognized and respected by his colleagues in the academic world. And for a conservative to find acceptance in that hostile atmosphere is quite an achievement. Jaffa hoped the speech would establish Goldwater as a candidate who revered the Constitution and recognized, respected, and understood the validity of the tripartite system which the founding fathers had given to the nation. And so it might. But under the Baroody-Kitchel system of organization there was no opportunity for any consultation between the candidate and the speech writers, other than Hess, who after Prescott made only minor contributions to the Senator's statements. Jaffa had been enlisted by Baroody because of his recognized excellence. Yet throughout the entire period, commencing ten days before the San Francisco convention and ending with the general election in November, Jaffa and Goldwater never met to discuss the speeches the professor of political science was authorized to write.

Jaffa did not pretend to be an authority on the management of political campaigns, but he was a student of the American voters' emotional response to certain charges. He believed the public would tolerate a politician who criticized the Court's decisions but would reject a candidate who appeared to attack the Court itself. He felt strongly that the person of the President and the personal actions of the President should not be attacked. In his view, it was quite proper to outline the misdoings of a Bobby Baker or a Walter Jenkins, but he held it was bad politics to call Lyndon Johnson a faker or to suggest that Johnson had amassed his great fortune as the result of political position. He believed the voters would instinctively react unfavorably to such charges even if they were true.

In the course of editing, Baroody, Hess, Kitchel—perhaps the Senator himself—inserted one paragraph in the Chicago speech, and Goldwater said: "Of all three branches of government, today's Supreme Court is the least faithful to the constitutional traditions of limited government and to the principle of legitimacy in the exercise of power."

The newspaper accounts we read seemed to imply an alignment between Goldwater and the far-right group which had been campaigning for the impeachment of Earl Warren, and all of the headlines said: "Goldwater Attacks Supreme Court."

The speech, except for that one unfortunate four-line statement, did question the opinions of the Court with powerful logic. Goldwater said the decisions in the school prayer case and the reapportionment case are defended implicitly or explicitly on the grounds that the results are desirable, that it really is not good for children to say prayers in school, that it really is desirable to have state legislatures in their entirety apportioned on a one-man, one-vote basis.

Goldwater questioned the claim that the Supreme Court "had to act because the states would not reapportion themselves." If this was a sound assumption, then he suggested, "It must be that all legislative power in the country is held at the pleasure of the Supreme Court. The Court just steps in and exercises it when the legislative body to whom the power was originally delegated by the Constitution fails to act in accordance with the Court's wishes." And he argued, "The job of keeping the law up to date should be in the hands of the legislators, the Congress and the common law courts, not just in the hands of the nine appointed Justices of the Supreme Court."

On the same day Goldwater spoke in Chicago, Mr. Justice Harlan of the Supreme Court released a statement saying:

> Recent decisions in the Supreme Court give support to a current mistaken view of the Constitution and the Court. This view in a nut shell is that every major social ill in this country can find its cure in some constitutional principle, that this Court should take the lead in promoting reform when other branches of the government fail to act. The Constitution is not a panacea for every blot upon the public welfare, nor should this Court, ordained a judicial body, be thought of as a general haven for reform movements.

On the second floor the Harlan statement was hailed as a weapon which could be used to demolish those who had criticized Goldwater's attitude toward the Court. But in the "think tank" it passed unnoticed. It was never repeated, never inserted in a Goldwater speech, never made part of a Goldwater press release.

On September 14th, the Goldwater campaign announced the formation of a seven-man Task Force on Peace and Freedom. This was described by James Marlow of the AP as one of the most "unusual tactics in the history of American politics." The Task Force plan had been under discussion for several days in the "think tank," and in the same release which told of the plan, Goldwater named the members of his seven-man group.

A bare three hours before the information on the Goldwater Task Force was given to the press, the White House announced that Lyndon Johnson had created a sixteen-man panel of distinguished citizens to consult with him on international probelms. The Johnson release did not name the distinguished citizens, but it took the headlines away from the Goldwater statement. And to a number of men on the second floor the Johnson move was too pat to be dismissed as a mere coincidence. We believed that someone in the Goldwater camp had revealed the Senator's plans to our opponents.

In the same week Walter Lippmann said the real question facing the nation was: "Is Barry Goldwater fit to be President?" And Holmes Alexander, a columnist whose articles had always been friendly to the Republican Senator, said: "You begin to get the idea that the Goldwater team has left its game in the gymnasium—that it was keyed up to win the nomination but doesn't know how to buck heads with the Democrats."

Long before the Senator was nominated in San Francisco, his opponents—particularly those in the Republican party and notably Senator Clifford Case of New Jersey—suggested the Goldwater strategy was to capitalize on the white backlash in the North and to exploit the vote of southerners who were disenchanted by the Johnson position on civil rights.

Burch, Grenier, Lichenstein, Guylay, and Kitchel have all denied the allegation that Goldwater was running on a racist platform. But the South was important. In every calculation of how victory might be won it was necessary to include the votes from some southern states which had in the past always gone to a Democrat candidate and Sam Claiborne, Director of Region VI, was pinning all his hopes on an effective southern tour.

The Senator, who was extremely sensitive to the charges of racism, had decreed that he would not go into Mississippi because of the tense situation in that state. Virginia was not on the itinerary because of Goldwater's warm personal relations with Senator Harry F. Byrd and the belief that Byrd-type Democrats would vote against Johnson anyway. But North and South Carolina, Florida, Tennessee, Alabama, Georgia, and Louisiana were all regarded as key states—second in importance only to Texas and California. Consequently, Goldwater's second tour was aimed at the South. It was to commence with a morning appearance at Winston-Salem, North Carolina, a noon stop at Orlando, and a night rally in the Tampa-St. Petersburg area of Florida, to be followed on the second day with major appearances in Knoxville and Memphis, Tennessee; Macon, Georgia; and Montgomery, Alabama. The third day's schedule commenced with Raleigh, North Carolina, then on to Greenville and Shreveport, Louisiana, with a major address in New Orleans on the night of September 18th.

Florida is the promised land in the minds and hearts of thousands of Americans who look forward to spending the final years of their lives in a mild, sunny climate. Many of that state's new residents are retired people drawing benefits from the nation's old age and survivors insurance programs. Sam Claiborne enlisted the help of Congressman William C. Cramer of Florida to emphasize the necessity of clarifying the Senator's position on Social Security in the speech planned for St. Petersburg.

Memphis is the cotton capital of the South. Residents of that area live, breathe, eat, and sleep with the production of cotton. And Claiborne brought in two members of the National Cotton Council to advise and assist the speech writers in the "think tank" in preparing a statement on agriculture which would assure the cotton growers that Goldwater was sympathetic with their problems.

Every state in the mid South has benefited from the water and power developments on the Tennessee River under TVA. Abundant, cheap electricity has attracted industry; miles of usable waterways appeal to the recreation-minded tourist. And while all of this has cost the taxpayers in the other states of the Union untold millions, the people of Tennessee and the adjacent areas become violently protective whenever the propriety of this vast governmental empire is questioned. Goldwater was on record as having said it would be good business to sell the TVA to private enterprise. Yet, Knoxville, Tennessee, is the heart of TVA country, and forty thousand people are employed in industry dependent upon TVA.

Claiborne, the politician, was sensitive to these local concerns. His home was in upper-middle Tennessee, and he had represented his district in the state legislature. He spent hours with Chuck Lichenstein from the "think tank," stressing the importance of a cotton speech in Memphis, a Social Security statement in Florida, and a clarification of Goldwater's views on TVA in Knoxville.

There was some confusion at 1625 Eye Street about the Senator's real viewpoint on these issues. Goldwater had consistently voted for measures to strengthen and improve the Social Security system. On one of his final days in the Senate (August 22, 1964) he had endorsed a bill to increase cash benefits by 5 per cent for twenty million persons. But he had also voted against Medicare and warned that the imposition of unnecessary new burdens on the Social Security program would penalize every senior citizen.

The Senator's position on agriculture was not so clear. On August 24th, he had said, "Price supports should be designed to help farmers achieve orderly marketing within the framework of our dynamic American market system—should be voluntary—and should be established for specific commodities in order to widen markets, ease production controls and help achieve increased family income." Dick Herman was carrying the ball on an acceptable agricultural statement, and this will be dealt with in another chapter.

The TVA record was a muddy, confused collection of statements, some of them contradictory. The most controversial one, although attributed to Goldwater, had actually been written by

Ted Kazy, one of the Senator's aides. In *The Conscience of a Conservative* Goldwater condemned the principle of vast government developments which proliferate and intrude into the private sector of the economy, a description which certainly fits TVA with its multitude of enterprises not directly connected with navigation, flood control, or the generation of electric energy from falling water. In an interview in 1963 with Stewart Alsop, Goldwater had said it would be beneficial to force TVA to dispose of some of these satellite operations. But the most widely quoted statement was a letter written over Goldwater's signature by Ted Kazy in response to an inquiry from Congressman Richard Fulton, Democrat of Tennessee. Fulton, after reading the Alsop piece, had written Goldwater to ask if the Senator was serious about disposing of TVA. Kazy's response: "Yes, it should be sold because it would be better operated and would be of more benefit to more people if it were a part of private industry."

Claiborne was not able to secure from the "think tank" an advance of the speeches planned for Memphis and St. Petersburg. But he and Lichenstein did agree on a three-page memorandum covering TVA. The words did not say that Goldwater was withdrawing his basic criticism of the operation, but they did indicate that as President he would not sell TVA or recommend its sale or even suggest anything beyond divesting this public corporation of some of its ventures, such as fertilizer plants operated in direct competition with private industry. Lichenstein was most cooperative and assured Claiborne the statement would be used in Knoxville. He also acknowledged the wisdom of Claiborne's suggestion that since the Memphis audience would be predominantly Democrat, the appeal there should be for bipartisan support, while in the eastern end of Tennessee the Senator could make a strong partisan Republican speech.

In Winston-Salem, North Carolina, Goldwater attacked Secretary of Defense Robert McNamara and the administration's policy in South Viet Nam. He did not mention cotton or peanuts or tobacco.

In St. Petersburg he addressed himself to the rising crime rate, terror in the streets, the "Mallory case decision," and the evils of Medicare. Not one word about Social Security.

In Knoxville, Tennessee, he appealed for the support of Democrats and did not use the TVA statement which had been agreed upon by Lichenstein and Claiborne.

In Memphis he made a partisan Republican address and did not mention cotton. In Montgomery, Alabama, he renewed his suggestion for ending the draft and repeated his proposal for a 5 per cent per year tax cut.

The slow fuse which had been smoldering among the politicians on the second floor since early August suddenly exploded. To Claiborne it seemed that the sabotage had been deliberate. The cries of anguish from Florida and Tennessee could not be ignored; the speech writers had gone far beyond the "honest politician" approach demanded in the Kitchel-Baroody directive. But Baroody in Washington and Kitchel on the airplane had ample opportunity to see the speech copy in advance. In his earlier campaigns in Arizona Goldwater had been especially sensitive to the local concerns of his constituents. He had been guided by continuous surveys. (See *How To Win An Election,* Chapter 11.) No one had wanted him to modify or compromise or change his previous positions on Social Security, the TVA, or agriculture. To most of the regional directors it seemed that Kitchel and Baroody were arrogantly ignoring the most fruitful opportunities to counteract what Goldwater's enemies were saying.

When I interviewed Chuck Lichenstein after the campaign was over, he explained that the speeches were usually prepared by two or three writers, then edited by others, and finally given to Baroody or Kitchel for approval. To many of the men on the second floor this was obvious—they had no beginning, they did not build to a climax, they had no conclusion, and they lacked the unity necessary for victory. As a result Herman and Claiborne, with the approval of Wayne Hood, began to work on a plan which they hoped would result in a radical change in the "think tank."

Meanwhile, the Johnson television spots were exploiting the fears and the ignorance of the voters. Nan Robertson in the *New York Times* wrote a vivid description of the first one:

Shortly before eleven Saturday night a little girl licking an ice cream cone appeared on millions of television screens all over America. While the little girl concentrated on ice cream, a woman's voice—tender and provocative—told her that people used to explode atomic bombs in the air, but the radioactive fallout made children die. The voice then told of the treaty preventing all but underground nuclear tests . . . now a man who wants to be President of the United States voted against it . . . his name is Barry Goldwater, so if he's elected, they might start testing all over again . . . a crescendo of Geiger counter clicks almost drown out the last words, then came the announcer's tag line: "Vote for President Johnson on November 3rd . . . the stakes are too high for you to stay home."

21

The temptation to argue with history is almost irresistible. It is sometimes easier to prove what might have been and should have been than it is to accept what actually happened, and when almost seventy million people express a political decision, the hindsight experts enjoy a field day explaining why this man had to lose and that one had to win, or demonstrating why the loser should have won and the winner should have lost.

In September, 1964, all of the pollsters were predicting a Lyndon Johnson victory, and in November the voters vindicated that prophecy. But the in-depth surveys made for the Republican National Committee by Public Opinion Research of Princeton, New Jersey, seem to indicate that Goldwater might have confounded his enemies and walked off with the brass ring.

For the staff at 1625 Eye Street and for a national meeting of Citizens for Goldwater-Miller held in Chicago on September 19th, Rus Walton developed a presentation supporting this possibility. Walton was a partisan Goldwater supporter, but not even the outcome of the election can destroy the hopeful logic of his demonstration, and any objective evaluation of the effectiveness of the Goldwater-Miller campaign effort requires careful consideration of the Johnson-Goldwater profiles so carefully developed by these experts in the field of public opinion sampling:

BACKGROUND RESEARCH DATA

Public Image of Lyndon B. Johnson

Favorable Qualities

Warm and friendly personality	57%
Good judgment	39
Serious and thoughtful	36
Speaks his own mind	35
Honest and truthful	33
Has strong convictions	32
Progressive and forward looking	32
Dignified, statesmanlike	28

Unfavorable Qualities

Too much of a politician	23%
Promises anything to get votes	16
Too liberal	10
Not very sincere	8
Too ambitious	7
Acts without thinking	5
Too inexperienced	5
Superficial, shallow	4
Vain and conceited	4
Too conservative	3
No image	6

President Johnson estimates his personal wealth at $3.5 million. The press at $14 million. With whom do you agree?

Press	20%
LBJ	40%
N.O.	40%

How would you personally rate the administration in Washington?

	Excellent	*Good*	*Fair-Poor*	*No Opinion*
Total public	9%	44%	38%	9%
East	14%	51%	27%	8%
Midwest	8%	47%	38%	7%
South	8%	27%	51%	14%
West	6%	57%	30%	7%
Democrats	16%	50%	25%	9%
Republicans	2%	37%	56%	5%
Independents	6%	39%	46%	9%

The Republican National Committee spent hundreds of thousands of dollars to obtain this information, and Walton attempted to apply it. Using slides and charts, he gave us a graphic picture of the possibilities.

The survey figures and percentages supporting the profiles Walton used had been compiled from samplings taken in the previous week. If the data were accurate, Walton had a sound foun-

Public Image of Barry Goldwater

Favorable Qualities

	Public	*GOP*	*Ind.*	*Demos*
Speaks his own mind	58%	71%	71%	46%
Has strong convictions	45	55	56	37
Honest and truthful	19	30	26	9
Warm and friendly personality	17	26	18	12
Progressive and forward looking	16	21	22	10
Dignified, statesmanlike	16	25	18	10
Good judgment	15	21	21	9
Serious and thoughtful	13	23	19	7
Unfavorable Qualities				
Acts without thinking	24	18	23	30
Too much of a politician	20	12	24	22
Promises anything to get votes	18	12	20	21
Too ambitious	16	11	17	19
Too conservative	15	10	17	19
Vain and conceited	11	10	11	14
Not very sincere	10	6	8	9
Too inexperienced	8	9	8	9
Superficial, shallow	6	3	5	5
Too liberal	4	3	5	5
No image	16	11	9	20

Goldwater: Public Familiarity

	November, 63	*Today*
Know great deal	8%	10%
Know fair amount	31	41
Know very little	61	49

Public and TV Debates

Question: Would you like to see the presidential candidates debate?

Yes 62%

One-third of those interviewed said they thought L.B.J. was purposefully trying to avoid TV debates.

dation for his contention that the Republican ticket could win in November.

The public image of Lyndon Johnson and his administration clearly indicated that on this date the voters had not made up their minds. Fifty-seven per cent of this sample agreed that Johnson had a warm and friendly personality, but only 39 per cent thought his judgment was good and only 33 per cent believed him to be honest and truthful.

On the debit side only 9 per cent rated the Johnson administration excellent; 44 per cent good; 38 per cent fair to poor; and 9 per cent held no opinion. When these figures were reported for the various sections of the country they became even more encouraging.

Twenty-three per cent of the body politic regarded Johnson as too much of a politician. Sixteen per cent said he would promise anything to get votes. This was the week when the figures on Johnson's wealth had been revealed, and the sampling included a question: "President Johnson estimates his personal wealth at $3.5 million, the press at $14 million. With whom do you agree?" Press, 20 per cent; L.B.J., 40 per cent; no opinion, 40 per cent.

When this slide was shown, Walton argued that it was obvious the public had not yet become fully aware of the Bobby Baker and Billie Sol Estes scandals, and 50 per cent of those sampled expressed a belief that the administration had deliberately concealed and whitewashed the misbehavior of Johnson's friends.

The composite picture of Goldwater is revealing—particularly when considered against a background of the knowledge that only 10 per cent of the American people said they knew a great deal about Goldwater and 49 per cent said they knew very little. Certainly those who said they knew very little were open to persuasion. The Senator's most favorable quality indicated by the survey was that "he speaks his own mind."

It should be noted that at this point only 24 per cent of those sampled said Goldwater "acts without thinking." And the Independents, whose vote was necessary for victory, gave an even better reading. Those who argue that conservatism vis-à-vis liberalism never became an issue in the campaign will find support in the survey's indication that only 15 per cent of the general public thought Goldwater too conservative and only 19 per cent of the Democrats shared that opinion. On the unfavorable scale of Lyndon Johnson, only 10 per cent found him too liberal.

Sixty-two per cent of those polled indicated a desire to see the presidential candidates debate, and one-third of those interviewed said they thought L.B.J. was purposely trying to avoid any television confrontation.

On the personality scale and the degree of public knowledge it must be argued that both candidates were in a positon either to win or lose the election between the middle of September and the day of decision in November. But when we look at the response to questions dealing with national issues, the Goldwater opportunity becomes even more pronounced.

ISSUES OF CONCERN TO THE PUBLIC

When given a list of issues and asked to rate them as to personal concern, the public responded as follows:

Living costs	58%
Segregation	57
Medical care for the aged	48
Employment	42
Government spending	41
Depressed areas	38
Aid to education	36
Tax reform	34
Cuba	30
Cold War (Win it)	30
Viet Nam	28
Government efficiency	28
U.S. prestige	26

Foreign Issues which "Bug" Americans

When asked specifically to rate foreign-affairs issues which concern them, they responded:

Stop spread of communism	78%
National defense posture	62
Viet Nam	59
Cost of Foreign Aid	47
Cuba	45

Defense Hardware

"The United States should give defense emphasis to" . . .

Manned Air Force	88%
Missiles	2%
No Opinion	10%

U. S. Policy Toward the U.S.S.R. Should Be

Tougher	45%
More friendly	38%
No Opinion	17%

In Matters Such as Viet Nam and Cuba We Should Take More Positive Action

Agree	69%
Disagree	17%
No Opinion	14%

Has Foreign Aid Helped the U.S.A.?

Yes	23%
No	63%
No Opinion	14%

The U.S. Should Trade with the U.S.S.R.

Yes	36%
No	51%
No Opinion	13%

The Administration and Civil Rights

Despite all the clamor and publicity on civil rights, the public is about evenly divided, pro and con.

	Favorable	*Unfavorable*	*No Opinion*
Total public, Nov., 1963	46%	45%	9%
Total public today	47%	43%	10%
Democrats	57%	33%	10%
Republicans	35%	56%	9%
Independents	41%	51%	8%

19% say the civil rights program will help in their community
22% say it will be harmful
44% say it will make no difference
15% have no opinion.

The Public Reaction to a $4.5 Billion Increase in the Federal Budget is Not Much Better Under Johnson Than It Was Under Kennedy

	Kennedy Nov. '63	*Johnson Today*
Unfavorable	50%	47%
Favorable	28%	32%
No Opinion	22%	21%

The Public Sees Less Need for Tighter Government Controls Over Either Business or Labor.

	Nov. '63	Today
Favor tighter controls:		
Business	36%	31%
Labor	54%	51%
For easing up controls:		
Business	38%	41%
Labor	21%	21%

On the Matter of Medicare, How Do You Think It Should Be Handled?

Social Security	30%
Joint Venture (gov't & patient)	42%

This indicates a slight shift in public opinion toward the joint venture plan.

Fifty-eight per cent of the Americans sampled were concerned about living costs, and Goldwater was the only candidate genuinely offering to reduce expenditures. It should be pointed out that Mr. Johnson carefully cultivated the image of an economizer, but his record before the election and since denies any validity to this image. Seventy-eight per cent of the Americans believed we must stop the spread of Communism, and 88 per cent expressed more confidence in the manned Air Force than in the missile system advocated and supported by the McNamara-Johnson administration. Forty-five per cent were in favor of a tougher policy toward the USSR; 69 per cent wanted more positive action in regard to Viet Nam and Cuba; 63 per cent said that foreign aid has not helped the United States; and 51 per cent were opposed to trade with Soviet Russia.

The civil rights issue which received so much attention and which was second on the list of significant issues was not, if the survey can be believed, a great albatross around Goldwater's neck. The public was just about divided in its opinion on the benefits of the civil rights legislation passed by the Johnson Congress. There was strong opposition to the budget increase under Johnson and a marked increase in sentiment for easing up controls imposed by government on business. And while there was great support for some kind of Medicare, 42 per cent of those polled expressed a preference for a joint venture between government and private enterprise to care for this need.

Political Party Affiliation, U.S.A.

	1940	*1950*	*1960*	*1962*	*1963*
Democrats	42%	45%	47%	50%	53%
Republicans	38%	33%	30%	28%	25%
Independents	20%	22%	23%	22%	22%

More People Consider Themselves Conservative than Republican:

Democrats	48%	Conservatives	41%
Republicans	26%	Liberals	31%
Independents	26%	In between	28%

Conservative/Liberal Split by Party

	Conservative	*Liberal*
Republicans	65%	14%
Democrats	30%	42%
Independents	41%	29%

These last three items deserve special attention. The Democrat Party had been growing steadily in preference since 1940 and was six percentage points ahead of the 1960 figure, while the Republican popularity had declined by five percentage points. But when asked to classify their political ideology under the labels "conservative" or "liberal," 41 per cent claimed to be conservative, and only 31 per cent classified themselves as liberal.

Rus Walton used all of these statistics to support his argument that the Goldwater campaign must move rapidly to improve the public understanding and acquaintance with the Senator, to identify Goldwater with the conservative cause, and to make it clear that the Senator was actually on the popular side of the major issues of the day. He also pointed out that it would be necessary to illuminate and emphasize the Johnson record as a spender, a political wheeler-dealer, and a candidate who would support a continued alteration of our national defense posture against the expressed popular will.

The literature which had been developed by Citizens under Walton's supervision was designed to achieve these objectives. One piece carried a photograph of Lyndon Johnson in contrast to a Karsh portrait of Goldwater, and then listed the documented philosophical positions of the two contenders. Two clever pocket cards, one on Johnson and one on Goldwater, offered the voter a chance to contrast the Johnson record on any issue with the Goldwater position on the same issue.

But what Walton really hoped to achieve by his presentation was the cooperation of the Goldwater speech writers. He argued that the Senator should start immediately to present the reasonable conservative alternative to the Johnson administration proposals. He wanted the Republican candidate to become an advocate rather than a critic, to recognize the problems existing in relation to our domestic economy, our social structure, our educational facilities, our national defense, and the operation of the federal government itself. And he believed that if the Goldwater campaign became a positive force, concentrating on three or four specific proposals which would promise an improvement over the solutions to problems offered by the Democrats, the opportunity clearly indicated by the statistical sample could be translated into a victory for the Republican ticket.

Most of the men on the second floor agreed with Walton, and there were indications that the strategists working under Bill Baroody had been striving toward the same end. The October *Readers' Digest* carried an eight-page insert printed in two colors under the title *Senator Goldwater Speaks Out on the Issues.* The copy prepared by Chuck Lichenstein, reiterated some of the old Goldwater contentions of peace through strength; offered a defense strategy based on the development of a "mixed arsenal"; called for action in Southeast Asia and Cuba and an implementation of the civil rights bill which would guarantee everyone the right to vote; dealt with fiscal responsibility, the maintenance of a strong social security system, and a complete restudy of the federal taxing practices.

The insert cost the Republican National Committee three hundred thousand dollars; yet in the middle of the first page of body copy in blue ink, these words appeared: "There is no greater political lie. . . ."—a line which certainly must have strengthened the belief of those who regarded Goldwater as a violent man.

In addition to the *Readers' Digest* advertisement, Baroody arranged for the publication of a new Goldwater book to be titled *Where I Stand.* Lichenstein did the editing and some of the necessary writing of transitional pages, but most of the content was taken from previous Goldwater speeches and statements. The National Committee bought one hundred thousand copies of the paperback edition for one hundred thousand dollars. These were intended for resale, and it was thought the committee could recover its investment. According to Ray Collett, who served as comptroller for the committee, only about 5,000 copies were sold; the rest were given away.

It must be assumed that President Johnson's managers were also sampling the public pulse—with similar results. The Democrat candidate refused to engage Goldwater in a discussion of any of the significant issues. He continued to ignore the Bobby Baker and Billie Sol Estes scandals, and his managers directed a careful buildup of the warm and friendly personality—the man who loved everybody, who wanted to help everybody, who projected better days ahead. The "Great Society" was appealing; like a cornucopia of cotton candy, there wasn't anything to taste, you couldn't bite into it, but it was going to be yours and for free. The voters were not asked to make any painful decisions or face the reality of the war in Viet Nam or the declining gold balance or the terror in the cities or Communism in the Caribbean, and the way to avoid all this unpleasantness was to vote for the warm and friendly personality.

22

To win the Presidency in 1964 it was necessary for Barry Goldwater to carry the Midwest and the Plain states, an area regarded as the heartland of Republican strength. The cynics suggest that the nation's farmers suffer from chronic discontent, are perpetually dissatisfied with their economic lot. In 1964 there were indications that a Republican candidate who would offer a reasonable alternative to the makeshift, hodgepodge administration program of subsidy and control (the farmers had rejected the wheat proposal of Secretary Freeman in a nationwide referendum) would prosper mightily at the polls.

Since the early days of the New Deal billions of dollars had been spent on subsidies by each succeeding administration in a vain effort to curtail production and increase the farmer's income. Surplus grains purchased by the government had been permitted to rot in storage, and the consumers paid for the waste. The latest Billie Sol Estes scandal involved manipulation of provisions of the agricultural act. Surplus cotton had been sold to our competitors overseas at a net loss to the taxpayer, and domestic cotton spinners suffered a competitive disadvantage. The artificial price maintained for feed grains had increased the cost of producing beef and pork, inflicting penalties on both the producer and consumer.

The farmers, often referred to as the last solid group of real free enterprisers, have never been united. One segment, represented by the American Farm Bureau Federation, has indicated opposition to both controls and subsidies. At the other end of the scale the Farmers Union and its spokesman, James S. Patton, constantly lobbies for increased subsidy and more universal control. But both groups recognize that the sudden elimination of all subsidy and all control would mean bankruptcy for millions of farmers. And Goldwater, according to his opponents, proposed an immediate end to a subsidy program.

The Democrats, quoting from *The Conscience of a Conservative* and other Goldwater statements, never missed an opportunity to tell the farmers that Goldwater's election would mean an immediate end to the program under which they had operated for the past thirty years.

The regional directors, especially Herman and Claiborne, recognized the problem. Victory was dependent upon the farmers' vote, and to get that vote it was necessary for the farmers to understand that Goldwater had never proposed an immediate or abrupt end to the present wasteful practices. He had in fact repeatedly stated that while his goal for the farmer was an ultimate return to the free market and the elimination of both control and subsidy, he recognized that to make such a transition would require a number of years and the cooperation of the agricultural economists to develop a workable plan. In discussing the agricultural problem in the preconvention days Goldwater had stressed the fact that the federal government itself was responsible for the farmers' predicament and must therefore assume responsibility for rescuing the farmer from the adverse situation which government controls had created.

Before the campaign was officially opened, Kitchel and Baroody decreed that Goldwater would not attend the annual plowing contest at Fargo, North Dakota. United States Senator Karl Mundt of South Dakota and Milton S. Young of North Dakota were furious over the decision. To these Farm Belt politicians the plowing contest was a must. They believed Goldwater's chances of carrying the Midwest depended upon his appearance and delivery of a detailed and specific explanation of the official Republican attitude toward the farmers' problem.

On September 9th, Kitchel and Baroody were finally persuaded that Goldwater should attend the plowing contest. Young, Mundt, and Herman were delegated to work with the speech writers from the "think tank" in the preparation of a statement which would be politically acceptable to Mundt and Young.

The two Senators, who were familiar with Goldwater's personal viewpoint on the farm problem, did not see any great difficulty in framing an acceptable statement, but Dick Herman, who was more familiar with the attitude of the "think tank," had reason to be concerned. Earlier in the campaign the *Philadelphia Farm Journal* had solicited a statement from Goldwater on the farm problem.

The Goldwater statement prepared in the "think tank" had been delivered to the magazine just two days in advance of the printer's deadline. Richard Babcock, president and publisher of the *Farm Journal,* and Claude P. Streeter, his editor, read the piece and found it totally inadequate. In the words of the magazine editor: "We were disappointed that the Goldwater presentation was not more vigorous in spots and did not take fuller advantage of opportunities to expose weakness in the administration's position as well as to state more forthrightly what Mr. Goldwater is for."

Streeter said, "I called Charles Lichenstein at the Republican National Committee to tell him it was our feeling that the copy was not as vigorous as it might be. Hoping that he might show an interest, I was ready to suggest some things, even to come down to work with him. Instead, he said that the copy was 'as vigorous as they wanted it to be.' At that I felt there was no point in debating the philosophy of the approach."

In a memorandum from editor Streeter to publisher Babcock the problem is carefully defined:

> Mr. Goldwater is allowing the impression to get around that he would wreck all farm programs forthwith. A lot of farmers are afraid he would. Mr. Goldwater needs to state forthrightly that (a) farm income is too low, (b) that he intends to do something about it, (c) that he favors support prices for price stabilization purposes, but low enough not to aggravate the surplus problem, (d) that he favors encouraging more industries located throughout rural America to offer good jobs to those who want to or have to leave farming, (e) that he favors more group bargaining power for farmers, (f) that he favors the continuation of the Rural Electrification program with some

changes, (g) that he is compassionate toward those having a hard struggle, and (h) that he intends to decrease the role of government in agriculture and turn more of the control of farming back to the farmers.

The two Republican senators from North Dakota and South Dakota wanted the Goldwater statement at the plowing contest to express essentially the proposals in the Streeter memorandum. Both Young and Mundt were critical of the administration's farm program and opposed in principle the policy which requires the taxpayers to subsidize the farmers. But they were also aware that any abrupt alteration of the present program would create chaos, and until a new plan could be devised and implemented which would permit the farmer to survive and prosper on the free market, they believed subsidies were essential.

At the first conference, attended by Young, Mundt, Herman, and Lichenstein, it was agreed that Goldwater's speech for the plowing contest would emphatically deny the false charge that he intended to make immediate and drastic changes in the farm policy, and Lichenstein promised to deliver a draft of the speech for Senator Young's approval before noon on September 15th. The date was fixed by the fact that Young intended to go to Bismarck, North Dakota, on the evening of that day. It was hoped that he would introduce Goldwater at Fargo, and this was an assignment he would not accept unless he could be assured in advance that the Goldwater speech would be acceptable to the farmers gathered at the plowing contest.

On Monday, September 14th, Herman contacted Lichenstein and was told the draft, while not completed, was taking shape. Herman suggested it would be wise to call Senator Young and report the progress and reminded Lichenstein of his promise to have the completed draft delivered to the Senator's Capitol Hill office before noon on Tuesday. Lichenstein did not make the telephone call, and the speech was not delivered. Senator Young left for North Dakota, and the speech writers were told to give the draft to Karl Mundt.

On Wednesday, Bob McCoy, Senator Mundt's administrative

assistant, tried unsuccessfully to reach Ed McCabe, Lichenstein's superior. When this failed, Senator Mundt called Dean Burch, who assured him the speech, in acceptable form, would be delivered by 6:30 Thursday. This timetable left no room for editing or changes, but it was the best Burch could do. Mundt finally received a copy at 10:30 that night. He reviewed it with Senator Carl Curtis of Nebraska and then asked for a conference with McCabe at 10:15 Friday morning, September 18th.

Dick Herman went to the conference; Ed McCabe did not appear. Instead, the Senators were required to deal again with Lichenstein. The draft was not satisfactory. Mundt and Curtis, speaking for Young, urged certain changes. Lichenstein was noncommittal.

At 4:30 that Friday, Mundt sent a draft of his requested changes to Dick Herman at the National Committee, who in turn gave the copy to Burch with a request that McCabe and Lichenstein be called down from the third floor to discuss the speech. At 5:15 on Friday the two men from the "think tank," the National Chairman, and Dick Herman met in Burch's office to discuss the proposed changes. The chairman told McCabe and Lichenstein that in his opinion the suggestions made by Mundt and Curtis should be included. He wanted the speech rewritten, and McCabe and Lichenstein went back upstairs to carry out the chairman's orders.

At six o'clock Friday, Dean Burch went to the Army and Navy Club where a reception was being given in honor of Bud Wilkinson, the Republican candidate for the United States Senate from Oklahoma. Senator Mundt was present, and Burch told him the appropriate and desired changes were being made and promised that the Goldwater statement at the plowing contest would be satisfactory to the three farm state Senators—Mundt, Curtis, and Young.

At 8:15 that Friday night Herman learned that the original speech, the one which Mundt and Curtis and Young believed totally inadequate, had been released from the airplane to the newspapers and would be used verbatim by the Senator at the plowing contest.

Goldwater in North Dakota delivered his expected condemnation of the administration's farm program. He reminded his audience that 17 per cent of the farmers' income, amounting to $2.1 billion, represented the federal subsidy, and asked, "Do you want that to continue?" Only three paragraphs of the entire speech offered any suggestion of what the Goldwater administration would do, and these were far from specific.

> Farm income certainly should be improved, but the question is: How should it be improved? By arbitrary handouts subject to the whim and caprice of an arbitrary farm boss in direct contact with the dealer in the White House, or by the healthy and fair forces of flourishing and expanding markets?
>
> We pledge a farm program good for the farmer, good for the rancher, good for the nation. We support the Republican farm platform plank by plank.
>
> We know in our hearts that you are plagued with your special problems, and we know they are serious problems. We will work with you toward solutions, not schemes.

Lichenstein and McCabe, Baroody and Kitchel may have been pleased with the speech; the farmers were not.

The regional directors who were involved, the three United States senators, and Wayne Hood might have given up, washed their hands of the whole affair after that first frustrating experience with the adamant speech writers, but they did not. And it was Doug Whitlock who suggested a possibility for correcting the situation in October when Goldwater was scheduled to attend the corn-picking contest in Sioux Falls, South Dakota.

Whitlock, Hood, and Herman proposed a meeting in Des Moines, Iowa, on October 14th, which would be attended by a committee of agriculturalists recruited by the Citizens for Goldwater-Miller. In Whitlock's outline of the plan he suggested the meeting be given great publicity. "We will announce that Goldwater is meeting with the farm leaders to develop a specific plan to solve the farmers' problems," he suggested, "but we won't tell them what the plan is. Then every day until he goes to South Dakota there will be another hint that the Senator is going to make a momentous announcement of interest to farmers when he speaks at the corn-picking contest."

The meeting was finally held, but in order to put it in the schedule it was necessary to cancel a part of Goldwater's Iowa itinerary. The publicity announcement did not come off in accordance with Whitlock's plan, and while the speech at Sioux Falls was far more specific in its guarantees, the important paragraphs were surrounded and obscured by more generalities from the "think tank." However, Goldwater did say:

> But let me make myself absolutely clear. I know, as you do, that the mistakes of the past cannot be corrected overnight and I will never try to correct them overnight.
>
> We must honor commitments already made by the federal government.
>
> We must keep faith with those who made plans and acquired property on the basis of those commitments. We must have the good sense to move slowly in making changes so that the citizens of this nation and indeed the economy itself can make smooth adjustments, adjustments that will cause nobody harm. Above all, we must not scrap existing programs until we are sure we have something better to substitute for them.
>
> I pledge to you as I have pledged before that I will never propose a change in the price support program until something better has been developed that can gradually be substituted for it.

Perhaps in the opening days of the campaign the farmers might have heard these reassuring words from Goldwater. But by the middle of October their minds were made up, and the Senator failed to carry a single state in the heartland of Republican strength.

23

By the end of September most of the regional directors on the second floor at 1625 Eye Street were convinced the National Committee telephones were bugged. The only thing we disagreed on was the identity of the eavesdroppers. The Johnson campaign committee had been able to anticipate Goldwater's task force to work for peace. Some of our most confidential conversations had been reported in the newspapers. Even the walls and the desks and the draperies seemed to be listening.

At one meeting held in John Grenier's private office with Hood, Hay, Herman, Whitlock, and the executive director present, it was discovered there was time on the schedule to insert an additional Goldwater stop. Sam Hay suggested that East St. Louis, Illinois, be included on the itinerary. Thirty minutes later Hay was called out of the conference to answer a long-distance telephone call from a newspaper man in East St. Louis, Illinois, who said he had heard Goldwater was coming to town and wanted to know the details.

Electronic eavesdropping threatens to end all privacy. In any political campaign it is helpful to know what your opponent is doing or planning to do. Telephone men had discovered one crude attempt to tap a line at the National Committee, but they had been unable to identify the perpetrator. Strange and mysterious clicks and noises on the telephones, repeated leaks of confidential information, all helped to create an almost intolerable situation. Believing our conversations were monitored was just as devastating as being able to prove that someone was listening, and many of the regional directors adopted the practice of going to a pay telephone to make their confidential calls. All this added to a feeling of uncertainty and mutual distrust which was not beneficial to the campaign.

At the weekly report session, presided over by Grenier, the regional directors listed the progress being made on the voter-canvass program, heard the week's itinerary explained, and were always asked to send suggestions for subjects and speech material to the "think tank." Despite continuing disappointment, we followed orders.

Fred Finlinson, the Goldwater chairman in Utah; Ray Child, Republican state chairman; and Ernest Wilkinson, who was running for the United States Senate, were most anxious to have Goldwater in Salt Lake City for a major evening appearance. Finally this stop was placed on the schedule for the second far western swing. It is impossible to overestimate the influence of the Church of the Latter-day Saints of Jesus Christ in Utah, Idaho, Arizona, New Mexico, and California. Lyndon Johnson made a nonscheduled stop to visit with the church president, David O. McKay, and the Goldwater itinerary was planned to give the Senator ample time for an hour with the Mormon patriarch before making his political appearance in the Mormon Temple on the evening of Saturday, October 10th.

Fred Finlinson, a good churchman and a smart politician, sent me a booklet containing reprints of speeches President McKay had made on the Constitution, the function of government, and citizen responsibility.

The Mormon church has always been fiercely independent. It has carried on an excellent welfare program for its members, and one time boasted that no deserving churchman need look to the federal government for assistance. President McKay's speeches were forceful expositions of the conservative viewpoint. He expressed the same reverence for the Constitution which had become Goldwater's trademark. I dictated five pages of excerpts from the McKay speeches and sent them up to the "think tank" with a notation urging their use by Goldwater when he appeared in Salt Lake. I was convinced that if the Senator identified his political philosophy with the published statements of the president of the Mormon Church, our cause would be immeasurably strengthened.

The Senator went to Salt Lake City, visited with the president at the Hotel Utah, rested, went to the Mormon Tabernacle, and delivered a speech on morality which had been written by Warren Nutter. There was no mention of McKay in the text, no quotations, no attempt to link Goldwater's conservatism with the political philosophy of the most influential and illustrious resident of Utah.

Following the third nationwide TV broadcast, Lichenstein's question-and-answer program which provoked such violent criticism, Cordiner, Hood, Herman, Claiborne, Hay, and Bob Mardian decided to try once more to push for a change in the "think tank." They wanted a politician in charge of the speech writing, and they wanted Goldwater to drop his personal attacks on the President and concentrate on a presentation of the positive steps he would take as President to correct the demonstrated deficiencies of the Johnson-Kennedy regime.

Hood, Middendorf, and Cordiner—knowing that I had written many of the Senator's speeches in that period from 1952 to 1962 when his philosophy and his personality were gaining such widespread acceptance throughout the nation—were hopeful that I would be permitted to take charge of the speech-writing effort. But it was impossible for anyone to see Goldwater privately in Washington. He was always surrounded and protected by Kitchel, or Baroody, or McCabe, or Lichenstein.

Ralph Cordiner decided he would fly to Arizona with the candidate on October 8th and hopefully be able to arrange fifteen minutes of private conversation with the Senator. Cordiner made the trip, but there was no opportunity to talk on the airplane where the Senator was guarded constantly by Hess, Kitchel, and Paul Wagner. When the party arrived in Phoenix, Cordiner tried to make a specific appointment and failed.

"It was obvious to me," Cordiner reported, "that Goldwater did not want to see me. I suspect he knew the purpose of my visit, and

I didn't think anything could be gained by forcing my ideas on him."

Bob Mardian boarded the Senator's airplane in Portland for the flight to Salt Lake City. He managed to find a seat near Goldwater, who was in a relaxed and friendly frame of mind. "You've been a very busy boy, Robert," Goldwater said accusingly, "and I want you to stop it."

"I've been doing nothing more than trying to help you win this election," Mardian objected.

"Well, whatever it is you say you're not doing, I want you to stop it," the Senator said firmly; "it's too late."

Mardian, Rosenzweig, Herman—and to a lesser extent Claiborne and Hood—had been the prime movers in the effort to change the third-floor operation. It was apparent that Goldwater knew of the movement, disapproved, and wanted it ended.

Perhaps it was too late to make any improvements. For all his faults—and they are not nearly so numerous as his enemies charged during the campaign—Goldwater is a perceptive politician. It is difficult for anyone who has known and worked with the Senator to believe that he was unaware of impending defeat. Indeed, in many of his speeches following October 10th he appeared to be rationalizing not only the conduct of his own campaign, but the anticipated action of the voters. Goldwater, who never truly wanted the Presidency for the reasons which motivate most successful politicians, was committed to the almost hopeless task of defending the American society against its own indulgence, slothfulness, and apathy.

The Walter Jenkins incident did not lose the election for Lyndon Johnson, but it provided a sanity-saving release for the tensions and frustrations on the second floor. It also raises a question which still begs an answer: How far can an ethical publisher go in suppressing news of a personal scandal involving an individual close to the President of the United States?

The news of Jenkins' arrest was whispered about in Washington for several days before anything was said about it by the news media. On the afternoon before the story broke an investigator for the Republican National Committee actually inspected the police blotter on which the arrest had been recorded. The next day the blotter disappeared.

Jenkins, a long-time trusted adviser of President Lyndon Johnson, was arrested by two detectives in the men's toilet at the YMCA on a "morals charge." The language on the police blotter left nothing to the reader's imagination. Jenkins was released on bail and then rushed off to the hospital. And two newspapers in full possession of the facts were persuaded by Clark Clifford, an old Washington friend of Lyndon Johnson, not to print the story. When one of the wire services finally moved the account of Jenkins' offense and prior arrest, no explanation was given for the delay in reporting an event which had taken place seven days earlier.

The change in leadership in Russia with Khrushchev being displaced by Kosygin and Brezhnev and the announcement of an atomic explosion in China blasted the Jenkins case from the front pages of the newspapers. Johnson wisely refused to make any comment, and the scandal died. Eyebrows were lifted across the nation when it was disclosed that J. Edgar Hoover had sent a bouquet of flowers and a get-well message to Jenkins when in the hospital. Subsequently it has been explained that the greeting was sent by an efficient secretary in the office of the FBI director and dispatched at a moment when Jenkins' hospitalization had not been connected with his arrest. The mystery which was never solved was how Jenkins had avoided discovery following his arrest on the first offense. And this was shuffled back and forth between the White House and the FBI for a number of days.

The Jenkins case became a great topic of conversation and produced hundreds of off-beat, risqué stories; it did not materially affect the voter's decision. But it did exert a profound influence on the attitude of the third-floor "think tank." Some members of the Baroody group seemed to become obsessed with the necessity of finding additional moral aberrations in men close to the White House, and for a period of about ten days the third floor lived on the optimistic hope and the mistaken belief that if they could just find one more Walter Jenkins, the trend against Goldwater would be reversed.

The Senator never shared this feeling. He refused to permit his speech writers to make an issue of Jenkins' misfortune. And while he continued to hammer away at morality in government—the Bobby Baker case, the transgressions of Billie Sol Estes—he refused every suggestion to make use of the Jenkins incident.

The revolt against the speech writers did bear some fruit. Charles S. McNally was enlisted to write Goldwater's script for the October 9th broadcast with Richard Nixon. The news was spread in whispers around 1625 Eye Street because it was said that McNally was a staff writer for the *Saturday Evening Post* and his superiors, who were violently anti-Goldwater, would punish him if his connection with the campaign became public knowledge. The speech, with Nixon's sincere introduction, was perhaps the best one Goldwater used in the entire campaign. It was a quiet, forceful discussion of the responsibilities of the President. But it also contained some rationalization. Goldwater told the nation:

> You have probably been reading and hearing about some of the unorthodox things I have been doing. I have gone to the heart of Appalachia and there I have deliberately attacked this administration's phony war on poverty. I have gone into the heart of Florida's retirement country and there I have deliberately warned against the outright hoax of this administration's Medicare scheme. I have gone into the heart of our farm areas and there I have deliberately called for the gradual transition from a controlled to a free agriculture.
>
> I have gone into an area of rapid urban growth and there I have deliberately leveled against the Supreme Court the charge that they have no business attempting to redraw the map of our state legislative districts.

As a sober commentary on the problems of America in the seventh decade of the twentieth century, the speech deserves to be reread, but as a vehicle to win votes, it fell far short of the intended mark.

On the following Tuesday the taped television program was repeated from Milwaukee in what might accurately be termed the most incredible foul-up of the Goldwater campaign. The Senator was returning from his western tour and was scheduled to be in Topeka, Kansas, Tuesday morning, Des Moines at noon, and Milwaukee, Wisconsin, that night. The party leaders of Wisconsin had planned a closed-circuit television broadcast of the Senator's appearance in order to be able to use two ballrooms for the anticipated local crowd. They were told on Saturday, October 10th, that Goldwater would make a live television address to the nation from Milwaukee on Tuesday night.

Kitchel was opposed to live TV broadcasts on the theory that an enthusiastic audience would, with its applause, consume too much valuable network time. He had decided to reuse the video-taped program from the Friday night presentation but no one in the ballroom was told about the change in plans. Some of them did not know it until Goldwater had concluded his remarks and the affair was breaking up. Actually, the Senator was introduced live, and for thirty seconds, or perhaps a minute at the most, the Milwaukee rally was on the air. Then the network cut to an isolated booth where Mrs. Clare Booth Luce, substituting for Dick Nixon, introduced the video tape from the earlier presentation.

When the Wisconsin Republicans discovered what had happened, all hell broke loose. Sam Hay, who had been so anxious to get Goldwater into Wisconsin, told us it would have been better if the 727 had never landed. The local reaction is graphically conveyed in a communication written shortly afterward by a volunteer who had been involved in planning arrangements for the Goldwater appearance and given to me by the PR department at Citizens:

> Obviously the committee was formed and the plans laid out three weeks in advance of the visit. All details were worked out. Then a little more than a week before the visit network TV was decided by national. It was not our choice. We had not asked for it. We had already planned to do the closed-circuit television in the auditorium. The meeting was in the arena and the people in the auditorium could watch on closed-circuit. When the announcement was made, we collaborated, changed many of our plans, naturally.

David Light, Goldwater's advance man, arrived a week ahead of the meeting. He is an excellent, capable person. We went through all the plans, any changes suggested we made. George Rogers, Goldwater's TV director, arrived on Friday. We ordered everything to his exact specifications and he was satisfied.

On Saturday, Dave Light and I worked with the hotel for two and a half hours on room assignments. At that point Dave had no manifest. It arrived Monday, the day before the meeting. Dave made a few changes.

All this time our people were working on the monumental task of trying to fill two huge arenas when people could watch the meeting at home on television. We provided Rogers with everything he needed, and in doing so we obscured forty per cent of our best seating behind the platforms. They were six feet high, forty feet long, with cameras on five-foot tripods. Many seats were lost for viewing. We hated to do this to loyal Goldwater Wisconsin contributors but we sacrificed for the greater good of the campaign and so millions of people could see the Senator on network television and the conditions for TV were excellent.

Rogers told David Light early on Tuesday that they had never worked in a finer arena. He repeated this to me later on Tuesday night when he left during the so-called TV program to go back.

Concerning the visit generally, the arrival time had been changed several times, but in spite of that we had two thousand enthusiastic people at the airport. Then on the way into town Paul Wagner took great delight in tearing apart the hotel plans. Rooms had been assigned, luggage was to be taken to the individual rooms and keys distributed before arrival at the hotel. Wagner messed things up so thoroughly no one got much sleep. At 1:00 a.m. Wednesday morning he was still making room changes.

As to Kitchel's part, he made the decision not to televise and we did not know this. We placed newspaper ads for live television from the arena. The local television station has threatened to sue the campaign for fraudulent advertising and they have every right to do it. My first inkling of the change came when the monitor behind the platform blacked out. Dan Parker, state finance chairman, was on the platform. He did not know about it until the speech was over.

The calls, telegrams, letters and stopped payments on checks have been fantastic. Kitchel gave a reason that stems from sheer idiocy—'crowd reaction would hold up the meeting and TV viewers would not have heard the end of the talk.' That is a complete admission of incompetency.

Two nights later Hubert Humphrey spoke in the same arena with an enthusiastic crowd. He was televised from 8:30 to 9:00 and he concluded his remarks at nine o'clock. It was a crime that Hubert Humphrey's campaign managers are so much more intelligent than Goldwater's.

Many people in Wisconsin feel that it is absolutely necessary that Kitchel and Wagner resign or be fired. This is owed the American people so that Goldwater will have a fighting chance to be elected. No one is accusing them of disloyalty to him. I am not in a position to know their inner feelings, but their incompetent performance. We have sixteen days left in the campaign and they have to be replaced by competent people.

Dave Light, the advance man, resigned the morning after the meeting. He agreed to continue through the Miller talk last night in Racine. I talked to him before he left Milwaukee and tried to convince him to reconsider because Goldwater needs men like Light. I hope he stays in the campaign.

Many people I have talked to here are very concerned that if Goldwater is elected, he will continue to surround himself with unqualified people. I think he has to show the voters that this is not going to happen and rid himself of these people before the election. The entire thing was an insult to everybody.

Goldwater lost Wisconsin, but a conservative Republican candidate for governor, Warren P. Knowles, defeated his Democrat opponent by a margin of 18,878 votes.

24

The Republican National Committee raised and spent more than twelve million dollars in its effort to elect Barry Goldwater President of the United States. Almost five million dollars went to pay for television time and related production costs. The results were disappointing.

When the Senator made his opening nationwide TV appearance on the evening of Friday, September 18th, most of the regional directors gathered in my quarters at the Jefferson. No one was happy with the speech Chuck Lichenstein had written. It was defensive, it dealt in generalities, and it opened with Goldwater's repeating the charges his opponents were making, i.e. that he was impulsive, imprudent, and trigger-happy.

The thirty-minute speech with Goldwater on camera almost the entire time concluded with a quotation from a speech by Winston Churchill. The strategists in the "think tank" wanted to identify Goldwater with Churchill and Johnson with Chamberlain, but this notion was discarded when someone pointed out that only a few American voters in 1964 would remember the man who went to Munich with the umbrella.

The Senator's second nationwide television presentation with General Eisenhower was entitled *Conversation at Gettysburg*. On September 14th, Goldwater, Lichenstein, Kitchel, Hess, McCabe, the camera crew from Erwin Wasey, Ruthrauff & Ryan, and the Senator's official campaign photographer, Don Dornan, went to Pennsylvania to make the film which everyone hoped would convince the nation that our candidate enjoyed the solid enthusiastic support of the former President. Eisenhower was still the most popular man in the Republican party, perhaps the most popular political figure in the nation. There was no script prepared; it was to be an ad-lib, off-the-cuff serious discussion of the great issues of the campaign.

The finished film never quite got off the ground. Ike spoke sixteen times, Goldwater fifteen. Ike began four speeches with a qualifying "well," Goldwater started six in that fashion, and the program rambled, beginning with Eisenhower's not-so-challenging question: "Well, Barry, you've been campaigning now for two or three weeks, how do you like it? And how does it seem to be going for you?" There was no crisp, direct, unequivocal declaration by Eisenhower in support of the Goldwater candidacy.

Don Dornan described the scene:

> The Senator was very distressed and at one point he got up and was trying to get across to the crew, Chuck Lichenstein in particular, that the General was missing the point, that he didn't like the take. All he got back from them was the typical Madison Avenue "It's okay, don't worry about it"—the soft-soap business, and they kept pushing him back, giving the impression that he was wrong, that they were right, and yet he knew he was right.
>
> The professional director took his orders from Baroody's men, and no one had the courage to say to Eisenhower, "Mr. President, we are not getting the point across, this is a political film, let's try again and make the dialogue more to the point and more positive."

At noon Ike went off by himself to have his lunch and his nap, and the Goldwater party climbed in a station wagon for the trip into town.

Conversation at Gettysburg was released to the nation on Friday, September 23rd. On this film Kitchel refused to permit a plea for contributions, a decision which Bill Middendorf said cost the campaign treasury at least five hundred thousand dollars.

The idea of tacking on an appeal for funds at the end of a political television film was opposed by Lou Guylay, Kitchel, and

Baroody. But on the other Goldwater presentations Cordiner overruled their objections, and the sixty-second clip voiced by actor Raymond Massey produced almost enough in contributions to pay for the time and the cost of production when it was used.

The next nationwide TV program almost brought the campaign to a grinding halt. It was called "America Asks Senator Barry Goldwater," and was the brainchild of Lichenstein, who had promoted a similar presentation in the final hours of the California primary.

Camera crews were sent to find and photograph people who wanted to ask Barry Goldwater questions. Subjects were suggested but the queries were not scripted. These clips were then projected in the studio on a back screen, and the Senator responded ad lib. Some of the answers were more than a full page long. All the subjects had been covered in other speeches.

Ralph Cordiner sent word to the "think tank" that he was not about to raise any money to repeat that kind of disastrous, dull television film, and the October revolt on the second floor came to its climax. Both Burch and Grenier were dissatisfied with the speeches, but they were not in on the effort to make a change in the "think tank." Mardian and Rosenzweig did meet but, as I have already mentioned, the request for a change was never presented to Goldwater.

On Friday, October 9th, Richard Nixon introduced Goldwater to the television audience, and the Senator delivered the speech which had been written by Charles S. McNally on "The Real Job of the Presidency." In spite of some poor transitions and movements not clearly motivated by the speech, this was probably the Senator's most effective television appearance. But it was not good enough to deserve repetition in place of the promised live TV presentation scheduled for Milwaukee, Wisconsin.

The October 20th television speech on morality in government was a repeat of the Senator's address originally delivered at the Mormon Tabernacle in Salt Lake City. The October 21st program was Goldwater's response to a change in heads of government in the Soviet Union. On October 22nd, Goldwater delivered his only forthright examination of the problem of civil rights in which he declared himself opposed to segregation and advocated that men must have the right of free association in every strata of our society. The original text, written by Harry Jaffa under the title "Civil Rights and the Common Good," was a scholarly discussion of the problem, liberally supported with quotations from Abraham Lincoln. When the "think tank" finished its editing process, they included a full page of attack on the administration which mentioned the shadow of scandal on the White House and terror in the streets. The concluding paragraph was a direct condemnation of the civil rights demonstrators. Goldwater said:

> I say that it is the responsibility of our national leadership, regardless of political gain or political popularity, to encourage every community in this nation to enforce the law, not let it be abused and ignored. It is *not* the responsibility nor is it a proper function of national leadership actually to *enforce* these local laws, but it *is* a responsibility of national leadership to make sure that it and its spokesman and its supporters do not discourage the enforcement or incite the *breaching* of these laws. Above all, no administration should, as this one has, call men into the streets to solve their problems.

The gentle logic of Jaffa's plea for the right of free association was overshadowed by these angry words directed specifically at certain actions which Goldwater regarded as transgressions, or perhaps it was Kitchel, or Hess, or Baroody who included this condemnation out of place and unconnected with the major portion of the speech.

The "Brunch with Barry" program offered to the nation on October 23rd was designed for a daytime television audience. Goldwater appeared with Senator Margaret Chase Smith of Maine; Mrs. Leo Agostini of Redding, California; Mrs. Edward Burke of Astoria, New York; Mrs. Charles Ranges of St. Petersburg, Florida; Mrs. Zaio W. Schroeder of Detroit, Michigan; and Mrs. Edwin Shank, Jr., of Winamac, Indiana.

Rus Walton had arranged the program, and he was particularly pleased when Margaret Chase Smith of Maine expressed her delight at being asked to help Goldwater. It was a happy, gossipy program ranging over Mrs. Smith's service in the Senate, the problem of busing children to faraway schools in New York City, the cost of living, the effects of inflation, finally providing Goldwater with an opportunity to declare his support for Social Security. Senator Smith conveniently brought to the studio Senator Goldwater's voting record as proof the Republican candidate had always been on the record in favor of strengthening the Social Security system.

The climax of the program was the dialogue between Goldwater and Mrs. Shank, who is the widow of Captain Edwin Shank, Jr., a victim of the war in Viet Nam.

The publication of the final letters from Captain Shank in *U. S. News & World Report* had provoked a wave of indignation directed against the administration which had permitted Captain Shank and other Americans to fly and fight in antiquated airplanes. Mrs. Shank read two excerpts from her husband's final communications and then confronted Goldwater with the direct question: "I would like to ask you why the American people are not able to be told the truth about the situation in Viet Nam. A number of times on TV I have heard that our country has the greatest arsenal weapons in the history of the world, so I would like to know why my husband and others die in airplanes that fall apart?"

Goldwater's response complimented Mrs. Shank, covered some of the dreary statistics from Viet Nam, complained that we have not produced any new airplanes for the type of combat encountered in jungle warfare, but he refused to make the one flat declaration Mrs. Shank was pleading for—that if and when he was elected President he would see to it that American fighting men were equipped with the latest and most modern weapons, including aircraft.

When the program was over, Walton, who was greatly disturbed, asked Goldwater if they could not remake the segment with Mrs. Shank and provide the Senator with an opportunity to reassure American mothers that his election would guarantee adequate equipment for our fighting men. For some reason Goldwater refused to remake the scene or to strengthen his response. He told Walton that all weapons are out of date when they come into the inventory, that it would not be honest to make such a statement.

The election eve broadcast featured the Senator and his family in Phoenix and Congressman Miller and his family in New York State. It was a pleasant, disjointed, pointless collection of reminiscences, none of which could have persuaded anyone, anywhere to switch from Johnson to Goldwater.

Lichenstein, Burch, Baroody, and a number of others who participated in the decisions of the "think tank" will argue that under the circumstances the Goldwater television campaign was successful. It produced millions of dollars in contributions, the voters had a chance to see and hear the candidate, and nothing could have prevented a Johnson victory.

On October 27th, Ronald Reagan, a staunch Goldwater supporter, delivered a speech of his own composition entitled "A Time for Choosing" on nationwide television. Thousands of Republicans have classified this as the most effective program of the Goldwater campaign. Local committees in most states secured film or video tape in order to rerun the Reagan program under local sponsorship. The Republican National Committee published the text in a special pamphlet, and the incredible fact is that Baroody and Kitchel tried their best to block and black out the Reagan television program.

"A Time for Choosing" was filmed well in advance of the projected release date, and a handful of men who believed the message had impact raised the funds to pay for a nationwide TV release. With the film made and the money in hand to buy the network time, Kitchel and Baroody were advised of the project. After reading the script they both urged cancellation. They even persuaded Goldwater to telephone Reagan in Los Angeles on Sunday, October 25th, to ask him to withdraw the film. Reagan was distressed. He asked the Senator if he had seen the script or the film.

Goldwater said, "No."

"Well, it's not really that bad, Senator, and I don't think it will do you any harm," Reagan replied. "Please read the script or see the film. If you are then of the opinion that it will hurt your campaign, I'll abide by your decision and cancel the release."

When Goldwater did not call on Monday, Reagan concluded the Senator had withdrawn his objection and the film was shown on schedule. But as late as 5:30 on Tuesday afternoon, Kitchel and Baroody were still attempting to persuade Reagan's sponsors to cancel the showing. The Goldwater campaign bosses opposed the Reagan speech principally because it discussed the inadequacies of the present Social Security program and linked Goldwater once again to the sponsorship of some "voluntary features which would permit a citizen to do better on his own."

Reagan's speech was by far the most effective exposition of conservative concern for the future of the nation offered by anyone in the 1964 campaign. As one of the regional directors pointed out, it sounded like the old Goldwater. Since the election thousands of Republicans have asked: why didn't we have more speeches in the same vein as Ronnie Reagan's?

The differences of opinion which produced a conflict between the practical politicians on the second floor and the elite members of Bill Baroody's "think tank" on the third floor were not the only causes of dissention in the campaign. On October 27th, finance chairman Ralph Cordiner wrote an angry, detailed memorandum to Dean Burch, beginning:

> In view of the accusations and acrimonious criticism made at the meeting you called on Monday, October 26, I want to make some factual statements for the record in this memorandum:
>
> 1. The function of the Republican National Finance Committee, and particularly the Chairman, is the overall responsibility for the collection of funds, of the Republican National Finance Committee, and as you are aware, there are many individual Republican Finance Committees acting independently toward the goal this fall. Unless specifically designated, neither the Treasurer of the Republican National Committee nor the Finance Coordinator of the Republican National Finance Committee speaks for, or with the authority of, the Chairman with regard to the actual financial position of the Republican

> National Finance Committee, or authentic forecasts of anticipated funds to be received at any specific date. As far as the Chairman is concerned, this relationship will continue to be in effect until November 3, 1964, at which time I am resigning as Senator Goldwater and you have been advised.

Cordiner went on to point out that he was first presented on July 19th with a budget asking for $9,398,000. On August 10th, this was raised to $10 million. On August 20th, it was raised to $12 million, and on September 5, it was raised again to $12,166,000. He said, "On September 19, I received a copy of the budget of $11,991,983 with an item under activity 421 entitled 'TV and Radio' of $4,853,472, which had not been discussed with those involved in the work of the Republican National Finance Committee."

These five separate budgets, Cordiner continued, "were issued without concurrence." The potential income to finance the expenditures was a reasonable expectation in the opinion of the chairman of the Republican National Finance Committee. But Cordiner was disturbed over a meeting called by Kitchel and Baroody for October 24th, at which time they tried to force comptroller Ray Collett to authorize funds for expenditures outside the budget.

In addition, the relationship between the Citizens for Goldwater-Miller and the Republican National Committee, which started on shaky ground, was further disrupted when Kitchel and Baroody ordered the cancellation of the announced showing of the documentary *Choice*. The film, produced in Hollywood, based on a concept developed by Rus Walton, was rejected because Baroody believed it was racist and vulgar. He and Kitchel had been appraised of the project when it was undertaken, the script had been approved by the staff at Citizens. The trouble started when a newspaper columnist, Drew Pearson, attacked the film. Pearson had somehow managed to gain possession of the confidential stenographic notes made at a story conference in California, and Democrat Chairman John Bailey joined the attack.

Walton and White had announced plans for a press preview

showing in Washington prior to a nationwide release on television to be sponsored by Mothers for a Moral America. The film was a put-together documentary consisting of news clips of teenagers in honkytonks, burlesque show marquees, riots in the cities—all reflecting the moral deterioration of America. Intercut were shots of a big black sedan traveling over a country road at high speed with the driver, or someone in the car, throwing out empty beer cans. No one denied that these scenes were intended to remind the voters of the high-speed drive of Lyndon Johnson in Texas, which had been reported in full detail in the national news magazines, even down to the brand of beer being consumed.

If *Choice* had been shown as scheduled, it would not have won the election for Goldwater, but the announcement of cancellation was accepted as a confession by the candidate that Rus Walton and his helpers had produced a vile, offensive, immoral, racist movie. Since the election I have shown my copy of the film to many people. While the viewers have not all been enthusiastic and many have said the intended message was somewhat obscured, not a single critic has classified the documentary as racist or vulgar.

25

> *And I think also the press has probably planted the seeds of its own destruction because there isn't any question in my mind that at least forty per cent of the people in the country feel subconsciously or consciously that the press jobbed Goldwater.*

There is no way of determining how many millions of Americans share this opinion voiced by Dean Burch in December of 1964, but certainly the attitude of the press exerted a major influence in the presidential campaign.

The chairman of the Republican Party also said:

> I don't think they particularly tried to distort statements or change wording or use trick quotations, but nevertheless the press—particularly the columnists, the so-called thought controllers, *Life* magazine, the *Saturday Evening Post,* etc.—were not only against Goldwater, they were absolutely hysterical about Goldwater. It's not a question of honest reporting; it's a question of what is chosen to be reported and what is chosen not to be reported.

From the day Goldwater announced on January 3rd until he was defeated on November 3rd certain columnists and certain newspaper editors constantly charged the Republican candidate with being an extremist in his thoughts, his philosophy, and his associations. Those who know Goldwater believe the charge was unfounded. However, the repeated accusations persuaded many of the voters to accept the charges as true; yet some of the most violent actions of the campaign were taken by supporters of Lyndon Johnson. These "extremists" were not criticized nor condemned by the press.

The September-October issue of *Fact* magazine came out with a statement on the cover in black type: "One thousand one hundred eighty-nine psychiatrists say Goldwater is psychologically unfit to be President." The tortured logic advanced to support the cover statement is an insult to any thoughtful reader. The magazine on its inner pages stated that a questionnaire had been sent to 12,350 psychiatrists in the United States asking, "Do you believe Barry Goldwater is psychologically fit to serve as President of the United States?"

The magazine claims that 2,417 replies were received. Five hundred and seventy-one who responded said they did not know enough about Goldwater to answer the question. Six hundred and fifty-seven said they thought Goldwater was psychologically fit, and 1,189 said he was not. The 9,939 men and women who failed to respond to the magazine questionnaire were at least being faithful to the ethics of their profession. Those who presumed to reach a medical and psychiatric conclusion about Goldwater without ever having seen him, questioned him, or followed any other of the normal procedures required in a patient-physician relationship betrayed themselves as men unfit to practice any profession. It would have made as much sense and been just as valid to address the internists of the United States soliciting their opinion on whether or not Lyndon Johnson had an ingrown toenail.

The publication of the magazine statement was sufficiently offensive to have called for universal condemnation by the press, but the affair did not end here. Full-page ads in metropolitan newspapers blared forth the statement that "Eleven hundred eighty-nine psychiatrists said Goldwater was psychologically unfit to be President." Ralph Ginsberg, the editor and publisher of *Fact,* was at the time under conviction in a federal court for printing and distributing pornography.

Successful magazines such as the *Saturday Evening Post* or *Life* or *Look* have rarely found it profitable to use full-page newspaper ads to attempt to sell their magazines. Why did editor Ginsberg follow a practice not generally accepted in his trade? Who put up the money for the newspaper campaign? One cynic suggested that Ginsberg, who was out on bond awaiting the results of an appeal, might have hoped to secure friendly treatment from the Department of Justice.

The lead article inside the cover entitled "Goldwater the Man and the Menace," published under editor Ginsberg's by-line, quoted from published Goldwater biographies without permission from the authors and owners of the copyrights and then used the quotations to substantiate his personal opinions of the Senator. What did the liberal press do? It ignored the publication or in some cases called attention to the subject by repeating the charge that Goldwater had once suffered a nervous breakdown.

Perhaps Ginsberg was inspired to produce his vicious issue by the story of a reporter who interviewed Mrs. Goldwater and quoted her as saying that in the early 1930's her husband had suffered, in her terms, a "nervous breakdown." When the item was first published it was quickly exploded as a colloquial Indiana description for exhaustion. Holmes Alexander, the syndicated columnist, made a trip to Phoenix, Arizona, examined the Senator's entire past medical record, interviewed his personal physician —a reputable internist whose opinion and integrity could not be questioned—and then stated unequivocally that Goldwater had never suffered any kind of mental difficulty. Even more conclusive, Alexander quoted the Air Force medical report. No man with a history of mental instability or a tendency toward a nervous breakdown is certified by the Air Force to fly a Mach 2 aircraft, and each year the Senator had passed with flying colors the intensive medical and psychometric examination given to Air Force pilots.

It is possible for defenders of the press to quarrel with the conclusions voiced by Dean Burch, but no man of good will can overlook or forgive the failure of the press to condemn the Ginsberg publication.

The second act of violent extremism was perpetrated in St. Louis during the triennial convention of the Protestant Episcopal Church of North America. William Stringfellow, a New York lawyer who has achieved some recognition as a theologian, circulated a petition among the clergy and the laity of the Episcopal Church gathered in St. Louis, then called a press conference and released the statement suggesting that the church had condemned the candidacy of Barry Goldwater, an Episcopalian.

Under a two-column head, "Barry Accused of Using Racism," the story had a vicious implication.

> *St. Louis, Missouri, UPI*—A statement accusing Senator Barry M. Goldwater of "transparent exploitation of racism" has been signed by seven hundred and twenty-six Episcopalian bishops, clergy and laymen, it was announced today.
>
> Episcopalian layman William Stringfellow, a New York attorney, revealed the terms of the statement at the Episcopalian General Convention in St. Louis.
>
> Stringfellow said he had mailed the statement to one thousand one hundred Episcopalians throughout the country Wednesday. He said signers were from forty-one states and included ten Episcopalian bishops. He said he had received only two outright rejections.

Stringfellow, an ardent liberal, went through the motions of issuing a disclaimer saying that his petition did not represent an official action of the General Convention. But he did arrange to circulate his petition and release it in the shadow of the church's meeting, and it must be assumed it was a deliberate attempt to cloak his unauthorized action with the imprimatur of the official church. A handful of the controversial figures within the church signed the statement, notably Bishop Pike of San Francisco.

This action was one of the great ironies of the campaign. The official church, which sanctimoniously proclaims its dedication to a division of church and state, found itself maneuvered into a position where it appeared to be taking corporate action and voicing the official position of the church in a political campaign.

As an elected lay member of the National Council of the Episcopal Church I was shocked when I read the first story from St. Louis. It was still coming off the wire when the Right Reverend Arthur Lichtenberger, Presiding Bishop of the Episcopal Church, sent word to me regretting Stringfellow's action. The General Convention took notice of this attempt to mislead the American public by issuing an official statement denying that Stringfellow's attack on Goldwater represented the official opinion of the church. But it is very doubtful that the denial ever caught up with the charge. Stringfellow and Ralph Ginsberg, erstwhile pornographer and publisher of *Fact,* must be recognized for their achievement in extremism in 1964.

Had the Roman Catholics denounced Kennedy in 1960 or the Christians (Disciples of Christ) denounced Johnson in 1964, it is easy to imagine how the press would have reacted against these attacks. In Goldwater's home state he was defended, and the Right Reverend Joseph Meakin Harte, Bishop of Arizona, expressed his disapproval of the Stringfellow petition. But the casual readers across the land, particularly those who were being taught to hate Goldwater, noted with reassurance that the Senator's fellow churchmen found him unfit for the job he sought.

The scandal magazine *Confidential* added its voice to the chorus of violence in an article under the by-line of Graye Oliphant, entitled "Commie Tactics Are Selling Barry Goldwater" and subtitled, "His Brain Trusters have broken every basic rule of political life and are brazenly following those laid down by Mao Tse-tung, China's Red dictator."

The Oliphant piece was based on his interpretation of my book, *How to Win an Election,* in which I described the creation of a basic organization in each community, a necessity for victory which had been recognized by Mao Tse-tung, who once said: "Give me two men in a village and I will take the village." All political campaigns are based upon the successful enlistment of volunteer citizens. But when employed on behalf of Goldwater they became deplorable tactics. The same piece quoted Drew Pearson as saying, "The smell of Fascism is strong at this convention (San Francisco)." And Charles Bartlett, who wrote, "The evidence of hate at the convention in San Francisco and the sharpening of the racial issue have raised new fears that it will be physically perilous for President Johnson to campaign extensively. Security experts are keenly aware of the danger to the President from fanatics."

In the 1964 election there was not one authenticated incident of a serious threat to the President's life. The Goldwater campaign featured a succession of threats. At one midwestern city the security detail lined up all the press photographers, ordered them to aim their cameras at the crowd and fire their flashbulbs as the Senator left the hotel in order to blind the fanatic they believed was lurking in the shadows with murder in his heart.

The *Reporter* magazine in its August 8th issue devoted eight full pages to an editorial by Max Ascoli, a by-line piece by Gerald Ter Horst, an article by Meg Greenfield, and another by William Lee Miller—all attacking Goldwater and his associates.

Fred J. Cook rushed into print with a paperback attacking and deriding the Republican candidate. On one page Cook calls the Senator "a Phoenix Country Club McCarthy"—and this from a liberal who decries guilt by association!

The Democrat National Committee published hundreds of thousands of copies of what it called *A Goldwater Inconsistencies Primer*—a happy device for quoting out of context. And the editors of *The New Republic* put out a collection of articles by Murray Kempton, Gilbert Harrison, Milton Viorst—all illustrated by the violent anti-Goldwaterites, Robert Osborn and Bill Mauldin. A typical piece by Murray Kempton begins with this: "Barry Goldwater opened the last month of his wait for the Republican nomination by allowing his son-in-law-elect to throw him into the family swimming pool. In theory he embodies all our stern and unfashionable principles; by nature he defers to all our slack and modern heresies of which the most pervasive is the notion that Father Knows Least." If Kempton's logic is to be believed, Goldwater committed a cardinal sin when he was pushed into the swimming pool in a moment of frolic with the young man who was going to marry his younger daughter!

There were others. The official organ of the AFL-CIO purported to print a comparison of Goldwater and Johnson. The Communist party's number one theoretician, Herbert Aptheker, published a vicious attack on Goldwater in the September issue of *Political Affairs*. Mike Newberry, a staff writer for the Communist party newspaper, *The Worker,* put out a fantastic book entitled *Goldwaterism,* sponsored by Marzani and Munsel of New York

City, which suggested that all of the Goldwater supporters were native fascists.

The same combination of Marzani and Munsel put out the *Goldwater Coloring Book,* with the Senator attired in a Napoleonic uniform pictured as a leader of the Ku Klux Klan. *The Christian Century* did its bit with a by-line piece by William Stringfellow who had authored the resolution at St. Louis.

Indeed, there was extremism in the 1964 campaign! It reached a violent and unequaled high for American politics.

Evets Haley, a respected Texas historian, published a paperback called *A Texan Looks at Lyndon,* and the liberal press literally took the hide off Haley's back. John Stormer wrote a paperback called *None Dare Call It Treason,* and his effort was likewise categorized by the liberals as unfair, dishonest writing. Neither Stormer nor Haley had any connection with the official Goldwater campaign, and no one purchased full-page ads in the metropolitan newspapers to push the sale of these writings.

The *New York Times* on Sunday, October 4th, ran a by-line story by Donald Janson with a Houston dateline. The headline was "Extremist Book Sales Soar Despite Criticism in GOP," and the subhead, "Attacks On President Assailed as 'Smut' and Scurrilous." The story dealt with the distribution of the Haley book, *A Texan Looks at Lyndon, None Dare Call It Treason,* and Phyllis Schlafly's *A Choice Not an Echo* and claimed that more than sixteen million copies of the books had been printed. Janson honestly reported that in some Goldwater headquarters the books were not sold, and he also quoted Lee Edwards as saying, "The official policy of the committee does not recommend nor endorse publications prepared outside the committee."

Janson does not mention the *Fact* magazine attack, but he does state that the Democrat National Committee "had sold more than 50,000 copies of the Cook paperback and received a commission from the publisher for each sale."

A careful reading of the *Times* article shows that the anti-Johnson books enjoyed tremendous public acceptance, but they were not subsidized or sold or recommended by the Goldwater campaign headquarters, whereas the Cook book, equally violent, had been sponsored and sold by the official Democrat National Committee.

In the *New York Times* Sunday edition for October 11th, in the section entitled "The News of the Week in Review," there were four political ads. Two of them were full-page statements directed against Goldwater, one sponsored by the New York Scientists, Engineers and Physicians for Johnson-Humphrey, Inc.; the second by the Council for a Livable World. The third—smaller in size—was published by Americans for Democratic Action with the headline: "You can do something about the Goldwater threat." That same week three hundred thousand throwaways were printed on newsprint in the South, repeating the *Fact* magazine libel. The headline: "1,189 Psychiatrists say Goldy is Unfit," by Science Service, dateline Washington.

A part of the answer to the question "What happened to Goldwater?" must be found in the violence of those who opposed him. The election did not hinge on the popularity or ability of Lyndon Johnson. He was a secondary figure, and the "great mandate" became his inheritance. It was not a testament to his wisdom or leadership, but rather an indication of the violent dislike for Goldwater generated largely by the hundreds of magazine articles, the derogatory remarks of the columnists, the unexplained errors (such as the UPI report of Goldwater's statement on the Howard Smith ABC television appearance), and the scathing attacks of people such as William Stringfellow, Ralph Ginsberg, and Fred Cook.

Dean Burch said:

> I think that most of the reporters, if they would ever let their defenses down, would agree that taken as a whole the press was so violently antagonistic to Goldwater that even if they had wanted to be honest about it, it was impossible for them to be honest because they were so busy looking for weaknesses. In other words, the press in this particular campaign performed the function of the opposition. They took a look at what Goldwater advocated and then they looked for whatever was the weakest link in that chain and that became the issue.

On the other hand, with Johnson, anything that was against him they ignored. For example, if Senator Goldwater during his twelve years in the U. S. Senate had accumulated $14 million as a personal fortune, I am sure that the press in a period of three months could have made his name synonymous with Benedict Arnold, whereas with Johnson it was just one of those "Well, boys will be boys things and everyone is entitled to make a living."

Secondly, if I or someone close to Senator Goldwater had been called before the Senate Rules Committee and then taken taken the Fifth Amendment, that subject would never have been dropped. At every press conference Goldwater would have been asked to explain in detail what my role was, what he planned to do about it, whereas the Bobby Baker case was stressed only by Goldwater. The press never discussed it with the President.

Thirdly, if I had been picked up in the men's room of the YMCA, the stories that would have been written on it would have lasted for two or three months and the conclusion would have been that obviously Goldwater knew about it and obviously, possibly, he was a little bit peculiar.

Yet these techniques were only used on one side of the campaign. They were not used on the other. Goldwater was accused by the press for not articulating well what his positions were. On the other hand, President Johnson did nothing but talk about the Great Society—whatever that is—and wander around climbing on and off cars, shaking hands and kissing babies. And yet this was set forth as one of the greatest campaign efforts any human being had undertaken, whereas the Goldwater campaign was categorized as amateurish and boorish and racist and on and on.

So far as I am concerned, I don't care to have any open arguments with the press because you don't win that kind of an argument. But I think someday these people are going to have to sit back and examine their consciences.

26

There is no way to prove that Barry Goldwater might have won the Presidency in 1964. Perhaps the Johnson victory was inevitable, but thousands of Republicans believe their candidate should have made a better showing.

The delegates to the 1964 San Francisco convention were all concerned party members, and their opinions are offered here as an expression of politically minded citizens qualified to speak the Republican point of view.

Immediately after the election I sent a questionnaire covering 78 separate subjects having to do with the nomination and campaign to the 1,308 official delegates. Each state and section of the country is proportionately represented in the replies received. Seventy-nine per cent of those responding said they were supporters of Barry Goldwater in San Francisco, and 68.9 per cent admitted they were in Goldwater's corner before he officially announced his candidacy.

A number of questions were designed to determine what factor or factors prompted these delegates to choose Goldwater as the 1964 Republican candidate for President.

Seventy-two per cent said they had heard Goldwater speak, 82 per cent had read *The Conscience of a Conservative,* and more than 50 per cent had read the Senator's newspaper column *"How Do You Stand, Sir?"* Certainly an overwhelming majority of the delegates were acquainted with the Senator and his beliefs before he became a candidate for the Presidency. Many of them indicated they were attracted to Goldwater because of his position in favor of reducing federal expenditures and the size of federal government.

Ninety-nine per cent were in favor of a more vigorous foreign policy; 94 per cent agreed with Goldwater's position on Cuba. A handful of delegates admitted they supported Goldwater because they were opposed to Rockefeller, Scranton, Lodge, or Margaret Chase Smith, but the bulk of his votes at the convention were positive pro-Goldwater votes.

The value of the Senator's work as chairman of the Senatorial Campaign Committee is emphasized in the replies—80 per cent said Goldwater had helped Republicans in their state. Eighty-four per cent said Goldwater's withdrawal speech at the 1960 convention caused them to regard him with favor.

When asked to classify themselves as liberals, moderates, or conservatives, 64 per cent claimed to be conservative, 33.9 per cent moderate, and only 1.4 per cent liberal.

During the campaign the opposition in the primary elections bitterly attacked Phyllis Schlafly's book *A Choice Not an Echo;* 92.8 per cent of the delegates said they had read the book, but only 25.6 per cent said it influenced them to support Barry Goldwater. And 80 per cent of those who responded approved the 1964 Republican party Platform.

Throughout the year 1964 Goldwater supporters were bitterly condemned as extremists, and when Eisenhower mildly rebuked the columnists and commentators in his speech at the Cow Palace, the delegates applauded enthusiastically. In the questionnaire, 82.3 per cent said they resented the label of extremism. We asked the direct question: "Are you now or have you ever been a member of the John Birch Society, the Ku Klux Klan, or the Minutemen." Of those who responded 1.6 per cent admitted they belonged to one of those three organizations. It can be argued that perhaps the delegates were not truthful, but the questionnaire was designed to protect the identity of those who replied—no signature or return address was required—and there is no valid reason for questioning their honesty.

One segment of the questionniare called for the delegates' opinions about the conduct of the campaign. Eighty per cent said they heard Barry Goldwater in person sometime between July 15th and November 3rd. Ninety-nine per cent said they saw one or more of the Goldwater television programs. This figure is surprisingly high, but it must be borne in mind that all of these people had paid their own way to San Francisco to participate in the convention, were keenly interested in the outcome of the election, and would logically have followed the campaign closely.

Seventy per cent believed Goldwater's personal appearances were effective, but only 55 per cent held the same opinion of the Goldwater television. Their opinions on specific programs seem to corroborate the judgment of the regional directors.

Only 38 per cent thought the opening studio program effective and convincing. Of all the Goldwater shows his statement on "The Job of the Presidency," when he was introduced by Richard Nixon, rated highest. Seventy-two per cent thought it effective and convincing. *Conversation at Gettysburg* was seen by more of the delegates, but only 20 per cent expressed approval of the content. The Madison Square Garden rally rated next to the highest, with 61 per cent saying it was effective and convincing.

When asked to name the opposition charge which most adversely affected Goldwater's chances for success, the delegates rated "trigger happy" as the most damaging. The claim that Goldwater would abolish Social Security was only slightly less harmful; "reckless and irresponsible" was third, and the fear that he would sell TVA fourth.

The delegates were asked if they thought Goldwater the candidate lacked warmth, and 54.5 per cent said "yes." Sixty-nine per cent are of the opinion that Goldwater failed to discuss the conservative issues in depth. And to 46 per cent of these Republicans, it seemed that Barry Goldwater in 1964 was somehow different from the Republican worker who had won their affection in the earlier years.

There was an overwhelming belief in the minds of the delegates that Goldwater should have discussed the civil rights problem openly and frankly, devoted attention to an explanation of how deficit financing was harming the country, and hammered away on the need for a change in foreign policy.

The Jenkins scandal, which created such a furor in mid October, had, according to the opinion of these practicing politicians, almost no effect on the outcome. Seventy-six per cent believed the 1964 election was decided on the personality of the candidate rather than on the issue of liberalism versus conservatism.

Eighty-two per cent expressed disapproval of the conduct of the 1964 campaign, and 77 per cent said that Goldwater's election tactics hurt other Republican candidates. A bare majority—53 per cent—were in favor of retaining Dean Burch as national chairman.

Like most questionnaires, ours called for "yes" or "no" answers. But many of the respondents volunteered explanatory comments. The residual effects of the bitter primary contests were frequently mentioned.

A Wisconsin delegate said: "The Goldwater campaign never got off the ground. We were on the defensive from the start. Rocky's charges on Social Security; Scranton's trigger-happy claim—these are the things that Demos used on us to great advantage. The TV scenes from our San Francisco convention and the tearing up of the Social Security card on TV were very effective."

A former Republican governor, Cecil Underwood, who was running for re-election in West Virginia said:

> I am at a loss to understand why Goldwater sidetracked all the first team which had helped him win the nomination. These loyal, capable men appeared to have been shoved entirely to the sidelines.
>
> Beginning with his acceptance speech he was on the defensive and losing ground. The candidate of the minority cannot hope to win with a defensive campaign. He never did get around to spelling out conservative philosophy for which all the country waited.
>
> In Charleston, West Virginia, he completely snubbed eighteen men who had paid $1,000 each to have coffee with Goldwater. He left them at the airport in a private dining room while he shook hands in the lobby and boarded his plane without so much as a "hello" to the waiting contributors. It took us the rest of the campaign to recover from this blow.

The delegates who replied referred frequently to Rockefeller, Romney, Lodge, and to a lesser degree William Scranton as "The Spoilers," responsible in part for Goldwater's defeat. They commented that many voters must have taken a cue from these party leaders who refused to support the nominee wholeheartedly.

In Michigan the Romney headquarters circulated pamphlets explaining how it was possible to vote a split ticket for Johnson and Romney. And in New York state the Goldwater leaders were bitter in their condemnation of the Keating-Javits-Lindsay-Rockefeller refusal to help.

When the campaign was over, I explored this subject with Dean Burch, asking him if Governor Rockefeller had been requested to take an active part in the Goldwater campaign. Burch told me that he contacted Rockefeller only once, and then it was to ask him to go to Montana for a Republican rally honoring Governor Tim Babcock. No formal request was made to Romney. And while Scranton did what he could, he was committed to remain in Pennsylvania, and the Goldwater people in that state felt the governor never put his heart into the campaign. His endorsement was always qualified by the words, "While I disagree with Senator Goldwater about. . . ."

Dean Burch admits the campaign might have been handled differently, perhaps better, but he feels much of the criticism is "nit-picking" on the part of professional politicians, and he told me that in politics everyone is an expert. "One hundred and ninety-million people," he said, "think they know all about campaigns and elections. They don't have to have any qualifications or any experience."

Chuck Lichenstein, after the election was over, told me he recognized some deficiencies in communication between the politicians on the second floor and the speech writers in the "think tank," but he blames this in major part on the pressure of the campaign. "There were so many speeches to write, so many statements to issue," he says, "there wasn't time to do all the 'consulting' and all the 'clearing' we might have wished."

Burch suggests that the ideal political campaign should be entrusted to a decision maker who would remain anonymous, someone who would not be bothered by the telephone calls and the letters and the conferences. To most of the regional directors on the third floor the great deficiency was the failure to establish this clear line of authority.

The Republican National Committee is a line organization served by staff members. During the campaign we found the staff members making many decisions independently of the official line of authority. Kitchel traveled constantly with the Senator and thus was not available. Burch was harrassed by the many problems of operating the committee, and most, but not all, of the policy statements and speeches were created in the "think tank" controlled by Bill Baroody.

Doug Whitlock was nominally in charge of tours, but each weeks' schedule had to be approved by the strategy group which met on Sundays. Frequently decisions were delayed until it was too late to implement them effectively. The same lack of coordination affected the television programs. Cordiner's condition that no money be spent until it had been raised prevented the advertising agency from making firm commitments for television time in advance; consequently some of the programs went on the air without the proper publicity necessary to attract an audience.

The decision to concentrate the spot television on clips of the candidate seriously hampered the agency's effort to attack the issues dramatically. Erwin-Wasey, according to Rudy Etchen, submitted seven different concepts for a TV spot on Viet Nam, and they were all disapproved by Baroody and Kitchel.

All during the campaign Kitchel, Baroody, Justice, Hess, and McCabe were overly protective of the candidate. Goldwater was not permitted any contact with advisers outside the official group. On the airplane, Judy Rooney and Karl Hess along with Justice made sure that Goldwater was not available to traveling VIP's. Only on very rare occasions did the Senator go back into the press section of the aircraft, and most of the contact with the working press was left to Paul Wagner and Karl Hess.

After one meeting in the South when a reporter, in the opinion of Hess, underestimated the crowd, the Senator's speech writer purchased a small, crude symbol and presented it to the reporter as his first prize for "crowd estimating."

According to Don Dorman, who rode the airplane constantly, there were many reporters sympathetic to Goldwater, but they never had an adequate opportunity to explore the Senator's mind. Most of the Goldwater team developed a feeling of animosity toward the press and particularly toward the television news commentators because of what they felt was unfair treatment of the candidate and the campaign. For the most part their reporting was accurate, but to the Goldwater conservatives it seemed unfair that their candidate should be interpreted to the public by men whose political philosophy took them to the other end of the scale.

Almost every unfortunate incident of the campaign could have been prevented by adequate advance planning. In the confusion and uncertainty which actually prevailed, it is perhaps miraculous that Goldwater did as well as he did.

Some Republicans did try to help, notably Richard Nixon, but even his participation was a mixed blessing. When the Nixon tour was being arranged, the former Vice-President called Senator Hiram Fong in Hawaii and asked if there was anything he could do in the island state to help the Republican party. Fong, a liberal, had been battling the Republican ticket. The suggestion that Nixon would come across the Pacific for an appearance to be arranged by Fong caused great consternation in the minds of those Republicans who were trying to help Goldwater win the Presidency.

The very nature of political campaigns denies the maintenance of secrecy, but the lack of security at Republican headquarters built animosities and suspicions impossible to overcome. Sam Claiborne told me that he once sent a single-copy confidential memo—*destroy-after-reading*—to the third floor. The next day he found a Xerox copy in a congressman's office on Capitol Hill.

In early September, Grenier ordered the door into the working headquarters at 1625 Eye Street locked. The regional directors and the other staff were given keys; everyone else had to be cleared by a receptionist in an office opposite the elevator. This action was taken to prevent the leaks, and it was probably Grenier's concern over the lack of security which led him to be trapped into an effort to buy information from a man named Fax, who claimed to be working for the Democrat National Committee. What Fax promised to deliver was the name of a traitor in the Republican National Committee. What Fax did was notify the newspapers, arrange to pick up his payment, and then denounce Grenier. There is an old axiom in politics—those who will sell to you will sell you to someone else. Dean Burch approved the payment, but Grenier took the blame in the press. When Goldwater was asked about it, he said the real moral offender was the man who attempted to sell.

One week before Election Day Wayne Hood asked me to write a Social Security ad. Using Goldwater's record which had been prepared by the "think tank," we laid out a full-page ad in which the Senator said he had voted specifically by date for each new Social Security proposal. On Monday, November 2nd, someone in the research division gave us the information that our ad was not correct—Goldwater had been absent when the vote was taken on the final item of our recital. At least we were consistent—he was misquoted on the day before he was defeated.

Millions of Americans heard Goldwater say on Tuesday morning when he came out of the polling place that he had split his ticket, and thousands of Republicans shuddered when they heard it. Parties strive to build loyalty. While Americans always tend to vote for the man, party allegiance is necessary to a successful operation of our form of self government. Anyone in Arizona could accept the remark without question because there are a number of offices for which no Republicans were running. The choice is either to split the ticket and vote for a Democrat or just not vote for the office. However the effect of Goldwater's off-hand remark was not beneficial in those eastern states where the polls were still open.

By four o'clock eastern time the outcome was obvious. Johnson had been re-elected. Len Hall tried to put through a call to Denison Kitchel. Hall wanted to urge Kitchel to have Goldwater make a gracious statement of concession. Kitchel refused to take the call.

Goldwater promised he would offer to the nation "a choice, not an echo." Eleven months and one hundred thousand miles later the choice and the candidate who offered it were rejected by forty-two million Americans, accepted by less than twenty-seven million. Yet in the same fortnight when Lyndon Johnson was elected with a new record of popular support the pollsters reported that more than 60 per cent of all Americans were deeply concerned over the growth and expansion of a bureaucratic federal government. Eighty-five per cent of those polled believed the militant, aggressive, sometimes violent supporters of civil rights had gone too fast. A majority of Americans were worried about continuing federal deficits. Almost no one exhibited any faith in American foreign policy.

Perhaps the choice Goldwater offered was never clearly understood. His position on foreign affairs was a direct and straightforward attack on what Frederick D. Wilheimsen, professor of philosophy at the University of Pomplona in Spain, has called our "Theology of survival—a subconscious acceptance of the belief that it is 'better to be Red than dead.' "

Goldwater strongly condemned those who were willing to borrow from the future earnings of their children's children in order to support themselves in luxury. He said that free men must have the right to choose *not* to associate as well as the right to associate. He said it is self-defeating to renounce in advance the use of force to protect American interests. He stated that some of the liberal solutions to social problems encourage immorality and irresponsibility.

The tragic history of the Grecian, Roman, and Florentine Republics supports every charge Goldwater made. But who wants to listen to history? The beguiling promise of something for nothing is so much more pleasant, and anyway Goldwater was "reckless and trigger happy. . . ." the commentators said so. Goldwater would "destroy Social Security . . ."; Rockefeller said so. Goldwater wanted to "use an atomic bomb in Southeast Asia"; the UPI said so.

As the campaign neared its dreary climax, Peter O'Donnell said that Goldwater had an atomic thorn in his heel which prevented him from walking into the hearts and minds of the American voters.

Who can say with authority what it was that persuaded the American voters to reject Barry Goldwater? Whatever the reasons, this man and the principles he espoused cannot be dismissed or ignored or categorized as an expression of the temporary insanity of the Republican party. When sufficient time has passed to permit the historians to view objectively this decade in American politics, it seems certain they will find two notable figures—John F. Kennedy and Barry Goldwater.

Kennedy won the Presidency by appealing to the vague discontent of a materialistic society with such imprecise phrases as the suggestion "We've got to get the country moving again." Goldwater, recognizing the sources of that discontent, chose to attack and condemn the causes and lost.

Goldwater spoke of painful things. To reform society it was necessary for him to attack society. A Goldwater victory would have required the voters to make an official confession of their past failures to face reality, to deal firmly with such matters as deficit financing, nonproductive foreign aid, and am ambivalent foreign policy and selfish self-indulgence.

And in the year of Goldwater's defeat the people were in a mood to escape responsibility, not accept it. The murder of Catherine Genovese in New York City, witnessed by thirty-seven householders who refused to become involved even to the extent of calling the police, reveals the temper of the people. Muggings and robberies on crowded subway trains, committed in front of witnesses who not only refuse to interfere but also refuse to report the incidents or appear in court, reveal a sickening unwillingness to participate either physically or emotionally. A people too cowardly or too timid to defend themselves or their fellows against such acts of personal violence could not be expected to face the moral decisions of the 1964 elections.

If Barry Goldwater's concern for the future of the United States was based on a valid understanding, then what he said will re-echo until the citizens of the Republic either heed his words or the Republic itself disappears.

Index